ONE HELL OF A LIFE

ONE HELL OF A LIFE

Brian Close:
Daring, Defiant and Daft

Stephen Chalke

FAIRFIELD BOOKS

fairfield books

Fairfield Books
Bedser Stand, Kia Oval, London SE11 5SS

First published 2024

ISBN: 978 1 7399293 6 7

Printed and bound in Great Britain by
CPI Antony Rowe, Chippenham SN14 6LH

Contents

	Introduction	9
1	Too old?	10
2	Could not be beaten	18
3	Too young?	28
4	Let the blighter stew	44
5	Out of the wilderness	56
6	At the wheel	71
7	Champions again	77
8	Give him marks for trying	90
9	The prodigal is forgiven	99
10	Pure, unalloyed joy	109
11	An artist's eye	119
12	There to win the game	126
13	Changing times	138
14	Defiant or daft?	148
15	The end of an era	166
16	Just what Somerset needed	183
17	A rum fellow, the hemperor	200
18	Behold you live, Grandad	207
19	Just a great soft thing really	215
20	One hell of a life	226
	A brief statistical digest	230
	Acknowledgements	234
	Index	237

Dennis Brian Close

CBE, 1975

Left-handed batsman, right-arm bowler

Born: 24 February 1931
Rawdon, Yorkshire

Died: 13 September 2015
Baildon, Yorkshire

First-class Cricket

Yorkshire (1949–1970)

Somerset (1971–1977)

England (1949–1976)
22 Tests, 3 One-Day Internationals

Captaincy

Yorkshire (1963–1970)
4 County Championships, 2 Gillette Cups

Somerset (1972–1977)

England (1966–1967 and 1972)
7 Tests: Won 6, Drawn 1
3 One-Day Internatiomals: Won 2, Lost 1

with warm thanks to

the late **Ken Biddulph**

for starting me on this journey

and to

Ken Taylor and the late **Frank Keating**

who long, long ago encouraged me to write this book

I have got there at last

INTRODUCTION

This book has been forming in my mind for more than twenty years. The story of Brian Close's life in cricket is such an unusual one, with so many ups and downs, and the man himself is quite the most fascinating character in post-war English cricket. I admire greatly his spirit of adventure, his self-belief, his refusal to back down in the face of adversity, yet these qualities were accompanied by a surprising inability to see danger ahead and to protect himself from it. For an intelligent man, who could have studied mathematics or medicine at university, he could be a fool at times, never fulfilling the potential of his great talent. His judgement was questioned repeatedly, he suffered numerous setbacks and he made important enemies among those in power. Yet somehow his indomitable spirit kept seeing him return.

In my interviews with cricketers over the years his name has come up more than any other. Everybody has had a story about him. I met him a few times, notably interviewing him about his life for a 90-minute film organised by the Archives Committee of Yorkshire County Cricket Club. During our talk he relived the highs and lows of his long cricketing career, becoming emotional at times. For a man known for his hardness he was quite soft underneath.

In the opening chapter I quote the cricket writer Alan Gibson on Brian towards the end of his career: 'What the very dickens and the devil of a cricketer Close ought to have been for England. The historians, in the future, will be puzzled about it all. Was it his own fault? Very possible, though others might also be to blame.'

This book is my attempt to reflect on Alan Gibson's question and to put in some shape all that I have been told. There is some truth in Brian's own despairing verdict after the last of his great cricketing disappointments, that his career was 'a series of cock-ups', but I prefer his last words in the filmed interview with me: "It's been one hell of a life" – followed by that croaking laugh of his.

Stephen Chalke
Bristol, September 2024

1

TOO OLD?

> Close would bat on a broken leg if he had to, and that's the way
> we have to look at a Test match we daren't lose.

So spoke Tony Greig, England's South African-born captain, when
justifying the surprise recall of the 45-year-old Brian Close for the First
Test of 1976.

> When you are pushed for alternatives, then all you can do is
> back blood and guts. That's something Close has never been
> short of, and I happen to think it's worth the gamble on his
> age.

It was indeed a gamble, one with no precedent in the modern game.
Only once since the Second World War has England taken the field with
an older man – the amateur Gubby Allen, also 45, who was appointed
to captain a second-string Test team in the Caribbean in the winter of
1947/48 – and that was not a success, as *Wisden*'s damning report of his
tour makes clear:

> He pulled a calf muscle while skipping on the ship deck on the
> way out. That caused him to miss the first three matches in
> Barbados, and at no time was he completely fit. In fact, at the
> age of 45, Allen was too old.

What was it about Brian Close, this most remarkable of cricketers, that
made the selectors, or at least some of them, think that he was capable
of defying the realities of age, of overcoming the inevitable slowing of
reflexes to withstand the pace of a young West Indian bowling attack?
Were there really no younger men better suited to the challenge?

Test cricket had entered an era dominated by fast bowling. In the
previous two winters both England and the West Indies had been
badly beaten in Australia, whose attack of Jeff Thomson and Dennis
Lillee was as fearsome as any world cricket had seen for many years.
Now West Indies, hardened by their defeat, had arrived in England

with their own high-pace attack. With Andy Roberts, Wayne Daniel and Michael Holding, they had the firepower to test the best English batsmen, which they made abundantly clear with a string of early tour victories. If England were to win the series, they needed batsmen with the courage and the technique to play such bowling. In the eyes of most observers, such men were in short supply.

The England team for the First Test at Trent Bridge was to be chosen on Friday 28 May during the last day of a trial match, England versus The Rest, at Bristol. If the selectors had hoped to learn anything of the ability of the batsmen to play pace, they could have hardly chosen a worse venue, for the square at Bristol was notoriously slow – so slow that on the last day the spinners Derek Underwood and Geoff Cope took nine wickets for 37 runs in 29 overs, as The Rest were bowled out for 48.

The best batting of the match had come in England's second innings from Dennis Amiss and Graham Roope; yet this was little comfort to the selectors, for in the previous match, playing for an MCC eleven against the West Indians at Lord's, both had struggled badly against Holding and Roberts, as had all the batsmen. In the words of Robin Marlar in the *Sunday Times*: 'The past week has been blue-black with bruises for English cricket, and reputations have been scattered like skittles.'

To add to the selectors' headaches, their number one batsman, Geoffrey Boycott, who did have the necessary technique, was in the midst of a three-year self-imposed exile from Test cricket. Angered that Kent's Mike Denness had retained the England captaincy, he had missed the Lillee/Thomson tour of Australia. Now, with Greig at the helm, the selectors tried to talk him round but to no avail. Time has not made his reasons entirely clear but, whatever those reasons, England would be facing Roberts and Holding without him.

Meanwhile, as the selectors pondered in Bristol, the West Indian tourists were fifty miles away in Taunton, notching up an emphatic victory over Somerset. Their batsmen, all scoring freely, declared on 389 for eight, then Roberts and Daniel set to work, reducing the hosts to 70 for five. There followed a blazing knock from a young Ian Botham, who took 16 off an over from Roberts, then 16 off one from Daniel, hitting each of them for mighty sixes. Henry Blofeld in the *Guardian* was not slow to appreciate the potential of the youngster:

It was a marvellous innings, for it revealed great character. It was completely fearless, and it marked out Botham, who is only 20, as a cricketer who one day soon England will surely be grateful for. He showed characteristics which are seen all too seldom these days.

At the other end, playing a supporting role, was the balding Somerset skipper, Yorkshireman Brian Close, nearing the end of a long career that had started in 1949 when at the age of 18 years and 149 days he had become the youngest man to play for England. It was a record he held till the end of his life, in fact till December 2022 when the Leicestershire leg-spinner Rehan Ahmed, 23 days younger, made his Test debut.

Close, 16 not out at the start of the morning, took his score to 88 at tea, falling immediately afterwards when he skied a high full-toss from the off-spinner Albert Padmore into the hands of slip. For Henry Blofeld, it was 'certainly the most romantic innings played on one of the most pleasant of county grounds for some while':

> It may seem fanciful to suggest seriously that Close, at the age of 45, should be brought back nine years after his last Test.
>
> The plain truth is that for just over four and a half hours he showed that his eyesight and his reflexes have scarcely dimmed, that he is as courageous as ever and that his technique is admirably correct against fast bowling. His first movement is always back and across his stumps, and every time he is right behind the line of the ball.
>
> Admittedly Holding was not playing, but Close almost always looked to have time to spare against Roberts and Daniel. He drove when the ball was up to him. Sometimes he hooked when it was short, and he repeatedly tucked the ball away off his legs.

Alan Gibson of *The Times*, though a long-time Westcountryman, was a Yorkshireman by birth, one with great feeling for Close, and his report of the day grasped more emphatically the case for his England recall:

> What are we to make of this man Close? He stood there yesterday, not scoring quickly, though always ready to give the bad ball a bash, and the good ball a successful snick. He was the valiant warrior ...

Not, mind you, that he played Padmore very well. He is not at his best against spinners. He only rises to his majesty when the bowlers are trying to kill him. When you think of the past few years, and the way that England's batsmen have ducked and dodged among the bouncers, it is absurd that we have deprived ourselves so often of the services of the Old Bald Blighter. He ought to be captaining England next week. Possibly he might do something outrageous, but then England's current imported captain has also been known to do outrageous things.

I was sad when Close failed to get his hundred. He was out just after tea, from a bad stroke to a bad ball. I suppose this, too, is part of his character. The pitch was slower than on the first day. When the West Indians went in again, they scored runs without difficulty. Bang-bang went Greenidge's sixes to long leg and fours to square leg. The Old Bald Blighter stood steadfastly at short leg, for as long as it was useful. Then, as evening clouds and shadows drew round the Taunton ground, he dropped back a little, ruminating like a Wharfedale bull who is trying to remember spring. He nevertheless made one marvellous, sudden, stooping stop.

Oh bring back yesterday, bid time return! What the very dickens and the devil of a cricketer Close ought to have been for England. The historians, in the future, will be puzzled about it all. Was it his own fault? Very possible, though others might also be to blame. Even now, from the shadows, if we really want to beat the West Indians next week, this dour, difficult and daring man might be recalled to the sunshine.

Oh bring back yesterday, bid time return! Alan Gibson, the most literary of cricket writers, was slightly misquoting a line from Shakespeare, from the scene in which Richard the Second, assembling his army on a Welsh beach, learns that the promised Welsh forces have been told he is dead and have switched allegiance to his rival Bolingbroke, the future Henry the Fourth. The Earl of Salisbury breaks the fateful news to his king:

One day too late I fear me, noble lord,
Hath clouded all thy happy days on earth.
O call back yesterday, bid time return,
And thou shalt have twelve thousand fighting men.

One day too late. Such moments of ill fortune can turn the course of history, and ill fortune was never far from Close's lips whenever he told the story of his cricketing career. Was he as unlucky as he claimed? Was Richard the Second unlucky? Or did the fault, as Alan Gibson suggested, lie as much with himself?

The next day at Taunton, Close top-scored in the second innings, holding up the West Indian victory with an obdurate 40. It led Gibson to return to the theme of his England recall:

> The Somerset innings was dominated, morally even more than numerically, by the Old Bald Blighter. Several people who spoke to me appeared to think that, in suggesting his recall to the England team, I was making one of my little jokes. Not so. If I may purloin a phrase from Sir Neville Cardus, I would never dream of making a little joke about a Test match. I think in the present circumstances Close would be a rational selection. He might not be a success, his reflexes are slower, but he would die in the breach against the fast bowlers rather than run away.

Other cricket writers were less inclined to take the idea seriously. Some, in speculating on the team to be selected, did not mention him at all. With the all-rounder Greig going in at number six, there were five batting slots to fill, and the consensus was that the top four in the order would be John Edrich, Barry Wood, the uncapped Mike Brearley and David Steele, all of them well into their thirties. Only the 28-year-old Bob Woolmer, their choice at number five, offered anything resembling youth.

Those who addressed the possibility of Close's recall were without enthusiasm. The West Indies had just been badly beaten in Australia. Did England really need to react so strongly to the failure of their batsmen at Lord's? Michael Melford, cricket correspondent of the *Daily Telegraph*, thought not:

> To pick a 45-year-old batsman who has not played for England for nine years, apparently for the qualities of entrenchment which he demonstrated so stoutly this week, seems a defensive move smacking of apprehension and of panic – and premature panic at that.

John Woodcock, the cricket correspondent of *The Times*, used the same word 'panic':

If we were playing a single match, and playing it for our lives, it would make more sense to bring back Close. To start off a series of five matches by doing so would be a desperate measure. It would smack of panic. It could come to it later in the series, but only a Jeremiah would think so yet.

Fred Trueman, for twenty years Close's team-mate at Yorkshire, put it with trademark bluntness in the *Sunday People*:

Bringing him back to Test duty would be final proof that our international reputation has sunk to rock bottom.

But Brian Close was not one day too late. The timing of his Taunton batting was perfect, and he had one advocate, the most important of all: the England captain Tony Greig, a man who, like Close, had a maverick streak. The previous summer he had taken over from Mike Denness after the first Test against Australia, and at his first selection meeting he had successfully argued for the inclusion of Northamptonshire's David Steele, a silver-haired, bespectacled figure whose guts against the fast bowling of Lillee and Thomson had made him the highly unexpected success story of the year. He had so caught the public imagination that he was voted the BBC's Sports Personality of the Year, only the second cricketer after Jim Laker in 1956 to achieve the accolade.

Greig had a theory about beating the West Indians. He suspected that their morale would collapse if they did not achieve early success. Using an ill-chosen word, the racial implications of which were heightened by his South African accent, he said: "If the West Indians get on top they are magnificent cricketers, but if they're down they grovel."

His best strategy for making them 'grovel', he reckoned, was to blunt their fast bowling at the start of the series, then get on top as their spirits wilted. So he was not looking for flashy batsmen at the top of the order; he wanted hard men who would get behind the ball and not be intimidated. And who better for the task than that old warrior Brian Close, a man whose mad bravery was legendary on the county circuit?

At the selection meeting at Bristol Greig argued his case forcefully. His four fellow selectors were Alec Bedser (the Chairman), Ken Barrington, the umpire Charlie Elliott and Sir Leonard Hutton, the Yorkshireman who had captained England to victory in two Ashes series in the 1950s. Normally Greig would have had to win over two of his four fellow selectors, but Hutton was away on business in Germany and the casting vote in the event of a 2-2 split lay with the captain.

Had Hutton been present, Greig would have had a formidable opponent. A cautious and conservative man, Hutton was not over-impressed by Greig's self-confidence nor his accent. "He was a little too sure of himself for my comfort," he wrote some years later. "I helped to make him captain, and it did not take me long to realise my mistake." It seems that at selection meetings Greig was not inclined to show much respect for the combined wisdom of his fellow selectors – or, as Hutton put it, "I suspected that he regarded us as surplus to his requirements."

Hutton went back a long way with Close; he admired Brian's determination and spirit but knew he had never quite reached the highest class. To bring him back at the age of 45, in preference to a younger man, was in his view a thoroughly backward move.

With Hutton absent and the casting vote in the hands of the captain, Greig had only to persuade one of the others, and it seems that he managed to win over Ken Barrington, a contemporary of Close who had witnessed the Yorkshireman's bravery in Test match battles of old. Hutton was 'more than a little surprised' when he heard what had happened, while a perturbed Bedser immediately set to work to get the regulations changed. In future he as Chairman would have the casting vote.

Once more, in a career that had been dogged by controversy, Close was dividing opinion.

In those days players learned of their selection by tuning in to the lunchtime news on the radio. Brian Close was staying with the Somerset team in a Portsmouth hotel when he got a call from Brian Scovell of the *Daily Mail*, asking him how he felt about his England recall. It took him by surprise. If he was to play for England again, he had always assumed it was to be brought back as captain, but Tony Greig's appointment had ended that dream.

"You know, lad," he told his Somerset team-mate Peter Robinson on the way to the ground. "It's the first year I haven't put the dates in me diary."

John Woodcock saluted his courage.

No one has ever questioned his talent; only his judgment has been in doubt. He is absolutely fearless, the sort of man to have won a Victoria Cross had he ever gone into battle.

Nevertheless he was appalled by the decision:

> What a tribute to his indestructibility his selection is, what an indictment of the younger school, what a step in the wrong direction, what an act of despair.
>
> I am not sure who will be laughing loudest at the moment – the West Indians, for having prompted such hysteria among the English, or the Australians, on hearing of England's reaction to their dilemma. Close and the selectors may yet laugh last. I only hope so. If he does succeed, and he has the character to do so, a film will have to be made of his astonishing career.

'The Life of Brian', perhaps, though that title would be taken by the end of the decade.

Michael Melford in the *Daily Telegraph* was also scathing of the decision, saying it 'smacks of defeatism, panic and apprehension which can only boost the opposition's suspect morale'. He ended his withering verdict: 'Colin Cowdrey at 43 must be wondering why he retired so early.'

Tony Greig, never shy with his opinions, countered their scepticism: "Close is a man of proud character and technique, and this is what we need. If we can stop the West Indians getting off to a good start, then I think we can go on to trounce them."

Two years later, in his autobiography *I Don't Bruise Easily*, Brian Close, a more sensitive man than his tough exterior let on, recalled his feelings as he made his way to Trent Bridge:

> The press reaction was either lukewarm or downright critical, so the pressure was on. Once again I was on a hiding to nothing. If I succeeded I would be regarded only as a temporary measure for this series and one who had been introduced only because I didn't get out of the way of fast bowling. If I failed ... I honestly dare not think of it. I so desperately wanted to do well – desperately, awfully, terribly. My career had to end shortly, and after all those years of knocking this was my chance to go out at the top.
>
> No one will ever know just how much it meant to me to do well, but I think a few people have some idea.

So began another chapter, almost the last, of Brian Close's life in cricket.

2

COULD NOT BE BEATEN

Closey was a funny man – a brilliant genius and thick at the
same time.

Ken Biddulph was not one of the greats of the game. He was a good
enough fast-medium bowler to hold his place in the Somerset side for
three or four summers in the late 1950s and early 1960s, but nothing
more. He was, however, a sharp-eyed observer of his fellow cricketers, as
bowlers often are, and in later life he became an outstanding coach.

It was in this last role that I came to know him, attending a group
net that he ran each Friday afternoon in winter, at the Stratford Park
Leisure Centre in Stroud. I was 45 years old when I started with him,
wondering how much longer my mediocre talent would yield enough
runs and wickets to make my cricketing days worthwhile. So effectively
did he fine-tune my game that twenty years later I was still playing, still
looking forward to every game.

Ken did much more than that for me, though. He inspired me to
become a cricket writer. After every net I would stay behind to listen
to the stories of his days as a county cricketer, and I was enchanted. He
had a way of bringing alive the players of his time, not just as cricketers
but as characters, and that human side of the game was so much a part
of what I enjoyed about playing – the test of character, the revelation of
character, the quietly building tension, the humour.

In the autumn of 1996 I found myself wondering if I could make some
sort of article out of Ken's stories. Would anybody publish it? Maybe not.
But I came up with the idea that I would get him to talk about the best
game of cricket he ever played, and I would recreate it as a short story,
weaving his voice into the narrative of the match.

At the Old Fleece Inn, south of Stroud, we settled at a wooden table
with our pints of beer, and I turned on my cassette recorder. Little did
I imagine that the article would become a chapter in a book, that the
book – *Runs in the Memory: County Cricket in the 1950s* – would catch

the fancy of so many readers and that I would become the writer of more than twenty cricket books, the publisher of many more. If Ken had not been such a good raconteur, none of it would have happened.

Ken chose a match at Bath in August 1959, Somerset versus Yorkshire. Yorkshire were top of the County Championship table, hoping to end Surrey's seven-year reign, and Somerset, unfancied Somerset, had not beaten them since 1903. Those were days when the counties had distinctive identities, and none was more distinctive than Yorkshire, with its proud tradition of playing only Yorkshire-born men. Ken caught the feeling of that perfectly.

> Yorkshire were a hard team to play. The atmosphere was always a bit different from other counties. We used to laugh at the way they all strutted around like they were something special, but you couldn't help having respect for that attitude, that self-belief. They could not be beaten.
>
> When you went in to bat, they never used to look you in the eye. They used to look at your boots, as if to say, "What are you doing? How dare you come out here!" That was the impression they gave. You felt very much unwanted.

I had the relevant *Wisden Almanack* with me: 'At Bath, August 19, 20, 21. Somerset won by 16 runs.'

> In those days it was a great achievement to beat Yorkshire. It was the only occasion I was ever on the winning side against them. And I was awarded my county cap at the close. So that makes it memorable for me, too.

Ken happily talked about the characters in the match, notably Somerset's Bill Alley, the ageing Australian who never stopped talking. But the first person to come up in our conversation was Brian Close, who hit a century in Yorkshire's first innings, as my *Wisden* confirmed: 'D.B. Close c McCool b Biddulph 128'. Ken began by describing what it was like to bowl to the left-handed Yorkshireman:

> I never put anything near his legs. As soon as you put the ball anywhere near his legs, he was whipping you round square leg, behind square, anywhere on the on-side. "If you bowl at me legs, lad, it's got to go."

Then, noticing Ken's contribution with the bat – 'c Binks b Close 0' – I asked him about Close the bowler:

> Unpredictable. Sometimes he would bowl rubbish, sometimes he would bowl very well. Closey was a competitor. He was always trying to take wickets. Sometimes he'd lose patience with the rest of the bowlers. "Give me the ball, I'll take some wickets." He liked to put a few round the bat, probably more than he ought to have.

And as a character?

> A great opponent. If you played against Closey, you knew you were going to have a tough game. Later on, when he went to Somerset, he did their young players a hell of a lot of good. He taught them how to play cricket, how to really play cricket. Before that, I think they were playing at it a bit. There'd never been a lot of discipline at Somerset.
>
> The thing about Closey is that, if you talked to him or listened to him, he was never wrong about anything. You tended to get into the habit of believing everything he said was right. Most of it was, mind you, but not all of it.

On the last afternoon of the match Yorkshire, chasing 255 for victory, were 133 for two, with Brian Close and Ken Taylor looking in control. Then, with the third-day pitch showing signs of wear, wickets started to fall, most of them to Somerset's off-spinner Brian Langford, who regularly enjoyed success at Bath.

Ken Biddulph did not have precise memories of this passage of play, but my plan was to weave in newspaper reports and extracts from books. I found to my delight that the game had been recalled not only in *I Don't Bruise Easily* but by the Yorkshire captain Ronnie Burnet in *Champion Times*, a book compiled by Don Mosey.

Burnet, a 40-year-old chemical engineer, was some way short of the standard required of a first-class cricketer, but he had been appointed captain of the county the previous year, partly because he was the only available amateur (and Yorkshire had to have an amateur captain), partly because he had done well bringing on the young players in the second eleven and partly to introduce a greater discipline into the team. In Burnet's first season in charge Johnny Wardle, the great left-arm slow bowler, had become so frustrated by what he saw as his skipper's tactical naïvety that he spoke his mind too plainly and found himself sacked. Yorkshire ended the summer in 11th place in the championship, their lowest position ever; yet now, with a younger team pulling together, they were on the verge of winning the title.

The game was on a knife-edge, and Burnet was not happy when, in the cramped Bath pavilion, Close forcibly argued that the best way to counter Langford's spin was to plunge the front foot forward and sweep him. It was a shot that Close himself deployed throughout his career and, as Burnet observed, he had some well-publicised disasters with it:

> It might be a touch uncharitable to recall one or two occasions when Closey himself had employed the sweep with a spectacular lack of success! The fact was that up to that time the only first-class player to play the shot with any degree of consistent success was Denis Compton. As a "business" stroke, the sweep was virtually unknown, unlike today. So Closey gave us all a demonstration, there and then in the dressing-room, on how to execute it ... the art of sweeping.
>
> We needed to score 255 on this crumbling pitch and three of us (including, I am ashamed to say, myself) were bowled while sweeping, and we lost by 16 runs. I am convinced, to this day, that if we had batted in an orthodox manner we should have won.

Needless to say, Brian Close put it differently:

> We were still in with a chance of winning when Ronnie Burnet went in at number ten. I said, "For God's sake, get your left foot down the pitch and hit Langford anywhere between mid-on and fine leg. He's hardly likely to get you lbw, and you can pull him anywhere in that arc with reasonable safety." Well, Ronnie got his leg down the pitch all right but somewhere outside the line of leg stump! The whole lot went over – and he blamed me. "You told me to do that," he complained.

There I was, down in the West Country, writing a short piece with Ken Biddulph. Little did I comprehend how much this all mattered to folk in Yorkshire.

For *Runs in the Memory* I met up with old cricketers of the 1950s, and I did the same in a sequel on the 1960s. One was Don Wilson, Yorkshire's slow left-arm bowler in the 1959 match in Bath.

Not long before I visited Don at Ampleforth College, where he coached, he had attended the funeral of David Bairstow, the Yorkshire and England wicket-keeper who had shocked the cricket world by taking his own life. Don told me how during the wake he had approached Brian. "Here, Closey, have you seen this book *Runs in the Memory*? It's got about that game we lost at Bath, when you had us all playing the sweep shot."

In the midst of this most mournful of occasions Close responded by launching into a loud justification of his strategy, complete with foot movements and the waving of an imaginary bat, demonstrating how none of them had played the shot properly. "What I said was to get your foot across like this," he insisted, lunging his leg forward as the room around him fell silent. "Not down the line like this."

The day after the game in Bath Yorkshire were playing in Bristol so some of them, including Close, stayed for drinks with their Somerset conquerors. The scene in the bar provided the final paragraph of my account of the match:

> It was a wonderful opportunity for Brian Close to talk through the game, to explain to the Somerset lads how his batsmen could have swept Brian Langford with ease, how the victory was there for the taking. Yorkshire have been beaten after 56 years, and Ken has a county cap to add to the glow of these post-match drinks. "But after half an hour of listening to Closey, we thought we were the ones who'd lost. They were unbeatable. Yorkshire had lost the match, but he didn't believe it. They could not be beaten."

'They could not be beaten' – that became the title of the chapter. It was true of all the Yorkshire cricketers, but of none was it more so than Brian Close.

I toured the country writing these two books about county cricket, interviewing dozens of former players. Several of them chose matches against Yorkshire, especially ones when they achieved victories. These rare triumphs stood out as special in their memory, often rich with incidents and characters, and no character caught my imagination more than Brian Close.

He had fascinated me in the 1960s, when I was a young follower of the game. His daring innings against the West Indians at Lord's in 1963, when he had countered the high pace of Wes Hall by coming down the wicket to him and taking repeated blows on the body, was the stuff of schoolboy fiction. Then came his hugely successful stint as England captain and his controversial sacking – and, years later, that most romantic of recalls to the England team. Now he was being brought to life as a human being by his fellow cricketers – as a brilliant, brave, yet flawed personality, a genius and thick at the same time as Ken so beautifully put it.

The stories kept coming, and always with the observation, "There's no malice in him." Roy Booth, the Yorkshireman who had left to play at Worcester, chose a victory over his old county, having some fun at the expense of Fred Trueman and Brian Close. When I sent him the chapter for approval, he was anxious about Fred's reaction, knowing how the fast bowler could breathe menace when he took offence. "I don't know what Fred is going to make of it," he said, rather dreading the phone call. He had no such worries about Brian Close.

By the summer of 2001 I had set my heart on writing a book about Brian. My idea was to capture him through a series of matches, recalled by other people, not to speak to him at all, not to get drawn into the world of his justifications and excuses. Ken Taylor, who had provided superb illustrations for my first two books, thought it a grand idea, as did the sports writer Frank Keating who shared my opinion that Brian was the greatest character in post-war English cricket.

To my dismay I discovered that Alan Hill, a well-established cricketing biographer, was starting work on a book with Brian. So I set the project aside. I return to it now, not to write a definitive biography, just to share my take on Brian. Somehow I have never been able to let go of my need to write about him.

*

I met Brian a few times over the years, but I cannot claim I knew him well. In many ways he is most alive for me through the stories others have told me about him. They were all told with great affection for the man and mostly with admiration. Yet almost always there was this streak of daftness. There is no better word. For an intelligent man, one who if he had not been a sportsman would have studied mathematics at Cambridge or medicine at Leeds, a captain with great tactical acumen, he could be surprisingly daft.

In 2006, following Fred Trueman's death, Yorkshire County Cricket Club initiated a project to film interviews with their senior surviving players. At the insistence of Bob Appleyard, with whom I had recently written a book, I was asked to conduct the interviews for eleven films – nine with living subjects, plus tributes to Len Hutton and Fred Trueman.

First up was Brian Close, after a lunch at which we had celebrated the centenary of George Hirst's unique feat of scoring 2,000 runs and taking 200 wickets in a season. I had written a little monograph on the subject, and it fell to me to make the speech at the end of the meal. I closed by reading the words Hirst had spoken from the balcony at Scarborough on the occasion of his retirement from the game:

> What can you have better than a nice green field, with the wickets set up, and to go out and do the best for your side? I leave first-class cricket to those who have got to come. I hope they'll have the pleasure in it that I have had.

In the lift going up to the room in which our interview was to be filmed, Brian asked, "Did George Hirst really say those words? I must admit, lad, there was a tear in my eye when you read them." It was the perfect start for an afternoon together, getting him in the right mood to reflect on his life, which he did with feeling. At one point, when he came to his sacking as Yorkshire captain, we had to pause the camera for him to wipe the tears from his eyes and to recompose himself. At heart, beneath the image of the tough competitor, he was an emotional man. I liked that about him.

Geoff Cope, who joined the Yorkshire team as a young off-spinner in Brian's last years with the club, had a similar experience when he spoke at a dinner in 2001 to celebrate the 70th birthdays of Trueman and Close. With his wife June ill, Geoff took along his son Andrew, who had no interest whatsoever in cricket.

> I said to him, "You know Fred Trueman?" "I've heard of him." "And Brian Close?" "No." "Well, if I put it politely, he's probably the hardest man I ever played with."
>
> I got up to speak. I did Frederick Sewards Trueman. Then Brian. I told Arthur Milton's story about his time with Brian at Arsenal: how they got Brian to practise heading the ball down and in the next match he headed the ball so far down it bounced over the top of the goal. Then how he was a legend with Yorkshire.

"We used to look at the fixtures, and we'd say, 'Somerset, that's two wins for us.' Then he went down there, and suddenly two wins weren't taken for granted." I went on a bit.

When I sat down, Andrew said to me, "I thought you said he was hard. He's been crying through most of your speech."

"Physical courage is easy," Brian once said to the *Yorkshire Evening Post's* John Callaghan. "I don't feel the pain because I'm so totally immersed in what I am doing. Mental courage is different. I get embarrassed by sympathy. It's sympathy that makes you soft."

Our filmed interview lasted an hour and a half, and it required no editing – though we could have done with his using the phrase 'no messing' less frequently. "No messing, they were a great side ... No messing, he was a fine bowler." He was on top form.

Watching the film now, I am struck by his accurate command of the details of his career, how he knew exactly the dates of all his infrequent Test appearances. I am also struck by his class consciousness. I have heard old amateurs distinguish themselves from the professionals by using first names for their fellow 'gentlemen', surnames for the 'players', but only Brian have I heard do this in reverse. It was Les, Raymond, Wes when he spoke of Les Jackson, Ray Illingworth, Wes Hall, but when it came to the amateurs it was Cowdrey, Dexter, May.

Brian attended the launch of the first set of films at Headingley. He had discharged himself early from hospital, and during the taking of a group photograph his mobile phone went off three times, each of the calls from a bookmaker. A short film had been compiled, containing extracts from the interviews, and it included a section in which Vic Wilson, Brian's predecessor as Yorkshire captain, talked about the secret of close-to-the-wicket catching, something at which he, like Brian, was a master. He compared the markedly different experiences of standing close to the bat when Appleyard and Close were bowling:

> You have to have faith in your bowler. With Bob Appleyard you had the confidence to be ready to move, to anticipate when the batsman was picking the bat up. But fielding like that when Brian Close was bowling, it frightened you to death. You wouldn't know if it was going to be a long hop or a full toss.

I was too far away from Brian to observe his face as Vic spoke the words.

Two years later I returned for the next set of interviews, and Brian appeared again, this time contributing to the tributes to Len Hutton and Fred Trueman. Despite a sprinkling of no messings, he spoke with thoughtfulness and feeling.

Another six years on, in June 2014, writing a history of the County Championship, I arranged to spend a morning with Brian at Headingley, in the Hawke Suite where the club's dignitaries watched the cricket. He took me through his years as county captain, explaining how, in the seasons when Ronnie Burnet and Vic Wilson led the side, he had made most of the critical decisions in the field.

The history books record that Ronnie Burnet led the team to the title in 1959, Vic Wilson to two titles in the next three years, then Brian to four in the following six, making an impressive total of seven Yorkshire championships in ten years. Brian, however, saw it differently. "I did all bloody seven really," he told me emphatically before reliving once more the pain of his sacking at the end of 1970.

Throughout the two hours we sat together, there loitered in the background, occasionally eavesdropping our conversation, Geoffrey Boycott, Brian's successor as Yorkshire captain. A man rang me once, ordering a book, and he told me how as a medic he had once had to administer an anaesthetic to Brian Close. "Do you have any allergies?" he asked, only to receive the gruff reply, "Just the one: Geoffrey Boycott."

When Yorkshire celebrated its 150th anniversary at an evening at the Crucible Theatre in Sheffield, Geoffrey Boycott was Master of Ceremonies. His appointment as Yorkshire President led to a shunning of the event by almost all the players of the 1960s, yet entirely typically Brian turned up with his wife Vivien, loyal to the club, not one to embroil himself in the row. At one stage, when Geoffrey was explaining to his interviewer Michael Vaughan how he came to open the batting, a loud voice came from the dark bowels of the audience: "No, that's not what I said, Geoffrey. I said if you didn't bloody open, you'd be twelfth bloody man."

After Brian left the Hawke Suite at the end of our session, Geoffrey approached me. "You're not going to print all that rubbish, are you? I'll put you straight why he lost the captaincy."

"No, I don't want that," I said. "I'd rather you told me your view of the current state of the County Championship."

"Right, we'll do that then," Geoffrey said, and I heard no more about the 'rubbish' Brian Close had told me. Nevertheless this book will not duck the circumstances which led to Brian's loss of the captaincy.

Later that month I was back in Yorkshire for Bob Appleyard's 90th birthday, which Brian and Vivien attended. It had been raining in the morning, and we were told not to sit on the sofas that had been shifted into the garden, to make room in Bob's daughter's house for the forty or so of us to sit and eat. I hardly need to complete the story. I went outside to find Brian, sitting on his own on one of the sofas, puffing at a cigarette. I went to sit alongside him, but the sofa was much too wet.

He died of lung cancer the following year, at the age of 84.

*

I return to Brian now, more than 27 years after that session with Ken Biddulph in the Old Fleece Inn. Yorkshire cricket has moved on – moved on in ways that Brian would have struggled with. Yet my fondness for him remains undimmed.

I remember, when I first read his autobiography, being struck by the amount of pain it revealed. The title was *I Don't Bruise Easily*. That fitted his public image. Brian wanted to call it *I Took the Blows*, but the publishers over-ruled him.

> For what is a man, what has he got?
> If not himself, then he has naught.
> To say the things he truly feels
> And not the words of one who kneels.
> The record shows I took the blows
> And did it my way.

Brian, as a true-born Yorkshireman, never knelt, and he took repeated blows. He was left with plenty of unhealed scars.

No messing. Brian Close was, in the words of Frank Keating, 'the most appealing and exceptionally talented' of cricketers, his career full of 'zany gusto, glooms, glories and cock-eyed courage'. His is a story like no other.

3

TOO YOUNG?

The first time I saw Brian, I said: "This is the best 18-year-old I've ever seen." And I don't think I've seen anything since to change my mind. He should never have been out of the England side. If he hadn't gone to Australia when he did, he'd have got in the England side and stayed in. That Australian tour did him in. The promotion was too sudden.

That was the view of the wise old owl Ted Lester, who witnessed Brian Close's long Yorkshire career, first as team-mate, then as county scorer. And Brian himself did not disagree. "I was too young," he said in the interview we filmed. "I hadn't had enough experience. I was a naïve young lad."

His selection in 1976, at the age of 45, divided opinion. And so did his selection in 1950, at the age of 19, to tour Australia. Even when events were entirely beyond his control, it seemed that his life was destined to be mired in controversy.

In the summer of 1950 Signalman D.B. Close was in the middle of the obligatory 18 months of National Service. He had had a magnificent summer of cricket in 1949, becoming the youngest man ever to do each of three things: to achieve the season's double of 1,000 runs and 100 wickets, to make a Test appearance for England and to win a Yorkshire cap. Yet in the following summer, stationed in Catterick, he hardly played any first-class cricket.

Not long before his selection he had turned out for Leeds against Hull in a league match at Headingley. According to a Hull man who wrote to the *Yorkshire Evening Post*, he had bowled badly, taking only one wicket and being hit for 21 runs in one over:

> Close is a fine player with a great future, but at the moment he lacks regular practice. To ask him to tour this winter is not fair, either to himself or to the man who may have been chosen in his place.

To add fuel to the debate, his selection took place in the middle of a fast-developing international crisis. The Communist regime in North Korea had invaded the South, the United States had gone to war in support of the South, and the British government on 26 July announced that it was sending troops, with Prime Minister Attlee appealing to young men to enlist. Yet five days later, with the country filled with foreboding about another war, it was reported that Close, an able-bodied soldier, was to be allowed seven months of leave to play cricket.

Many, keen for England to do well in Australia, welcomed the flexibility shown in making an exception for Close. Others, believing in one rule for all, did not, sending angry letters of protest to the newspapers.

'Here we are at war! Yet a country which is shortly to send troops to die on the battlefields of Korea is calmly discussing, through responsible and accredited bodies, the propriety of releasing a 19-year-old (presumably hale and hearty) to play cricket!' wrote one man. Another called the decision 'a gross insult to the rest of the National Service men'. A third insisted: 'No favours should be shown to any boy called up under National Service. Let Brian Close do his time out, the same as every other mother's son.'

It was ironic that none of this, neither the glories of his summer of 1949 nor his selection for Australia, would have happened at all if an army doctor in February 1949, when Brian turned 18, had passed him fit for an immediate call-up.

He had left Aireborough Grammar School the previous summer, with his headmaster keen for him to go to university, either to study mathematics, his best subject, or medicine, his own preference. National Service had to be completed first, making university a distant prospect, and his teenage passion for sport led him to sign as a professional footballer with Leeds United, spending the winter playing in their youth and reserve teams.

At this stage professional cricket was not on offer, though he was on the county's radar, attending nets the previous winter and being selected for a 2nd XI game at Worksop. The match did not, however, advance his cause. Rain arrived on the first afternoon with Yorkshire only two wickets down, and he never set foot on the field of play. The following week he went on a southern tour with the Yorkshire Federation side, a youth team that also included Freddie Trueman and Ray Illingworth. In the last of their three two-day games he scored a confident century against a young

Sussex side, an innings which had one reporter comparing him with a dash of hyperbole to the great left-hander Frank Woolley.

When he reported for his National Service medical in February, he was carrying a slight football injury. "We'll delay your call-up a month or two, give it a chance to get right," the doctor said. "We don't want you joining when you're half-fit."

The injury cleared up within days, but the follow-up medical did not come as promised. So in May, when the football season was over, he was available to play league cricket for Guiseley. Then came the invitation to join the Yorkshire team for their games against the universities at Cambridge and Oxford. Resting several senior players, they were taking the opportunity to look at three youngsters; Frank Lowson, a 22-year-old who had completed his National Service, and two 18-year-olds, both born in February 1931, D.B. Close and F.S. Trueman. The *Wisden Almanack*, in a never-lived-down mistake, reported: 'Yorkshire gave a trial to three young players, Lowson an opening batsman, Close an all-rounder and Trueman a spin bowler.'

Freddie Trueman, a raw fast bowler, was a miner's son from South Yorkshire, with a home life that was rough-and-ready and at times chaotic. He had left school at 14 and already gone through several jobs. Brian, by contrast, was a weaver's son from the West Riding, one of six children in a close-knit, stable family, and had enjoyed the advantages of a grammar school education. They say Fred's mother had 'something of the gypsy' about her, whereas Brian's had aspirations, taking trouble to speak well and, within her means, to dress smartly. Cricket would throw Fred and Brian together for twenty years, but they were never to become bosom pals. Their differences were clear to Brian from the start:

> I was a very shy youngster. I had hardly spoken to a girl by the time I was sixteen – and the only thing I knew about the opposite sex was that, as far as I could make out, they didn't play cricket or football. Fred wasn't exactly my cup of tea. I don't suppose then that he knew any more than I did, but he was, shall we say, a little less shy.

During the first years of his cricket, before their houses had telephones, Brian wrote regular letters to his best friend from school days, John Anderson. 'Just a few lines,' his letters would often start, though they were rarely short. It was clear from the letter he wrote from Cambridge that he was experiencing a world well beyond any he had known: plenty of food at a time when wartime rationing was still in force ('You ought to have seen what some of the lads, Alec Coxon in particular, ate'), 'grand' living in a hotel ('especially when you have a very nice chambermaid to bring you a cup of tea and a paper in the morning'), and the 'lovely' scenery when they walked around on the first evening ('lawns, tennis courts and the colleges themselves were a sight to see').

He shared a room with Frank Lowson, quickly forming a bond with the older newcomer. There were trips to the cinema and games of snooker in the hotel. Brian may have been shy in the company of the Yorkshire team but, writing to his friend back in Yorkshire, he was not slow to boast when he got the chance:

> Oh! of course I won, I beat him three times running, and then at nine o'clock we retired to our room and I had a lovely hot bath and now here I am writing to you.

A brief profile in the *Yorkshire Evening Post* told of his father Harry's fine record in club cricket and quoted his old headmaster, Mr McDonald: "Brian has a first-class brain and could have gone to Oxford or Cambridge, not with the Yorkshire team but as an undergraduate."

He had a decent first game. He scored 28 in his only knock and, with medium-fast swing, took two wickets in each innings, though it seems he could have had at least two more victims:

> I bowled Dewes with a beauty and then in the same over Halliday missed Doggart in the slips in one of the simplest catches I've seen, right down his 'cake hole', and then the following over Trueman missed Morris so that if I'd had any luck at all I would have had three wickets for about ten runs that night.

He did better still at Oxford, taking four wickets in each innings, mainly with off-spin, and scoring 22 and 36. Along with Lowson but not Trueman, he remained in the side for the final game of the tour, his first County Championship match, against Somerset at Wells. There, bringing home to him the speed of his cricketing progress, he found himself playing for the first time with the great Len Hutton, as he reported in his next letter to his friend:

> Frank and I have just been introduced to the one and only Len. He seems a very nice fellow, quiet, not too talkative. We

spoke to him for quite a while about cricket and who we had played for.

The summer of 1949 brought week after week of fine weather, with more dry days than any other summer in the 20th century, and Hutton was in golden form. In June he hit 1,294 runs, an all-time record for one calendar month, and in August he became only the third man – after Ranjitsinhji and Herbert Sutcliffe – to hit 1,000 runs in two separate months. In all, he scored 3,429 runs, batting on occasions with Close as his admiring partner. Almost sixty years later, when we made the film tribute to Hutton, Brian arrived at Headingley more casually dressed than any of the other contributors. There was no casualness, though, about what he sat down and said:

> I think the greatest influence I ever had with my cricket was playing with and watching Sir Leonard Hutton. He was magnificent, the best batsman I ever saw.
>
> There's the saying that it's bowlers who win matches, but in 1949 he won games for Yorkshire. I had the opportunity of batting with him a few times that summer, and I saw his ability to move into the right place and steer the ball where he wanted it to go. He had a wonderful defence, and he knew what he could do with a delivery. He was a great cover-driver; that was his most wonderful shot. He could play it late, and it would go square; he could play it early, and it would go through extra cover. If you were batting with him at the other end, you couldn't help but be influenced.
>
> He'd cover up, and at the last moment he'd shape a little thing. And if the bowling was good, he'd get a one to get to the other end. *(A cackling burst of laughter)* That's what you call a good batsman.

It was often remarked that Frank Lowson bore the mark of Hutton in his strokeplay, but the influence of Hutton on Brian Close's batting was less obvious to the eye. Close was physically mature at the age of 18, a tall man with a powerful pair of arms, but unlike Hutton he was happy to take risks, to put the ball in the air when he struck it. This he did most notably in an innings of 88 not out in late May, when he hit the Essex leg-spinner Peter Smith back over his head and all the way onto the roof of the rugby football stand at Headingley. The towering strike astonished Essex's young amateur Trevor Bailey, who for many years believed Close to be the best young cricketer he had ever seen, a view he held till 1990 when he first set eyes on the 17-year-old Sachin Tendulkar.

Jim Kilburn, the magisterial cricket correspondent of the *Yorkshire Post*, was impressed by this innings, not only for the power and the quality of its scoring shots but for the calm that followed each boundary, with no youthful 'rush of blood to the head':

> Close has cricket born in him and is a remarkably mature young man. It is a long time since anyone looked so promising, although Denis Compton established himself quickly. Close has had a more immediate success in first-class cricket than any other young player for a long time.

After just six matches, with only that one fifty to his name and one five-wicket haul, he was selected for the summer's first Test Trial, the North versus the South at Edgbaston. Here, despite scoring only two runs and not taking a wicket, *Wisden* picked out his 'obvious all-round ability' for special mention.

In those first summers after the six-year-long Second World War the cupboard of young English players was almost empty. In the winter of 1946/47 England went to Australia with an ageing side and lost 3-0; in the summer of 1948, still with a side most of whom had established themselves before the war, they lost 4-0. The country, suffering the privations of rationing, was desperate for new heroes, and the young Brian Close looked certain to be one.

He wrote in his autobiography that the English County Championship at that time was 'the hardest school in the world' where he was 'learning everything from scratch'. Yet, when I asked him in the film interview whether he was conscious of the big step up from school and club cricket, he replied: "No, it was just a great thrill. I just enjoyed it. Every single moment was marvellous."

His letters certainly convey that joy. He marvelled at Lord's: the rubberised floor in the pavilion, the pictures everywhere on the walls and the quality of the practice wickets. He told of fan letters from 'ardent' female admirers. He was amazed by Denis Compton's approachability: 'He's quite a cheerful chap ... He's always coming over and talking to you, you know just friendly ... I got quite pally with him.' He described the sights he saw when on the Sunday he and Frank Lowson walked all round the capital. They started at eleven in the morning and, with

Brian's eyes agog with it all, they did not stop till six: 'Frank was on his knees long before four o'clock but I kept dragging him on.' He was in dreamland, on a journey that was introducing him to worlds far beyond his family's crowded council house in West Yorkshire. All summer he collected autographs in two books, one for his friend, one for himself.

Yorkshire's schedule was relentless. There were 26 three-day championship matches, and in the gaps between them there were always fixtures: the two universities, the touring New Zealanders, MCC, a Minor Counties XI, the Army, Scotland, even a trip to Dublin. After eight weeks in the team, Brian had had only one three-day rest, and he had passed 600 runs and 60 wickets.

In early July, against Surrey at Bradford, he had his best game yet, taking nine wickets in the match and hitting his second fifty for the county, an exhilarating 66 in just an hour. Jim Kilburn called the knock 'good and gallant cricket'; Brian relived the thrill of it in a letter to his pal:

> I went nice and slowly for about four or five overs, then they put Laker on at the Pavilion End. His first ball, a half volley, went straight back into the pavilion, his second and third went to square leg for fours but, anyway, he steadied himself for the rest of his short spell. Then Parker came on and he sent me a half volley which I hit over his head for a four. He evidently thought it was just a flash in the pan. He laughed when their skipper said "Have we to have a man behind?" Next ball I blocked and then the third ball I hit him clean into the pavilion or just in front of it. You ought to have seen his face, and then he quickly despatched two of his men to parade in front of the wall.
>
> Well I thought I had better not do that again so I remained quiet for a while until I got to the other end against Eric Bedser. I got my 50 with a hook off him and then I hit him for a six over by the football offices and dressing rooms. That completed my knock because somehow I hit one into someone's hands and unfortunately this someone wasn't in the crowd.

Was he becoming swollen-headed, an accusation often aimed at successful young sportsmen in those years, or was he simply a gauche teenager amazed at his own success? "I never got big-headed or anything like that," he said firmly in our filmed interview, but unfortunately his youthful exuberance led to that being said of him.

His letter then recounted the detail of his wickets before reporting a conversation with Bill Bowes, the former Yorkshire and England bowler who was now a cricket writer.

> Bill was saying to me "Do you think you can bowl New Zealand out? Would you like to play for England?" I don't know what I said but anyway he said "You'll probably be in the Gents v Players match and it will depend on that."

The annual Gentlemen/Players fixture at Lord's, pitting the best amateurs against the professionals, was a prestigious event, a game played in front of the selectors that was thought to test the big-match temperament of the 22 chosen men. Among the professionals it was seen as a great honour to represent all those who earned their living from the game, and that honour came to Brian very young.

In the midst of all this, the issue of Brian's deferred National Service reared its head. With all Yorkshire willing the youngster to a unique first-season double, a Bradford MP Maurice Webb, Chairman of the Labour Party nationally, lobbied successfully for his Service to start after the end of the season. By this reckoning he would miss the summer of 1950 but be back for the following one.

Brian rose to the occasion at Lord's superbly. He bowled his off-breaks with skill, he fielded splendidly in the covers, and he batted with a calm maturity. With the Players reduced to 63 for four in their first innings, he batted for two hours 40 minutes before being last man out for 65, the highest individual score of the match. The only blot on his card came when, on completing his fifty, he received a cheerful "Well done, Brian" from the Gentlemen's wicket-keeper Billy Griffith, who was at the time the Sussex Secretary, later to be a leading figure at Lord's.

"Thank you, Billy," Brian responded without any special thought, a reply that got him admonished some days later by Brian Sellers, the autocratic former Yorkshire captain who ruled the roost at Headingley for many years. "In future, when you address an amateur, you call him Mister."

Tom Graveney related a similar experience after greeting David Sheppard with the same familiarity, while Micky Stewart ran into trouble when he went to the Surrey Secretary's office to sign his first professional contract. Peter May, like Micky a public school boy, was in the room, and Micky greeted him cheerfully with a "Hallo, Peter". But, when he left, his "Cheerio, Peter" brought a sharp rebuke from the Secretary. "You mean Mister May. You're a professional cricketer now." Such was the strange world in which Brian was having to find his way.

Writing of that innings for the Players, Jim Kilburn was impressed by 'the calm way he tackled the astute bowling of Brown'. Freddie Brown was to prove a pivotal figure in the story of Brian Close's career. A 38-year-old all-rounder who played for England in the early 1930s, he had returned to full-time cricket that summer after an absence of ten years, lifting the fortunes of the lowly Northamptonshire as a larger-than-life captain.

With George Mann standing down as England captain, unable to spare time from his family's brewing business, Freddie Brown was a natural choice to take over for the next Test at Old Trafford, and he fulfilled Bill Bowes' prediction by ensuring that the twelve-man squad included the name of Close.

News of his selection reached Brian while he was watching a Sunday cricket match at Rawdon, his home village. He did not rush home, but when he did get there he ran into a world he had never experienced before, as he told his pal John:

> I don't think there was a minute when there wasn't a newspaper chap in our house until the last one left just after ten. Talk about cars, there were Buicks, Chryslers, Packards, queuing up to get in. Anyway, I survived it all, only to start again the next morning.
>
> I have had letters and telegrams galore, more than Len, thousands of them from all over the country. I have had an invitation from the Lord Mayor of Manchester to dine with him, an invitation to appear at a sportsmen's service in a church in Wakefield and to read a passage of scripture ...

His father, not one to get excited, told reporters that his son was only in the twelve which included another off-spinner, one already a Test cricketer. "He hasn't played for England yet," he said, trying to calm down the fuss. "It's unlikely they'll play both Brian and Laker."

On the day it was Jim Laker who missed out, making Brian the youngest cricketer ever to play for England. Initially, with cricket record-keeping in relative infancy, it was thought he was the youngest of any nationality, but it was soon discovered that the West Indian Derek Sealey had played against England at the age of 17 in 1930.

Also in the eleven, making his debut, was Derbyshire's fast bowler Les Jackson, a former miner with a low, slinging action. County cricketers of the 1950s all spoke of what a great bowler he was, moving the ball both ways off the pitch and rarely bowling a bad delivery. Yet he played just two Tests, this one in 1949 and a second at the age of 40 in 1961. Some say his low arm offended the purists at Lord's, others that his broad accent and his dour personality did not fit with their ideal of an England cricketer.

The four-match series against New Zealand was not a success. The matches, each scheduled for three days, all ended in draws, with a limited New Zealand side content not to lose. At Old Trafford, where the visitors batted through the first day to score 276 for eight off 123 overs, Brian bowled 25 tidy overs for 39 runs, taking one fortuitous wicket – from a full toss caught at deep square leg. "It was an accident," he admitted to a reporter. It was perhaps a harbinger of what was to come, as in time he would gain a reputation for the accidental full-tosses that took wickets.

Brian did not get to bat till the third morning when England were 419 for seven. After slow scoring early in the innings, they were now trying to force the game. "Have a look at a couple, then give it a go," Freddie Brown cheerfully instructed, and Brian did as he was told. He swung his bat at the third delivery, connecting well but not quite well enough to clear the fielder on the square-leg boundary. According to the older Brian, a man who was never slow to come up with mitigating factors, the match was using the full extent of the arena, "not just a reduced field as they do now", and the man who caught him, stretching up, was the tallest in the New Zealand side!

For the final Test at The Oval, Jim Laker took Brian's place, with the *Guardian*'s Denys Rowbotham not surprised by the decision: 'Though Close has shown remarkable promise this season, he did not flight the ball so deceptively for England as often he has done for his county. Close, indeed, scarcely presented New Zealand batsmen with a problem.'

Yet the season did not end in anti-climax. Yorkshire shared the County Championship title with Middlesex, and Brian, a vital part of the triumph, completed his historic double. In 31 first-class matches he hit 1,098 runs, with four fifties, and took 113 wickets, with six five-wicket hauls. There were also 19 catches. No one doubted that a great future lay ahead.

*

Brian played just once for Yorkshire in 1950 – in the Roses match held over the Whitsun weekend at Sheffield. These post-war contests between Yorkshire and Lancashire, played to packed crowds, were often grim, no-nonsense affairs, with the two teams more concerned to avoid defeat than to press for victory. Indeed, in the first 17 matches after the war, there were 16 draws and just one victory – by Lancashire in this 1950 game.

Geoff Edrich, the farmer's son from Norfolk, brother of the England cricketer Bill, joined Lancashire at the end of the war, having spent several harrowing years as a prisoner of the Japanese. He remembered his first coach at Old Trafford, Harry Makepeace, one of that rare band of sportsmen who played both football and cricket for England:

> He was like a father to the young players, a real good coach. He always said if a Lancashire player beat Yorkshire twice in his career, he'd done well. We beat them twice in my career there, but the one at Sheffield was my first. The turning point was the Brian Close run out.

Brian did not bowl well — 'unbelievably badly' was the verdict of the *Daily Telegraph*'s Jim Swanton – but he took seven wickets, and his 22 in the first innings was a handy contribution when they were looking to press on. But somehow he left behind only the memory of his second-innings dismissal.

In pursuit of 182 for victory, Yorkshire had slumped to 90 for five when he joined his captain Norman Yardley at the wicket. Fresh from his army cricket, he played without any Roses match inhibition and quickly the game seemed to be swinging back in Yorkshire's favour, as Swanton described:

> Young Close pulled his first ball, from outside the off stump, for a thrilling six to square leg, then sending Berry over extra cover to the boundary and giving his captain cause to hope that the improbable might after all be brought to pass.

Then, having raced to 17, came his downfall:

> Yardley declined a youthfully optimistic call for a second run. Close turned and could no doubt have made his ground, but slipped up badly (was he properly studded?) and a quick pick-up by Berry, followed by the slickest of returns, ran him out.

Was he properly studded? The answer was no, as they discovered in the pavilion after they had gone down to a 14-run defeat. The story goes that Norman Yardley, at the time captain of England, said nothing, preferring to write a note to Close after his return to barracks. The incident is often cited as an example to back up the commonly held view that Yardley was too nice a man to skipper a Yorkshire team with its share of awkward characters. He was certainly no Brian Sellers, the ferocious skipper of the side from 1933 to 1947.

According to Eddie Leadbeater, Yorkshire twelfth man that day, it was Sellers, by then a member of Yorkshire's Cricket Committee, who inspected Close's footwear. "If I had my way," he said in a moment of anger, "you wouldn't play again in this bloody team."

'I've never heard the end of the run out v Lancs,' Brian wrote to his friend John Anderson. 'Brian Sellers "had me on the carpet".'

Ted Lester never forgot his first encounter with Sellers, when he made his County Championship debut at Trent Bridge in 1946. He had heard the stories about him, and he was filled with trepidation when, before the start, he was summoned to the captain's room.

> For five minutes he talked to me like a father. I thought this can't be the same fella everyone's talking about, he's a different type altogether. It wasn't long before I realised the difference.
>
> We went out to field on the second day. I went down to third man, and he was in the gully. When a wicket fell, he beckoned me towards him. And I got the biggest mouthful I'd ever heard; I wasn't used to the sort of language that came forth. All that was wrong was that I was wearing my cap at an angle. "When you play for Yorkshire, you dress like a cricketer." It went on and on. When the batsman came in, I went back to third man. And I thought, if this is what you get for not wearing your cap straight, what will it be when I do something worse?

In time Ted Lester, the calmest of men, would forge a good relationship with Sellers, but Brian Close, himself a strong-minded character, would never find it easy.

Sellers and Brown were autocratic leaders, men who expected to get their own way. Norman Yardley and Billy Griffith were from a quieter school, more genial types. Yet in their different ways this quartet from the amateur class all played important roles in the unfolding dramas of Brian Close's long career.

*

Norman Yardley created a problem for the England selectors when he told them that business commitments prevented him from accepting their invitation to lead the side in Australia that winter. Their second choice, George Mann, gave the same reply, leaving them in a quandary. Should they opt for a young man, perhaps Hubert Doggart or Doug Insole, or an old one in Freddie Brown? Or even, though many trembled at the thought, turn to a professional as an interim measure, perhaps Tom Dollery whose ground-breaking captaincy of Warwickshire was receiving many plaudits?

The selectors were still uncertain when they gathered for the start of the Gentlemen/Players match on Wednesday 26 July. By the close they had their answer. Coming in at 194 for six, Freddie Brown seized the moment, hitting a blistering 122 out of 131 runs scored in 110 minutes, completing his hundred with a six into the pavilion. Dollery scored a fine century the next day, but the die was cast by then. Brown was undoubtedly their man for Australia.

Brown duly joined the selection panel and, just like Tony Greig in 1976, he knew what he wanted. This time it was not old men. As Alec Bedser scathingly put it, "He had this stupid idea that you could only beat Australia with youth. We could have won that series, but we left so many good players at home."

The selection process, late starting because of the delay in appointing a captain, was a muddle throughout. Altogether eleven men were involved in the process, not all of whom were present for all the meetings. It is said that two of them were shocked when they read in the papers of one selection.

At the end of the match at Lord's they announced only twelve of the seventeen names that were required. That went up to thirteen when it was established that the Army would release Close, then back down to twelve when Lancashire's Cyril Washbrook withdrew for business reasons. The last five were due to be added a fortnight later but, when the time came, there were only three more. It was almost the end of the month, with the season nearly over and the boat sailing in little more than two weeks, when the last two names were established: Washbrook, who had by this stage negotiated a late arrival, and the Cambridge University fast bowler John Warr.

The squad that toured Australia four years earlier had an average age of 33, with Godfrey Evans at 26 the youngest of only four men in their twenties. This time there were six under the age of 25, three of them from that year's Cambridge side. The three, having completed National Service, were all older than Close, who at 19 was the baby of the party.

Great concern about his selection came from those who knew him in Yorkshire. "They've picked Closey to go to Australia," Norman Yardley said to Ted Lester. "Brian Sellers and I told them he was too young." Bill Bowes was so concerned that he pleaded with Freddie Brown to change his mind. "He isn't ready. It's rushing him; he hasn't had enough experience."

Bill Edrich, one of the experienced players controversially omitted from the party, reported in a newspaper column what he had heard about the decision to select Close:

> A story is being told in the dressing rooms that when Close's name came up at the selection committee somebody suggested that there had been signs that Close's successes last season had made him 'big-headed'. "That's all right," snapped skipper Freddie Brown. "I want a few chaps with 'big heads' in my team."

Jim Swanton, knowing that Close had Brown's support, was optimistic about his prospects: 'One would imagine that the discipline and the experience of this tour might make him a truly worthy all-rounder.'

Others were more fearful, sensing that too much of the batting was in the hands of untried youth to the exclusion of seasoned professionals: not only Bill Edrich but Jack Robertson, Dennis Brookes, Harold Gimblett, men who had well-developed games.

John Arlott, not always a harsh critic, was withering in his assessment of the 17 men:

> The first striking fact about the party is that it contains seven players who have by no means proved themselves in Test cricket and two of whom must be regarded as promising but no more by county-cap standards. These two are Warr and Close.

The choice of Warr, one of three Cambridge men alongside John Dewes and David Sheppard, was a bizarre one. Was he really more likely to do well in Australia than Les Jackson or Yorkshire's Alec Coxon?

Coxon had taken more wickets that summer than any other quick bowler and had been in the England twelve for the final Test, but he was known to be a fiery character. In fact, Yorkshire let him go at the end of the season for reasons that have stayed in the realm of rumour. Some have whispered about an altercation with Denis Compton at a festival game, perhaps the throwing of a punch.

He was a blunt-speaking character. After moving to the north-east as a league professional, he played for Durham where his wicket-taking was inevitably accompanied by a few 'incidents'. Even in his eighties he was banned from his local pub for starting a fight with the barman. One obituary referred to his 'extreme political views'.

Les Jackson was a different type, not a man of many words. Perhaps the clue to the preference for Warr lies in the *Times'* description of the Cambridge man as 'a bowler of great promise, a keen fieldsman and a young man gifted with the valuable quality of a sense of humour'. An amateur with a good sense of humour fitted the bill better than a dour Derbyshire miner.

More seriously, John Arlott was worried about the effect the premature selection of the young players might have on their future development:

> Considerable harm might be done to their careers by subjecting their cricket to such a severe test while it is still in a fluid state. It is a side which could easily return with a crop of broken reputations of young men who might have succeeded if they had been allowed two or three more seasons to mature.

He argued that the choice of Close and Warr might have been justified, had they fitted into a well-structured squad, but on the contrary:

> This must be the worst-balanced team ever sent abroad. Certainly it contains two wicket-keepers, but there planning seems to end. It contains six opening batsmen, only one 'natural' spinner and not a single slip fieldsman.

*

All this passed Brian Close by. He was euphoric about his selection, another dream coming true, though news of it arrived at an awkward moment for him. The previous weekend he had been given permission to miss a Signals practice match to play a game in Roundhay Park, Leeds, raising money for charity.

I had a word with Captain Pocock, who was captain of the Royal Signals team, and he agreed. "Yes, we can let you off," he said. "Go home and play."

At that time I was opening the batting for the Signals, and in my absence the Brigade Major, normally number three in the order, moved up to open, and some silly bugger bowled him for a duck.

"Where the hell is Signalman Close?" he demanded.

"He's gone home," he was told.

"Then he's absent without leave."

It's remarkable how getting a duck can affect some people.

When I got back I found myself on a fizzer.

Despite Close's protests, the Commanding Officer issued a seven-day 'Confined to Barracks' order, a week of square-bashing in full uniform.

Often absent from camp playing cricket, and knowing that belongings had a habit of disappearing when left unattended, Brian was storing his Full Service Marching Order kit at a house outside the base. Claiming not fully to understand the literal meaning of 'confined to barracks', he caught a bus to collect it, staying for a bite of lunch while he was there.

It was at this point, while he was away, that the telephone call came through to Catterick with the news that he was going to Australia. The officer on duty sent for him, only to discover that he was nowhere to be seen on site. This time, with everybody delighted by his success, there were no repercussions. Yet, despite the best endeavours of the officers, the story of his confinement to barracks soon got into the newspapers, adding another colourful twist to the controversy of his release from National Service.

It could only happen to Brian Close.

4

LET THE BLIGHTER STEW

Lunch was approaching on the second day of the Melbourne Test. England, unlucky to be 1-0 down after the first match at Brisbane, had done well on the first day, dismissing Australia for 194. Now, however, their batting line-up was being severely tested. Simpson, Dewes and Washbrook had all gone cheaply, and the last over of the morning began with England on 54 for three. The young Gilbert Parkhouse, a stylish Glamorgan batsman playing in his first Ashes Test, was struggling badly against the unusual spin bowling of Jack Iverson, so much so that Len Hutton took it upon himself to face the final eight-ball over.

The ball pitched outside leg, and Hutton's initial instinct was to hit it. Then he opted to pull away his bat; the ball hit his pad and looped up to Don Tallon, the wicket-keeper. A lone appeal came from the bowler, wondering if perhaps the ball had grazed against bat or glove, and – to the evident disgust of Hutton and the surprise of the fielders around him – the umpire's finger shot up. England's best batsman, almost their only batsman in any form, was out, and Australia's total of 194 was looking a long way off.

In came the 19-year-old Brian Close to face his first balls in Ashes cricket. All he had to do, in the eyes of the senior players in the dressing room, was to play out the rest of the over and come in for lunch. For Iverson's first two balls he did just that, presenting a straight bat and looking in control. All seemed well. Then came the moment, the shot, that sealed his fate, not just for the rest of the tour but for some years afterwards. He tried to explain his thinking in his autobiography:

> I was tense, I was strung up. At that age – or, more to the point, with such a limited degree of experience – one doesn't appreciate the significance of certain field-placings and how they can affect what seems to be a bad ball.
>
> Iverson was bowling, and despite my tension I was conscious that I had played him well in our previous meeting; I was

confident he wasn't going to fool me. He bowled what I thought was a bad ball down the leg side. I didn't think about pushing and just surviving till lunch. If I had done, I could have established myself steadily afterwards, getting used to the pace of the pitch and the bounce and fixing all the field-placings on a radar screen in my mind. My thinking in those days was, you might say, imperfect, and no one had sought to improve it. It was, in my judgement, a bad ball and I decided to hit it.

In those years the cross-batted sweep, sometimes called a 'broom' shot, was not favoured in the English game, nor were batsmen encouraged to play attacking strokes before they had got used to the pitch and the bowling, especially not in a moment of crisis when lunch was imminent. But Brian was a young man of 19, on an exciting journey of discovery, and he was backing his own talent.

Alas, having spent so little time in the middle, he misjudged the bounce, sending the ball looping gently in the air. It was a disastrous choice of shot for which he was universally pilloried.

The *Daily Telegraph*'s Jim Swanton, a pillar of conservative thinking, called Close's arrival at the crease 'an awkward moment for the young man':

> If ever a quiet playing-down-the-line was called for, this was the time. The fact that he scooped blindly against the prevailing spin and spooned the easiest of catches to a backward short-leg stationed some fifteen yards from the bat admits of no comment. It is inexplicable in any cricketer, irrespective of age. And so 54 for five it was.

Lyn Wellings of the *Evening News*, often an acerbic critic, was more damning:

> It was the final over before lunch, the time when a new batsman, and even one well set for that matter, has his mind fixed on being there for the afternoon play. But not Close. Oh, dear me, no. Close chose that moment to perpetrate once again that dreadful sweep to leg of his, which had often cost him his wicket. Anyone with any pretensions to playing Test cricket would have eliminated it from his range of strokes long before.

Worse still came from the old Australian batsman Jack Fingleton, who was covering the series for the *Sunday Times*. He described the shot as a 'sickly, anaemic hit' and a 'nightmarish, incredible swish to leg', going on to list the times on the tour Close had already got out to 'this awful stroke':

> Words almost fail me about Close. Five weeks ago, on this very ground, I wrote that if ever he played his cross-bat "whoosh" again, he should be put on bread and water for a week. He has played it every match since, and today – of all days – he got out to it two minutes before lunch, before he had scored – and in his first Test match in Australia! Close should be made to work his passage home on a cargo ship.

A quarter of a century later, reflecting on his long years of watching cricket, Swanton wrote of the shot: 'I never saw a worse stroke played in a Test by a reputable batsman at such a moment. It was not easy at the time to accept Brian's youth as an excuse.'

The enormity of his shot selection was made even clearer to Brian when he returned to the pavilion.

> When I got back into the dressing-room, there was a deathly silence. I sat there through lunch nearly in tears. I was sick with misery.

Australia's off-spinner Ian Johnson saw what a lonely, disconsolate figure he was and spoke to Freddie Brown: "Young Close is a bit down. Go and have a word with him. He needs a little help." Brown was the man who had wanted the youngster on the tour, he said he was happy to have 'swollen-headed' men in his party, but his gruff reply contained no trace of sympathy: "Let the blighter stew. He deserves it."

Close had one opportunity to redeem himself. With England needing 179 for victory on the fourth day, he came in once more at the fall of Hutton's wicket, with the score on 94 for five. It was, in Fingleton's words, 'his chance of glory', but he did not seize it. After pushing a single, his first run in his third Test innings, he went back and across his stumps to a full, straight ball from left-armer Bill Johnston. Again eschewing orthodoxy, he tried to work it to leg and was unquestionably lbw. In Jack Fingleton's view, it was another 'bad stroke'.

Reg Simpson, one of the older men in the tour party, had no time at all for the young Close. Recalling the match more than half a century later, he said of the youngster's contribution to the Test: "He got 0 and 1, playing cow shots. Cyril Washbrook said to him, 'You don't play like

46

that when you come in. There's a batsman at the other end.' 'Oh, I shall do what I want,' he said."

England sank to a 28-run defeat and were now 2-0 down in the series. All the top-order batting had failed in the match; yet, when it came to the post-mortem, it was clear who in the eyes of his team-mates was the number-one culprit. Not for the last time in his chequered Test career Brian Close was the fall-guy for an England failure.

*

Back in September, when the boat had set sail from Tilbury, Signalman Close was in dreamland. After twelve months of army life in a Britain still in the grip of rationing, he was living a life of luxury, with food aplenty, activities on offer all over the boat and attractive women for travel companions. The other members of the tour party were all recovering from four months of six-day-a-week cricket, but he was raring to go.

He explored every corner of the boat with an almost childlike wonder. Never one to sit quietly, he filled every day to the brim, as he conveyed in letters to his pal John:

> We're on the go almost every minute of the day and have hardly a second to rest. Although many of us are getting slightly bored with the long journey, myself I wish it could go on for another few weeks.

Lyn Wellings was impressed by the talent of the young man in everything he tackled on the ship:

> Close is a magnificently built young giant with a natural flair for all games played with a ball and most sports unconnected with them. He quickly sorted out the mysteries of the deck games and in the pool showed himself to be unquestionably the best swimmer.

Brian was not a drinker and he did not engage that much with his team-mates, though his ability with arithmetic gave him a role when they staged a horse-race meeting with dice and a circular track drawn on the dance floor. When the bookmakers, Godfrey Evans and Denis Compton, got in a mess, he stepped forward to sort out their calculations.

Late in the journey, they had a second race night, and this time his horse, ridden by a New Zealand sports mistress to whom he had taken a shine, 'walked away from the rest of the field and won easily'. His bets that evening left him up by £15. It was only a dice game, but he could not resist a mock-boast in the next letter to his pal: 'I think my study of form was exceptional.'

Yet, for all Close's wide-eyed enthusiasm, it seems that his behaviour was already giving cause for concern among the senior players. He was off doing his own thing, he was not talking cricket, and he was paying no attention when he was given advice.

The age gap between the young Close and those senior players was not just a matter of years. It was also a question of the war years. Freddie Brown had lost four stone while a prisoner of the Italians and Germans, Alec Bedser had been fired on by a low-flying plane in his escape from Dunkirk, Trevor Bailey had witnessed the lines of emaciated inmates after the liberation of the Belsen concentration camp.

Brian, with none of that experience, was attracted to the daring and dangerous. Back in his school days he had developed a way of diving into the swimming pool from the top of a cubicle, taking no notice when the headmaster admonished him for it. So, faced with a pool on the boat, it was inevitable that he would look to do something similar, as Reg Simpson told me:

> He was a really naughty lad on that trip, very full of himself. On board ship, when we were going out, was a perfect example. Freddie Brown caught him running into the swimming pool and jumping over the rails at the side, straight into the pool. Fred said, "Cut that out. That's far too dangerous. If you slip, you'll hit the path on the other side." Next thing he did was stand up on the railing and jump in from there. You couldn't beat him. He was very, very naughty.

Brian's own view, expressed in *I Don't Bruise Easily*, was quite different:

> I was lacking in discipline in that I didn't know how to conform. No one told me what was expected of me so I just did my own thing, as they say. I was not inconsiderate; I had no desire to be a loner and I most certainly was not conceited as a youngster who had come a long way in a very short time. On the contrary, the senior members of the party were my heroes. I would dearly have loved *them* to take me on one side and talk to me ... about anything. I didn't know how to approach them because they were such demigods in my eyes.

Perhaps it didn't occur to them that I could be lonely, that I needed their company and their help and their guidance. As things were I had to make the best of things in the only way I knew – by taking part in everything I could. I had no inkling of the utter misery that was to come, of the treatment that was to leave its mark on me for the rest of my life.

*

His tour started well, with a century in the first game against a state side, Western Australia at Perth. It was his maiden first-class hundred, a chancy innings but one with an attacking intent that promised much for his prospects. Robertson-Glasgow, the most colourful of cricket writers, said that the innings 'lived in happy alternation between misprint and purple passage'. As a batsman who could serve as the fifth bowler, Close was promptly pencilled into the team for the First Test a month ahead, playing in all the major matches.

Unfortunately he had no further success. In the opinion of Wellings, 'He was liable to end the most promising innings by playing a stroke of reckless or shocking execution. He had not yet learned to use his natural attacking gifts discreetly, and he was mighty slow to learn.'

When it came to selecting the Test team, the batting options were thin, with both David Sheppard and Gilbert Parkhouse unwell. But, instead of sticking with Close for the last batting slot, England opted to play the reserve keeper Arthur McIntyre whose only significant score had been a century in Colombo on the way out to Australia. He had not bowled in first-class cricket for more than three years, but apparently his accuracy in the nets had impressed Len Hutton.

In the event his bowling was not required in the Test, which was arguably the most extraordinary in the history of Ashes cricket.

On the first day, a Friday, England did well to dismiss Australia for 228. Then came two days of heavy rain, leaving the pitch treacherous for batting when play resumed on Monday. England made 68 for seven, then declared to get Australia back in before conditions eased; Australia then made 32 for seven and also declared. It left England 65 minutes to negotiate at the end of the day, aiming simply to survive so that they could come back in easier conditions in the morning.

Hutton and Compton, the two star batsmen, were held back, and in a nightmare hour six batsmen fell for 30 runs. Simpson went first ball to a swinging yorker from Lindwall. Washbrook and Dewes created

45 minutes of calm before both falling, then in madness upon madness Bedser heaved the ball in the air to mid-off, Bailey was caught on the long-leg boundary, and McIntyre attempted a risky fourth run and failed to make his ground.

Little imagining that he would be the butt of such criticism in the next Test, Brian delivered his verdict on the pitiful fiasco to his pal John:

> Alec, who had been sent in as nightwatchman, took a swing and was caught skying one – the bloody fool. Then Trevor was out pulling a short one and to crown everything Arthur McIntyre was run out in the silliest run I've ever seen. He needs his head examining for such a thing but I blame the last three wickets entirely on Alec Bedser. Surely he should have had enough sense for a man of his experience not to have a 'blind swipe' at ten-to-six.

Mostly, his letters did not dwell on the cricket, being filled with his activities away from the matches: films, dances, golf days, a fishing expedition, a trip to the zoo and, above all, a day at the races to watch the Melbourne Cup. There he had a bet on a top-weight horse, Connie Court, that had never run two miles before and was an outsider at 30/1. Perhaps it was this race, after his success on board ship, that set off Brian's addiction to betting on horses.

> They came to the half mile post and all of a sudden Connie Court burst out of the pack, grabbed the lead and going like a thunderbolt charged into the straight. In the straight it just lengthened its stride and away it went, winning by four lengths.
>
> It was a marvellous thrill and it made my flesh go up in goose pimples as the crowd cheered it past the post and an even bigger cheer when the time was announced – an Australasian record over two miles and at top weight too.
>
> I didn't dash away to rob the bookmakers of my winnings straight away. I stayed and watched it being led into the winners' paddock and its owners being presented with the Cup. Oh! I could have given it a lovely big kiss (!!) then – it had won me £20. I went away that night feeling very satisfied with myself.

The quality of the writing in these long letters is outstanding. On top of his school success in maths and science, Brian had clearly had an excellent education. So what are we to make of David Sheppard's memory of him on that tour? 'People were amazed he'd got his Higher School Certificate because he didn't seem to be a very intelligent young man.'

Perhaps some of the answer lies with the reply John Dewes, another amateur, gave when asked late in his life about his contact with Brian:

> As amateurs we were not allowed, or encouraged, to mix too freely with the professionals. So I did not get to know Brian too well. Because of my Christian background, I did try to be approachable. But Brian did have a very broad accent, and this did not help him.

*

Brian was picked for two matches between the First and Second Tests, both two-day games against minor sides, not deemed first-class. These were opportunities for senior players to rest. At Toowoomba, against a Queensland Country Team, he got a pair of ducks and did not bowl. At Canberra, against the Southern Districts of New South Wales, he made one run in the first innings, bowled two wicketless overs, then – with the game drifting to an uneventful draw – struck a rapid 105 not out. Amid so much batting failure, it was enough to win him a place in the side for the Second Test.

During this century he strained, or perhaps tore, a tendon in his groin. Before the Test Freddie Brown asked him how bad it was. Keen to play, he made light of it. "It's only slight," he said. "I should be all right if I have it strapped."

> If I was ever big-headed in my life it was at that moment when I thought that my enthusiasm and the natural ability in which I had boundless confidence could take me through a Test in Australia with a groin strain, however slight. I paid for it later ... oh, how I paid for it.

With scores of 0 and 1 and indifferent bowling, it was no surprise when he was left out of the next Test which was lost by an innings, sealing Australia's retention of the Ashes. By this time there were mutterings among some of the team that Close was 'swinging the lead', happier with the off-the-field fun than focusing on the cricket.

The crunch came during a two-match trip to Tasmania. With senior players wanting a rest, he insisted that he was still not fit, which left them having to play Eric Bedser, Alec's twin brother who was travelling as a non-player with the tour party. Brown, staying behind, arranged for Brian to see a specialist on the island, booking the appointment for the morning of the first day.

So much had gone wrong on the tour, and much of it stemmed from the decisions made in selecting the party. None of the young batsmen had come good, nor in any of the Tests did either Cyril Washbrook or Denis Compton play an innings of any significance. Compton's contribution in eight knocks was a pitifully disappointing 53 runs. Should the selectors have prevailed upon Washbrook to tour when he refused their first invitation? And was it sensible to have entrusted the responsibilities of vice-captaincy to such a free spirit as Denis Compton? The questions were already being asked.

Compton, in charge of the team in Tasmania, was in no mood to hear about Close's groin or his appointment, instructing him to change and be available to field as twelfth man. Luckily Gilbert Parkhouse, Brian's room-mate and almost his only friend on the tour, agreed to stand in for him while he went off for the consultation.

Back came Brian with the specialist's report, which stated that he needed to rest for three to four weeks. He duly presented it to the tour manager, Brigadier Michael Green. "You'd better show this to Denis," he said. "He's planning to play you in the next game."

When the team left the field, Brian gave the report to Compton, who tore it in half, threw the pieces on the floor and said, "I couldn't care less what the fucking doctor says. You're playing in the next game."

The tour had two managers: Green for the playing side, John Nash the Yorkshire Secretary for administrative matters. In the opinion of Lyn Wellings, Close would have been better served if the roles had been reversed:

> He was not well handled – he was a difficult youngster to understand – and perhaps his story might have been different if John Nash had been the manager in charge of team affairs. Brigadier Green had comparatively small experience of cricket management. Handling cricketers is very different from commanding soldiers.

Close played the second match, as Compton demanded, and this led to another complaint against him. Put in to bat at number three, with

Parkhouse to follow at four, he suggested to his room-mate that he had better pad up as well, as he was not likely to be in for long. His own recollection in *I Don't Bruise Easily* is that what he said, and only in jest, was, "Get your pads on, I haven't had a bat for a month." When his turn came, he was bowled for 4, though Compton, not Parkhouse, came in next.

When they returned to the mainland he was summoned to Freddie Brown's room where the captain, lying in bed, interrogated him about his behaviour in Tasmania. Brown told him that he had been overheard – Brian thought by John Warr, an amateur with whom he had a 'less than cordial' relationship – saying that he was going to get out deliberately.

Who knows exactly what he said, and whether with his strong Yorkshire vowels it was heard correctly by Warr? What is clear is that he had reached the point of no return with many in the tour party. He was condemned to be an unwanted outsider.

In the final Test, with England 4-0 down, Reg Simpson hit a magnificent 156 to bring England victory over Australia for the first time since the war. Yet, while the players were celebrating their success, Brian was playing golf – and that, too, went down very badly. "I was no longer on speaking terms with the team," he said by way of explanation, many years later. "My presence would have been fairly pointless." Within days he was on the boat home, surplus to requirements for the New Zealand leg of the tour.

His letters to his friend John Anderson in Horsforth convey almost none of his anguish. Just once, after his failure in the Melbourne Test, does he reveal his inner turmoil:

> My memory seems to be going so if this letter takes quite a lot of understanding don't blame me. I can hardly think back a couple of days, let alone a week or so. My brain seems to be muzzy and keeps wandering into all kinds of thoughts and my nerves are on edge. Oh to hell with it all, I just feel like doing away with myself.

There then follow pages and pages of cheerful accounts of yachting, tennis, films, speedway, girls, even a description of the scenery at Hobart:

> Across the River Derwent, which is a continuation of the harbour, there is a floating bridge, the only one of its kind in the world, and it stretches across the river in a great arc and is

about a quarter of a mile long. It's a marvellous construction and has to be seen to be believed. In the background of the city there's Mount Wellington (lovely name, isn't it?) which, unless on a fine day, is always covered with clouds or snow. The cricket ground is a lovely place with the scenery blending in with the mountains to make it one of the most beautiful in Australia.

In his long career this was the only full MCC tour for which Brian was selected. Yet somehow, despite the setbacks and the misery, he still seems to be assuming, at least when writing to his pal, that he would be back in Australia in four years, as he revealed in his next letter, written from a hotel in Melbourne:

> Each morning we get up and before breakfast don a swimming costume and walk across the lawns in front of the hotel onto the beach. The water's lovely and warm, and all the girls in their costumes simply "stupefy" you, especially one (a daughter of one of the hotel managers) and she's simply marvellous. She's only 17 and still at school, but she certainly knows how to carry herself. And what looks, what a figure!! I'm getting her all lined up for four years' time. She'll be magnificent then.

When after Brian's death these letters were discovered, some thought the joy expressed in them gave the lie to his account of the tour in *I Don't Bruise Easily*. Undoubtedly, in the whirl of life away from the cricket, he had many happy experiences, but that is not the full story. Writing to his friend he was putting on a brave face, as a homesick boy at boarding school would have done at that time, not wanting to let on that this journey into dreamland had become a nightmare. Sitting on his own in his hotel room, he will have found solace in penning these reports of his activities, his well-controlled handwriting stretching over as much as ten sides of airmail paper, maybe 3,000 words in a single letter. It will have connected him with the loving world he had left behind in Yorkshire.

What a sad story it is. In the words of Alan Gibson, 'Was it his own fault? Very possible, though others might also be to blame.'

Trevor Bailey certainly saw fault in him: 'Unfortunately, Brian was under the impression that he knew everything. He was quite convinced that he was always right. If he made a mistake, it took him longer to realise his error. It did become very difficult for him.'

Brian himself, in *I Don't Bruise Easily*, saw it differently:

> I went out to Australia in 1950 a naïve and unworldly boy. Many times I retired dejectedly to my room at the end of the day, in sheer misery at the wall of hostility built by men I had hero-worshipped for years. Not one of them offered me one syllable of advice when I needed it. Not one of them offered a kind word when I was depressed. Not one of them sought to point out the error of my ways except by abuse.

In our filmed interview, he was more philosophical. "I hadn't had enough experience," he said. "If I'd have played in 1950, on top of my first year, that would have been a great help."

The happy lad who left Tilbury full of dreams in September returned in March a different man, troubled, almost broken, his natural confidence in ruins. What he needed was a summer with Yorkshire to regain his bearings, but that was not on offer. He had to serve the months of National Service which he had missed.

"What did the tour teach you?" I asked him in that interview.

> It taught me everything. By the time I'd played a number of years, I'd been through every experience a cricketer could go through.
>
> There's no messing. Cricket is a mind game. You've got to get your thinking right. The physical side is all right, that comes with having natural talent. In order to succeed, you need to have the right mental attitude.

For all Brian's grievances about the way he was treated on that tour, and he was undoubtedly handled badly, this was his way of admitting that he had not been tough enough mentally to do justice to his ability.

He did not forget his traumatic experience when twelve years later he was entrusted with the captaincy of Yorkshire. He may never have been an arm-around-the-shoulder leader, but he knew with an inner certainty that it was his job to look after and believe in every member of his team.

5

OUT OF THE WILDERNESS

Brian Close's one Test in Australia, in December 1950, proved to be his last for England for four-and-a-half years. He was no longer the boy wonder, the great hope of post-war English cricket. Indeed, when he was recalled for the final Test of 1955, against South Africa at The Oval, it seems that his 'nightmarish swish' in the over before lunch still hung over him.

Reflecting on his return to the Test team, the *Daily Telegraph*'s Jim Swanton, one always close to the thinking at Lord's, wrote:

> Close, the second and last time he played for England at Melbourne four years ago, batted in a manner that one might say, to be brutally honest, earned him a very long period in the wilderness.
>
> He is a young cricketer with touches of brilliance, hitherto lacking stability. Clearly he was brought on too soon. Has he acquired, by degrees, what previously was so palpably absent? Saturday's match may help to give the answer – for English cricket quite an important one.

In the years in which Brian had been absent from the Test team, England's fortunes had risen greatly, with two of his fellow Yorkshire professionals among the headlines: Len Hutton and Freddie Trueman, neither of whom – for different reasons – was in the side for the Oval Test in 1955.

Hutton, one of the few to emerge with credit from Freddie Brown's tour of Australia, had made history by being appointed England's first professional captain of the modern era. Though never appointed captain at Yorkshire, he made a great success of the England job. He won back the Ashes in Coronation year, 1953; his monumental batting secured a 2-2 draw in a highly fraught series in the West Indies; and he joined the not very long list of captains who have led England to victory in Australia. He was a quiet, introspective man, his batting took him into a cocoon of deep concentration, and the strain of the responsibilities involved in captaincy, especially on tour, was immense. With a recurrent back problem and perhaps some nervous exhaustion, he retired from the game during the summer of 1955. With his departure the captaincy of England passed back to an amateur, Peter May, and it remained with those of that class for the next eleven years – till the selectors, in their desperation, turned once more to a Yorkshire professional, Brian Close.

Freddie Trueman had made a slower start for Yorkshire than Brian. Indeed, by early in his third summer on the staff, he was close to despair. Eddie Leadbeater, a cheerful leg-spinner from the Huddersfield area, had two years in the Yorkshire side, filling in while Brian Close was on National Service, and he told me of a match against Middlesex early in the summer of 1951:

> Freddie didn't do all that well at Lord's. We were in the hotel bedroom at night, and Frank Lowson came in to us. We were all going to go out. And Freddie said, "I don't think I'll go out." He was really upset, was Fred, almost in tears. "I don't think I'll ever make it," he said. And I said, "Oh don't talk so silly, Fred. It's only one match."

Trueman played the next match at Sheffield, during which he was told he was out of the team thereafter. Then in the second innings, after the decision had been made, he took eight wickets, went off to be a sulking twelfth man for the second team at Grimsby and a week later returned to the Yorkshire side, full of resentful confidence. Within twelve months he was in the England team, granted leave from the RAF to terrify the Indian tourists. In four Tests he took 33 wickets. Post-war England had finally found what it was looking for: a bowler of high pace and, furthermore, one with that rare ability to swing the ball at speed.

The next summer, still a National Serviceman, Trueman took important wickets in the Oval Test that won back the Ashes, but his winter in the West Indies was not a success. In a tour beset with incidents on and off the field, when England became unpopular with both the white ex-pats and the black locals, he got a reputation for being a social liability, suffering the rare punishment of having his good-conduct money withheld.

It seems that he never stopped talking, and with his blunt turn of phrase, formed by a childhood amid the coalpits of South Yorkshire, he was regularly causing offence. There are so many stories about what he is supposed to have said on that tour, many of them doubtless elaborated over the years. Let me just stick with what the beleaguered manager Charles Palmer told me when I asked him about Fred:

> He'd been pulled out of Yorkshire and put in a context which was entirely alien to his upbringing. He spoke as a Yorkshireman would speak in Yorkshire. I remember in a bar one night. This fellow came up. He said he had a friend in Yorkshire and did Fred know him? And instead of Fred saying, "No, but I'll look out for him" or some such words, he said, "Never 'eard of the bugger." They were little things, but they didn't go down very well in a highly sensitive situation.

Just as Brian Close suffered for being a fish-out-of-water in Australia, so Freddie Trueman found himself cast aside by the selectors: no Tests in 1954, no place on the tour of Australia and just one match, at Lord's, in 1955. In the three years following that ill-fated tour he played only three of England's 26 Tests, watching with disgruntlement from Yorkshire as Frank Tyson, an even faster bowler, grabbed the headlines.

As Brian Close's recall for the Oval Test of 1955 was announced, JL Manning of the *Sunday Dispatch* spoke for many in the North:

> I ask once again: What must Freddy Trueman do to get into England's team? Will he spend as long in the wilderness as Brian Close? I expect so, and more's the pity. The trouble with cricket selectors is they develop lasting prejudices.

Close and Trueman had made their Yorkshire debuts on the same day at Cambridge, they had both blotted their copybooks on their first tours, and they both harboured a distrust of the men who ran Lord's in those years. But there the parallel should end. For the rest of his life Trueman bristled with indignation at the way he had been treated, the Test wickets that the "pompous buffoons" at Lord's had deprived him of, while Brian slowly processed the pain of what had happened to him, finding an outlet for his experiences in his years of captaincy.

When I was working on Bob Appleyard's book, I conducted a telephone interview with Fred. Within minutes he had diverted the conversation to the disgrace of the Test matches he had missed. He recalled how, when eventually selected to tour again, to Australia in 1958/59, he had been greeted by the tour manager Freddie Brown with the words, "One bit of trouble from you, Trueman, and you'll be on the next boat home." It was typical Brown, cracking the whip from the off, and as manager he was not a success. Popular from his tour as captain, he was greeted by the Australians with great warmth, leading him to drink far too much and at one stage to be sent away to dry out. As Geoffrey Howard, manager of the previous tour, said to me, "He was extremely easy to get on with, especially if you were thirsty."

When the telephone conversation with Fred ended, I rewound my cassette tape a fair way, pressed Play, and the first words I heard, emphatically articulated in Fred's elongated Yorkshire vowels, were "that drunken hound Brown". I confess it made me laugh. Fred had a good voice, and he relished the sound of it. For all his self-importance and his simmering bitterness, he spoke with a refreshing freedom.

Brian Close would never have spoken like that about Freddie Brown. Beneath the tough exterior his instincts were more generous. Fred and he were very different men.

*

Back in 1951, when Brian returned from Australia, his cricket was largely confined to services matches. He scored an unbeaten 96 for the Army against Oxford University at The Parks, 135 for the Combined Services against the touring South Africans at Portsmouth and 134 for the Army against the Royal Navy at Lord's. Fellow National Serviceman Micky Stewart, who would later play alongside Brian for England, remembers his Army team-mate less for these runs than for his expenses claims:

> The Secretary of the Army Cricket Association, Lieutenant-Colonel Kilgour, used to hand out the money. A lovely man. He gave us the expenses forms on the first day, then at the end of the match he would pay us out of a kitty. It didn't take us long to realise that, if we didn't get in before Closey, there would be no money left for us.
>
> "Now, Brian," he would say. "You are claiming a first-class train fare from Sandhurst to London. I've told you it's only Command Officers who have a first-class train fare."
>
> "But I did get a hundred, didn't I?"
>
> "And why on earth have you gone via Leeds?"
>
> "Well, I didn't have any clean shirts."

Discharged in October, Close spent the winter in London where he was on the books of Arsenal Football Club, playing in their reserve side.

His letters to John Anderson continued with regularity, and they now included reports of his first car. From the start his approach to driving was clear, as in this description of an outing soon after passing his test:

> We set off early in the morning, filled the car up and off we went, through Hatfield and on to St Albans. Once past St Albans we got onto the main road (Watling St) and it goes for miles and miles, as straight as an arrow. It was on this road that I got the car up to 90 mph and even then my foot wasn't right down. It was terrific. We almost flew along at times.
>
> When we turned off to take the road into Northampton one of my rear tyres blew up on me and we screeched to a stop. It didn't take us long to change the wheel and off we went again.

It seems that he was close to getting a game in the Arsenal first team. But once more, in a pattern that was becoming familiar, things went wrong for him. Arsenal's reserve side, holders of the Football Combination Cup, had at short notice to fit in a semi-final replay at Fulham, and this extra fixture coincided with the first day of Yorkshire's opening game against MCC at Lord's. Brian, keen to play in both, spoke to Norman Yardley, the Yorkshire captain, who in Brian's version of events agreed that he could slip away from Lord's at 3.30 in the afternoon.

At this point the story bears great similarity to the one in which he finished up confined to the Catterick barracks. Yardley, whose wife was about to give birth, stayed in Yorkshire, and the acting captain Don Brennan and county secretary John Nash, both at Lord's, knew nothing of the arrangement. With Yorkshire in the field, Brian was told firmly that he was a Yorkshire cricketer from this point of the summer and that he must stay till the close of play. As a result he did not arrive at the football till half-time, too late to take any part in the game, and the next day was told by Arsenal, a club renowned for its high standards, that he was to be released.

> Thus another branch of a promising career was summarily lopped off. I loved everything about Arsenal. The place was like a palace. You were immediately conscious of belonging to something really big, really important. Everyone at Highbury lived, breathed, talked, ate and drank Arsenal. Everyone believed in the club; everyone was proud to be part of it. It was just like playing cricket for Yorkshire.

That day at Lord's he took five wickets, and once more, after an absence of two summers, he was back in the thick of the Yorkshire team, completing the double with 1,192 runs and 114 wickets.

The county's bowling resources were thin that year, with Coxon exiled to Durham, Trueman on National Service, and Bob Appleyard, the great discovery of the previous summer, laid low in a sanatorium with tuberculosis. In their absence Johnny Wardle, the slow left-armer, bowled an extraordinary 1,857 overs, a season's total only ever exceeded by the little Kent leg-spinner 'Tich' Freeman in the early 1930s. Brian himself bowled 1,107 overs in 1952.

Here was the experience he had been lacking when he had toured Australia, his firm grounding in the game. Another season of such progress could see him back in the England side. Yet doubts remained about his character. Somehow he was not quite in the traditional Yorkshire mould, not a safety-first cricketer sticking to the tried and tested path. And, worse, he gave the impression to many that he was happy doing things his own way; he did not need their advice.

One who put into writing this negative view of the young Close was Lorna Smart, a civil servant in the Admiralty who wrote regularly to Bob Appleyard while he was laid up. She created statistical charts of how batsmen got out, which appealed greatly to Bob's analytical mind, and she accompanied these charts with lively comments on the Yorkshire players. She had her favourites, and Brian was evidently not one of them. In one letter she recalled an incident at the start of the summer, in the only match that Bob played before being hospitalised:

> Whether Master Close is learning more sense and unlearning his previous bumptious know-it-all errors, I don't know. That episode in the nets at Taunton didn't look very promising. You probably remember the way Master Brian hooked a ball over the back of the net out into the road, which you went to fetch. Eddie, I think, tore a brisk strip off Close for that stupid stroke but two minutes later, while you were still retrieving the first ball, the young chump did exactly the same again, with the air of a boy who thinks he has done something very clever.
>
> That time he really did catch it. Eddie took the bat away and made it clear that he'd had it, under the oldest rule in the world – "Six and Out". Serve him right.

At the end of the season she was a little more charitable:

> Brian Close's performance of the double again was a good thing (though faintly surprising when you saw some of the immaturity of odd bits of his play). He needs encouragement of the right sort, but newspaper agitation for him to play for England again is still, to my mind, unhelpful and a menace to his (we hope) gradually growing stability. I suppose one can forgive a Yorkshireman who fails doing his best, but never one who loses his head.

Brian was among several cricketers of that time who played football in winter, notably his Yorkshire team-mate Willie Watson, a double international who moved with a beautiful balance, and Ken Taylor, who would make his Yorkshire debut the following summer. That winter of 1952/53 Fred Trueman was on the books of Lincoln City but, not wanting to risk his cricket career with an injury, he took the county's advice and gave up playing professionally. No such caution was in Brian's nature, and in mid-winter, playing for Bradford City, he suffered a serious knee injury.

Lorna Smart was quick to make comparisons that were unflattering to her bête noire, 'Master Close':

> I am glad to see that Fred Trueman has had the sense to pack up his football, at least for the moment, on the suggestion of Mr Nash, but I suppose it would be too much to expect that Brian Close would ever listen to advice or remember that he has some responsibility towards Yorkshire. Willie seems to keep out of trouble on the football field, but he isn't clumsy like Master Close. Maybe that makes all the difference between injury and safety.

Was Brian clumsy in his movements? Not according to his wife Vivien, who always said how well he moved on the dance floor.

Brian tried to play for Yorkshire in May, but after two matches he withdrew, missing the rest of the summer. In five years he had played only two seasons of county cricket, and he was starting to believe that the Fates were against him, making clear in *I Don't Bruise Easily* how low his spirits were:

> I had regular treatment, but the knee never improved. I got a bit of a job as a rep, but there was plenty of time to brood. Was

I ever going to be able to play cricket or football again? Had I chucked away a decent education and the chance of a career in medicine, or accountancy? There were times when I was close to despair.

How interesting it is to set these sentences alongside the letter he wrote the previous June to his friend. Clearly John Anderson had wallowed in self-pity in his most recent letter to Brian, and Brian, waiting to bat at Worcester, responded with a full blast of home truths:

> For God's sake stop being so damned moody and enjoy life for a change instead of being sulky when things don't happen just the way you want them to. I was a great sufferer of that until a short while ago, but now I'm thankful to say that I learned my lesson ...
>
> Shake yourself out of this 'stupor' you're in. Believe me, it's the only way and if you don't enjoy yourself when you're young, you'll live to regret it for the rest of your life. After all, you can only expect back from life what you put into it so come on, John, pull yourself together and you'll be all the better for it ...

There was much more in the same vein before he signed off:

> I must close now as I'm next in to bat and I want to accustom my eyes to the glare. If you think of all I've wrote I shall be only too pleased, because I know that once you think of it you're bound to change your line of thought to all things and it will be very good for us all besides yourself.

So much was going on for Brian in these years, the roller-coaster of fortune in a world in which he was in many ways still an innocent lad. He wanted to live his life, as he drove his car, in the fast lane, and somehow, in a pattern that remained a thread throughout his life, he never seemed to see disaster on the horizon and to take steps to avoid it.

That day at Worcester, when he went out to bat, he was bristling with purpose, racing to a fifty in less than half an hour. Then two months later he was coping with the news that his friend had polio. It was some weeks before he could bring himself to write to John, struggling to 'assimilate the seriousness of it' and disappointed that he had been advised not to visit while there was any chance of catching the disease. All he could do was offer the kind of platitudes that perhaps he needed to be offering himself when he was down:

> Keep your 'pecker' up, laugh at things which go wrong and they'll soon take a turn for the better.

*

Close played almost no cricket in the summer of 1953, and his knee felt much the same at the start of 1954, or so he said. Yet he played all through the season, and somehow, as if confirming the view of those who thought he exaggerated his ailments, the knee grew gradually stronger. With Trueman and Appleyard back, and the summer's weather the worst of the 20th century, he bowled a little less, taking only 66 wickets, but he scored a new high of 1,320 runs, including his first two centuries for Yorkshire, against the Pakistan tourists and the Combined Services.

Then came the extraordinary summer of 1955. His bowling was in full use again, and in a warm year he finished only three short of the coveted 100 wickets. His batting, however, was a different story. An early century at Cambridge augured well, but soon he found himself in the worst trough of form in his life. In a sequence of six matches in June he recorded scores of 1, 3, 3, 2, 1, 10, 5*, 24, 3 and 0. He was complaining of migraines, severe headaches, blurred vision, to the point where he was dropped from the side at Lord's and Norman Yardley sent him off to see a London specialist.

> My vision became so blurred that I thought my sight was going altogether. I worried myself sick, to such an extent that I became afraid to play for fear of failing. At Lord's I went out to field as substitute, and I made a complete and utter mess of two straightforward stops. I go hot and cold every time I think of them now.

Was it a real physical problem, or could it have been psychosomatic? Although it does not fit with the tough-as-boots Close of later legend, there were those at Yorkshire who thought he was something of a hypochondriac, especially as throughout this time he was continuing to bowl long spells without difficulty.

Not for the first time his mind was in turmoil:

> Was I a coward, unable to face a loss of form and to fight to overcome it? Would I ever get back to those carefree days when

I had no problems and played every day for the sheer joy of
being involved in top-class sport? Should I go home and rest
and try to overcome my problems that way?

The team were moving on from Lord's to Taunton, and Yardley, a wise
and sympathetic man, asked Brian if he wanted to stay with them or go
home. He thought it through during a session of play and opted to stay.
Willie Watson had sustained an injury while batting, and Brian took his
place in the eleven against Somerset.

In the first innings he felt his form returning, scoring 30 before being
given out stumped – wrongly, he always claimed. Then, when they faced
a run chase of 285 runs in 3½ hours, a tough ask in those days, Yardley
surprised him by telling him to open the batting. With no time to think,
he quickly padded up, went out and hit a blistering 143.

It was the most marvellous feeling I had ever experienced – to
be back out of the wilderness.

It was his first century in a County Championship match, against the
weakest team in the competition. Yet, less than three weeks later, with
England short of reliable openers, he was named in the team for the Oval
Test. It was the most remarkable transformation of his fortunes. Fate, it
seemed, was smiling on him once more.

England were level 2-2 with South Africa, needing to win this last
Test, and the selectors boldly made seven changes to the eleven defeated
at Headingley, opting for a more attacking side. Close as opener was
replacing the more obdurate Trevor Bailey, a decision which raised some
eyebrows, not least those of John Woodcock in *The Times*:

To omit Bailey was a courageous decision. Many will be
waiting only for Close to fail, and England to face a crisis, to
take the selectors to task.

In the event Bailey was reinstated down the order when Cowdrey
and Tyson dropped out. Close was to open with another left-hander,
Lancashire's Jack Ikin, facing the testing new-ball pair of Heine and
Adcock, as fast and nasty an attack as any in the world at that time.
They batted first and made a good impression – 'more confident and
watchful than any English opening pair this season', according to Denys
Rowbotham in the *Guardian* – and together they put on 51 runs, 13
more than the sum of England's previous six opening partnerships.

Ikin was first to go, then Close in the over before lunch, to a stroke that Jim Swanton called 'not the most prudent'. Inevitably, given its timing, his dismissal in Australia was remembered, notably by John Woodcock:

> When Close carelessly lifted his head in the over before luncheon, driving at Goddard, they were 59 for two. Mansell jumped at first slip to take a fine catch at the full stretch of his right hand. One still carries a clear image of Close being caught at Melbourne in the second Test match of F.R. Brown's tour in 1950 off a wild stroke in the last over of the morning, and, regrettably, this latest folly lost him some of the good marks he had won. With his success it is so much a matter of temperament.

In a low-scoring game, his 32 turned out to be the highest score in either side's first innings, and there was no criticism of his dismissal for 15 in the second innings. 'It was a beautiful ball,' Swanton wrote, 'and not the slightest discredit attached to the batsman.' The Test was won by England, and Brian was back in the fold.

A further opportunity to establish himself came when he was selected in a 15-strong party for a three-month MCC tour of Pakistan. With the Australians arriving the following summer, he had every reason to believe that he would soon be opening the batting for England in the greatest cricketing contest of them all.

*

The tour of Pakistan did no harm to Brian's cause. MCC were keen to give the leading England players a winter's rest ahead of the Ashes series, yet they wanted to recognise Pakistan's emergence as a Test-playing country, so they came up with the new idea of sending an 'A' team, mainly consisting of younger players. Four representative matches, not Tests, were scheduled: Pakistan against MCC, not England.

Several of the tourists would go on to have lengthy Test careers, notably Ken Barrington, Jim Parks, Fred Titmus, Tony Lock and Peter Richardson. Yet not all of them prospered in the unfamiliar conditions of the Indian sub-continent, and the series of representative matches was lost 2-1.

'Few of the batsmen enhanced their reputations,' was the verdict of the *Wisden Cricketers' Almanack*. 'Exceptions were Richardson and Close, the left-handed opening pair, who often gave the side a good start, and possibly Barrington, although following his good season in England more was expected from him.'

Placed in charge of the party was the Lancashire Secretary Geoffrey Howard, who had made a great success of two full England tours: to India four years earlier and to Australia the previous winter. In 2001, at the age of 92, he sat down with me to share his memories in a book, and his accounts of these tours – in comparison with tours as they had become by the start of the 21st century – were breathtaking.

In India he went out with no support staff at all, just a party of players and two journalists, not even a baggage man or scorer. In Australia, when on arrival he went to the bank, he discovered that MCC had neglected to make any financial arrangements. Using all his charm, he managed to secure a flexible overdraft, running the tour from a personal account that at one stage, before the takings flowed in, was £20,000 in debt.

Reflecting on the experience, he said with a sigh, "How much easier I would have found it to manage the tour if MCC had provided me with the two things I didn't have – help and money."

In Pakistan he was again on his own with the players, of whom he was very fond in a fatherly way. He shared with me two memories of Brian Close. The first was of a trip by aeroplane when they had on board with them several copies of the *Kama Sutra*: "I was sitting next to Brian, and he sat and read it from cover to cover without a word. Then he put it down. 'Well,' he said, 'I've learnt nowt from that.'"

Then there was a shooting expedition: "We went out shooting samba, and you should have seen the way he was waving his rifle about. 'I know what I'm doing,' he said. 'I've done this a lot.' He frightened the life out of everybody."

With little in the way of entertainment to occupy them and full of youthful energy, the players started to let off steam by throwing water around. Brian's letter home to his friend describes the second evening of a match at Sialkot, when they were celebrating the manager's birthday:

> All of a sudden we started our aquatic sports!! Someone splashed a little water about and before long everyone was in shorts or trunks and buckets were flying around all over the place. I was writing, but realising what was going to happen I hastily put it all away and beat it. As each person got wet, they joined the 'mob' chasing the rest. They even broke into

the rooms and 'drowned' one or two sleepers including the Press. It was great fun.

I got changed into a pair of trousers and dark shirt so that I would be camouflaged in the darkness and laid low for a while in some bushes. There were three of us who escaped that night — Jim Parks, Pete Sainsbury and I — and eventually we took to the trees and watched in comfort all the goings and comings of everyone. They were dashing about all over the place with buckets or jugs but could find us nowhere. Later on, when they couldn't find us, they 'wrecked' our rooms and upset everything — I slept that night with half my bed missing, I had it supported on two armchairs. We had a great time and I might say that if we didn't do things like this at some of these places we'd go nuts.

There's nothing to do at night time except sit around in each other's company all the time, and of course the subject of conversation is always cricket. We have to find some diversion somehow and those are the things we do to let our 'hair down'.

As English teams often did at that time, they came to distrust the Pakistani umpires, particularly Idris Begh, who was something of a showman. "They come to see me umpire," Geoffrey remembered him saying proudly.

One night three of them, including the captain Donald Carr, hatched a plan. They would bring the umpire from his hotel, sit him down on a chair in front of a pillar, ask him if he would like some water, then pour two full buckets over him. The plan was duly executed, with the umpire quick to see the funny side of it, happy to be at the centre of attention.

Then, alas, it all went wrong. It seems that Begh could cope with the English players laughing at him but, when two of the Pakistan team came in and joined in the laughter, he became disturbed, returning to his hotel and reporting the incident to the captain Abdul Hafeez Kardar, who was outraged by the insult to his people.

Unfortunately I can't write everything down in a letter for several reasons – you'll just have to wait till I get home when I can tell you the lot!!

It was our 'greatest night' and so funny we burst our sides with laughing. Unfortunately it was an incident, a joke or piece of ragging which fell on stony ground. They've no sense of humour out here, although every one of their players except Kardar nearly wetted themselves with laughing and the other umpire did too.

The crisis escalated rapidly. Begh was pictured in the local newspapers with his arm in a sling, complaining that he had been manhandled violently. "They gagged me, twisted my arm up my back and sat on me. I thought my shoulder had been put out in the struggle, but the hospital said it was only strain and bruising."

The prank was no longer harmless horseplay; it was now a violent attack on an umpire. There was great local anger, and MCC were appalled. For a while it seemed the tour would be abandoned, but after high-level meetings involving the President of Pakistan a diplomatic rapprochement was achieved. In a fulsome apology the manager tried to downplay the episode, saying that 'a party of young men misguidedly thought that what they had once or twice found funny amongst themselves would also be thought funny by another.'

At the time we were working together on his book, 45 years after the event, Geoffrey still did not know who the two men were who had assisted the captain in the escapade. I drove him to Donald Carr's house in Radlett, where their identities were finally revealed to him.

"It was Swetman and Close. The problem was that Idris took a bit of fright when Closey grabbed him and put him in the tonga. Brian can be a bit intimidating. He's tremendously strong."

Donald Carr carried the can for the whole episode. With no attempt by the manager to identify the other culprits, Brian Close for once stayed out of the spotlight. He was able to start the summer's cricket with his reputation enhanced by a good tour, looking forward to the Ashes Tests.

If only Brian's life were ever that simple!

*

On Wednesday 9 May 1956, in their first big match of the summer, Yorkshire were due to host the Australian tourists at Bradford. Early rain washed out the day's play, and four of them – Ray Lindwall and Ian Johnson of the Australians, Bob Appleyard and Brian from Yorkshire – agreed to head off to the Halifax Golf Club on Ogden Moor. Brian went home to collect his clubs, making his way to the course via a short cut over Thornton Moor.

Brian's account of what happened is reported in Alan Hill's 2002 biography. He was driving a hired car, as his was in for repair. He was on an unfamiliar road. There was a hump-back bridge leading to a T-junction. Then: 'Approaching in the opposite direction was a monster obstacle – a three-ton lorry. He slammed on his brakes, but there was no avoiding the collision.'

The sub-text is clear. It was not his fault at all; he was just very unlucky. If he had been driving his own car, if he had known the road, if the T-junction had not been so soon after the bridge – and if he had not been confronted by such a 'monster obstacle', leaving him no room on the road? There was, as he put it, 'no avoiding the collision'.

The newspaper reports paint a different picture. He was driving a 'high-powered' car, which must have been going at some speed towards a 'lonely wind-and-rain-swept' junction:

> The lorry, weighing over two tons, was knocked over onto its near side, the cab door was dented inwards, the chassis was twisted and glass from the cab windows was strewn over the road.

Happily the lorry driver, a farm labourer, was able to climb out of his cab through a window, suffering only a few cuts. Brian, however, had damaged his knee, the same one on which he had been operated after the football injury, and was out of cricket for a month.

When he did return, at Bradford where the closeness of the crowd created the effect of a bull ring, he was soon reminded of the accident. "This catch went up into the sky," Yorkshire's keeper Jimmy Binks recalled. "Brian was under it, but it had the dreaded spin on it, and it dropped to his side. He never even touched it. There was a deadly silence. Then one of the wags in the crowd called out: 'You can't drive a bloody car, either.'"

England's openers for the First Test were Colin Cowdrey, promoted up the order, and Peter Richardson, Brian's partner in Pakistan. The two opened in all five matches, as England retained the Ashes.

Brian, meanwhile, had a poor season. In 27 matches he hit just 802 runs and took 24 wickets.

6

AT THE WHEEL

County cricket was a relentless schedule in the 1950s and 1960s. A three-day match would end on a Tuesday evening, and another – often many miles away – would start on Wednesday morning. The same thing would happen each Friday night and Saturday morning.

In 1961 Yorkshire were programmed to play six days every single week from 29 April to 5 September and, with seven home grounds around the county, not once did they stay put from one game to the next. Twenty of their journeys were longer than 100 miles, with their season starting at Lord's, then zig-zagging them from Cambridge to Bradford to Oxford to Swansea to Hull: nearly 900 miles by the middle of May. Later the schedule would send them to Taunton between matches at Chesterfield and Bradford. For Hull-based Jimmy Binks, their ever-present wicket-keeper, even the home games in Bradford and Leeds required a round trip of well over 100 miles for his little Volkswagen Beetle.

"It was a game of stamina," the Yorkshire batsman Bryan Stott says. "We weren't as finely tuned as they are now."

No one exemplified this season-long stamina better than Derek Shackleton, the phlegmatic Northerner who week in, week out for twenty summers opened the bowling for Hampshire. A medium-pace seamer of unrelenting accuracy, he glided to the wicket over after over, never a footstep varying in his run-up, never a ball off length, never a hair out of place. In the summer of 1962, turning 38 years old in August, he played 34 three-day games in 17½ weeks and sent down 1,717 overs.

His driving was just the same. There was petrol money for those who took their own cars, so 'Shack' was not going to accept a lift. Whatever the distance, he pottered along at a sensible speed, never one attracted by life's risks. Alan Castell, a young jack-the-lad in the team, recalls a journey with his senior professional:

> Shack had this Ford Corsair. He wouldn't let many people drive it but, if they did, it had to be at 45 miles an hour. There

71

was only once I got my hands on the wheel. He must have been totally knackered. There I was, I'd got this lovely car, and I'd got half an eye on Shack. I could have sworn he was asleep so I started putting my foot down. All of a sudden he's leant forward and tapped the speedo. "No more than 45, lad." "Sorry, Derek."

At the other end of the spectrum, embracing risk as one of the joys of living, was Brian Close. In the spring of 1968, writing for the *Sunday Mirror*, he listed the various cars he had been through, as accurate in the dates as when he went through his on-off Test career for our filmed interview:

> So far I've had a Jaguar, an Armstrong Siddeley, a Humber Hawk, a Dormobile, an Austin A-95, four Zodiacs and a Corsair. I haven't smashed all of them. Not quite.
>
> I wrote off the Humber Hawk in 1956. I hit a couple of trees with the Zodiac in '63 and rolled five or six times in the Corsair in '66. But the silliest thing that happened was when I was driving home to see my wife, Vivien, in late '66.
>
> Viv was expecting our first baby and I was anxious to get home. I swerved to miss an oncoming car, ran off the road and had to crawl out of the wreckage.
>
> A passing driver gave me a lift. I didn't want to worry Viv when I got home, so when I got in I pretended nothing had happened. Fortunately I'd noticed that my coat had been right torn down, and I had it carefully folded over my arm.
>
> "Where've you been till this hour?" she wanted to know.
>
> "The car broke down," I said off-handedly and gave her a peck. "I'll just put these things down and bring in my gear."
>
> But as I walked across the room, she saw my back. I hadn't realised that whatever cut my coat had sliced through my shirt, too. There was a great bloody cut down my back.

Needless to say, the list of his cars and accidents grew considerably in the years that followed. There is even a story, possibly apocryphal (though who knows with DB Close), that he collected a car that had been in for major repair, drove out of the garage and into the back of a van, limped it round a roundabout and straight back into the garage.

At the start of one summer, as a county captain, he received a sponsored car, a Ford Capri, that he wrote off the same day and had to go back for a replacement. Geoff Cope, a member of the Yorkshire team, described the accident to me, adding his own memory of being driven by Brian:

> There's a junction at Norman Cross on the A1 near Peterborough, where you go out at one o'clock. Well, Closey went straight on, and he wedged this Capri into a tree. I don't know how many of those Fords he went through.
>
> There was another time, we had a do at Fulford. "I'll pick you up," he said. He had this mat with rubber pimples on it on top of the dashboard. He was driving along, and he got a flask out, opened it up and got out a tea bag. We were racing up the A64, and he was mashing tea. "We're all right," he'd say. "Stop worrying."
>
> One day we had to go from Colchester to Lord's, and he said, "You can drive." So I was driving his Capri while he was reading the racing paper. "Where are we? … Get a move on … Oh for God's sake, stop this car and get out." It was frightening. "Do you realise this car's never been above 45 miles an hour all the way here?" He got in the car, and he went with handbrake turns and everything through London, by which stage I'd lost quite a bit of weight.

The cricketers' journeys increased further when the Sunday League was introduced in 1969. At first it was usual for the teams to play on Sunday at the same venue as the championship match on Saturday, Monday and Tuesday. Then, concerned that there was collusion occurring in some crucial games ("Go easy on us on Sunday, and we'll give you a good declaration on Tuesday"), the authorities decided to send them elsewhere.

In August 1974 Brian Close's Somerset side found themselves travelling from Nottingham on Friday night for a three-day game at Worcester that was punctuated on the Sunday by a 40-over contest 150 miles away in Torquay. Then on Tuesday evening, after the Worcester match was over, they set off on a 200-mile trip to Canterbury for a Gillette Cup semi-final.

I wrote a book with Tom Cartwright, who had worked in car factories in his home city of Coventry. He played alongside Brian at Somerset and was full of tales of the Yorkshireman's crazy driving:

73

I remember driving into Taunton one Saturday morning and, when I got to the bend at Burrowbridge, there was this car perched on top of the hedge, with about twenty or thirty yards of hedgerow before it all flattened. I thought, "That looks like Closey's car." I got to the ground, and there he was, with his pot of tea, his *Sporting Life* and a fag.

"Have I just seen your car?" I said.

"Is it still there, lad?"

Apparently, going round the bend, he'd been leaning across to grab his portable radio. And he'd come off the road and ploughed along the top of the hedge.

He needed the radio, apparently, to catch 'Wogan's Winners', a feature in which Terry Wogan gave out the day's horse-racing tips.

Another time we were playing a Sunday League match at Worcester, and I was driving home with Joan and the kids on the M5. It was dark, and the car in front wasn't lit up. "Look at that idiot," I said to Joan. I kept flashing it, and nothing happened. Then I saw the top of Peter Robinson's head on the passenger side, and I realised it was Closey. He was in the middle lane so I went out into the outside lane, got alongside him and looked across. And he'd got the Sunday paper spread across the steering wheel. I could see Robbo slumped back – probably praying. It took me ages to get Closey's attention.

The Yorkshire lads told me there was a time when they were going down the Edgware Road in London, and the inside lane was all dug up and cordoned off. And when they went past, there was a car down in the hole, with its top level with the road. "I bet it's Closey," they said. And it was. He'd probably been reading the paper and driven straight through the barrier into the hole.

Usually, when lifts were arranged, it was the juniors in the side who were assigned to Close's car. One was a young Viv Richards:

Coming back from the Scarborough Festival once with him I was holding on grimly to the arm rest. The Close foot was hard down, and he was strangely silent. I looked at him out of the corner of my eye and suddenly realised he was asleep.

Going fast through the night with a driver who has his eyes closed is a nasty feeling. I shouted, "Skip!" He jumped up in his seat, instinctively concentrated on the road ahead and gave me a long, withering look.

"It's all right, lad."

Another was Peter Roebuck:

I only travelled with him once. We spent most of the journey whizzing up the inside lane of the motorway, flashing past all these slow-coaches who were clogging up the fast lane.

I followed him once, too. Colin Dredge and I, searching anxiously for a route to Chelmsford, chanced upon Close's car. We tagged courageously onto his tail. He did not notice us, but we followed anyhow. It was when we ended up at the Brighton exit of the South Circular with Close waving his arms around at all and sundry that we realised something was amiss. We did not rely upon Close's concentration or sense of direction again.

Did he ever blame himself for any of the accidents? Or, like his cricketing disasters, were they in his mind all moments of extreme bad luck, caused by other people and by unforeseeable hazards? 'I swerved to miss an oncoming car' is not a turn of phrase that suggests any acceptance of responsibility. Fred Trueman, with typical embellishment, put this well:

Even though he has been one of the game's most colourful characters, he becomes positively surrealist once he is at the wheel of a car. Not that he's a BAD driver, of course; he's just unlucky. Trees, for instance, leap out into the road and savage him; engineers iron out bends in main roads without telling him.

His watchword is speed. I have known him leave a game at Grace Road and head north through the rush-hour traffic which was in three lanes going out of Leicester and one coming in. Out he went into the inward lane and screamed northwards, leaving a trail of city-bound cars up the grass verge.

One newspaperman was whisked from his hotel in Edgware Road to The Oval in eight minutes, and he was still shaking at the end of the three-day game.

Trueman was a fellow competitor in a celebrity sportsmen's race at Brands Hatch that Brian won:

He was more pleased about this than any ton he ever scored because he thought it proved he was the best fast driver in any sport. No chance. The rest of us just got out of the way to save our own skins.

Brian was not that big a drinker, but he liked his whisky. One evening in 1980, following a game for Scarborough, he had one tot too many and failed a breathalyser test on the A1(M). His final drink had been bought by Ken Biddulph, who had moved to the north-east after his Somerset days. In court Ken testified that he had bought a double when Brian had only asked for a single, and as a result Brian escaped with a fine. Ken told me the story, saying how before the hearing Brian had complained to him about being stopped, protesting that he had only been doing "about 80". When the evidence was presented in court, it turned out that he had been driving at nearly 90 with an out-of-control caravan in tow.

On a later occasion Brian was less fortunate, serving a ban for 'excess alcohol' and having to employ a driver for some months.

Perhaps the last word on Brian's driving should be left to Ian Botham, himself no dawdler at the wheel. I suspect there is not as much exaggeration in this account as you might imagine:

I will never forget my first experience of his driving. The first thing that hit you was his need for speed. Come shine or rain, day or night, crystal-clear visibility or pea-soup fog, to him all driving conditions were perfect for cruising at around 100 miles an hour.

The next thing you noticed was the open flask of scalding hot coffee pirouetting on the central console. Then there were the beef sandwiches made for him by his wife Vivien which, while steering the car with his knees and with seemingly little regard for what was happening on the other side of the windscreen, he would open up with both hands to make sure the meat content was acceptably high. And finally, to complete this nightmarish scene, he had a copy of *Sporting Life* folded in half on his lap, from which I swear he was studying the form as he drove along.

"Do you want me to drive?" I would ask hopefully.

His reply every time? "No, lad. Driving helps me to relax."

'Helps me to relax', what a wonderful insight that is into the inner life of Dennis Brian Close.

7

CHAMPIONS AGAIN

The car crash in May 1956 was a setback for Brian. Up to this point he had been a genuine all-rounder, arguably achieving more with the ball than with the bat. In the County Championship he had taken five wickets in an innings 19 times, but he had scored only that one century at Taunton. Troubled by his knee, his bowling became the lesser part of his game, with not one five-wicket haul in championship matches between 1956 and 1958.

What began to emerge in these years was Brian's fascination with captaincy, in particular his awareness of bowling changes and fielding positions in the challenge of taking wickets and winning matches.

The 1950s were difficult years for Yorkshire, a county that expected cricketing success. The team's predecessors, captained by Brian Sellers, had won eight championships in ten years on either side of the war, so the years from 1950 to 1958 when they won nothing prompted much grumbling, among both the supporters and the committeemen. When the next ten years, from 1959 to 1968, brought seven championships, it inevitably prompted the question: "What made the difference?"

As an outsider, interviewing many of the Yorkshire cricketers of those years, I have heard two radically different answers to that question. The first, given by Ray Illingworth and many of the 1960s team, was that the 1950s team, though they had more individual talent, were all playing for themselves, constantly arguing, creating a bad team spirit. The second, given by Bob Appleyard and many of the 1950s team, was that there was nothing wrong with the team spirit, the arguing was a healthy part of the Yorkshire tradition; the reason they never won the championship was that they were up against a Surrey team whom most cricket historians consider the best county side of all time. Interestingly, the one person who did not take sides in this argument was Brian Close.

There were several strong personalities in the 1950s team, none more so than Johnny Wardle. In many ways he was the ideal cricketer – a superb left-arm bowler who thought deeply about the game and was fired with a determination to win. He set the highest standards on and off the pitch, never one to drink late or play loose with his marriage vows. He could also be generous with his wisdom: passing on to the young Ray Illingworth everything he had learned in the game, and in later years taking Geoff Cope under his wing and seeing him through difficult times.

Yet those high standards could be accompanied by a sharp tongue, especially when catches were missed off his bowling, and by a selfishness that was not always conducive to harmony in the team.

The stories are plentiful: the youngster apologising for a dropped catch, only to be made to feel worse – "It's not your bloody fault, it's mine for putting you there"; the fielder told off for trying to run out a tailend batsman, thus depriving Wardle of a potential wicket – "You don't run out nine, ten, jack."

Eddie Leadbeater told me about a game at Worcester when, bowling leg spin in tandem with Wardle's slow left-arm, he achieved his best figures in the first-class game: eight wickets for 83 runs. In the second innings Wardle demanded a change of end, then started to offer his bowling partner advice, suggesting that he flight the ball more. The result was an over in which all six balls were driven to the boundary.

> Norman Yardley came up. "What are you doing?" I said, "Johnny said give it more air." "Well, what's Johnny doing? All he's doing is bowling maidens. Go back to the way you were bowling." Which I did. Then Johnny came up. "I thought I told you to give it more air." I said, "Get lost." He didn't want me to get wickets.

This happened in a tight game when Worcestershire, in a run chase, came close to winning. Perhaps Wardle meant well, and Eddie Leadbeater did him a disservice. Even so, what does it say about the spirit in the team that he suspected Wardle of intentionally encouraging him to bowl badly?

The same could be said of the row in an end-of-season game at Dover when Fred Trueman blasted through Kent's top order and looked briefly like he might take all ten wickets. Wardle, who was in line for the £100 prize for best bowling performance of the summer, nine for 25, proceeded to drop two catches at short leg, one a bad miss, then took two wickets to deprive Trueman of the prize. Trueman, never one to hold his tongue, was not slow to accuse his team-mate of doing it deliberately.

Then there was Bob Appleyard, a tough character who always wanted the ball in his hands. Ray Illingworth told of a game at Sheffield when Norman Yardley asked him to take over bowling from Bob. He arrived at the wicket to find Bob peeling off his sweater and telling the young Ray to "bugger off, I'm bowling." The captain's response, when Ray reported back, was to sigh and say "Leave it for now."

Ray's view was that Yorkshire under-achieved in those years:

> It wasn't a happy side. There were too many arguments, too many jealousies. That's the reason we didn't win things. Norman Yardley was a lovely man and technically a very good captain, but he wasn't strong enough with certain players.

Leicestershire's Terry Spencer described them to me: "Wardle, Closey, Fred, they were always getting on at each other. 'Get up there', 'I'm not fielding there', that sort of thing. They were an unruly team, and Norman Yardley wasn't a disciplinarian."

'I hate waving the big stick,' Yardley wrote. 'Somehow I can't get it into my head that it should be necessary in a game of cricket.'

"Norman Yardley was the nearest to a good captain that I played under," Brian Close said, "but he was very soft on the senior players." A lesson had been learned – it was not a mistake that Brian would make when he took on the captaincy and had to manage Fred Trueman.

Yorkshire finished second in four of Yardley's last five years – the exception being 1953 when they were deprived of three of their four main bowlers: Appleyard, Trueman and Close – so it is wrong to think that they were bad years for the county. Yet this was Yorkshire; second place was failure.

"Cricket to Yorkshire people is a way of life," Vic Wilson told me. "They want success. Yorkshiremen are good winners, but they're bad losers." Vic was a regular in the side through these years, and he was adamant that there was nothing wrong with their team spirit.

They were up against a Surrey side that won seven consecutive championships from 1952. As early as the autumn of 1954, on the boat to Australia, Len Hutton told Bob Appleyard that the Surrey team were better than Brian Sellers' Yorkshire team of the 1930s:

> We were chatting after dinner, and he came out with this statement. It flabbergasted me. He'd been thinking, and he felt that the present Surrey side would have beaten the pre-war

Yorkshire one. You see, they had one international bowler more than any other side had ever had. They had Bedser, Loader, Lock and Laker. Four. And all different styles for different wickets. I doubt if any county side in the whole history of the game has had four like they had. And they were playing at The Oval, which was a result wicket at that time, where we had to go all round the county, taking the pitches we were given.

The summer of 1955 was a good example of what Yorkshire were up against. Three-day championship cricket produced plenty of draws, but Yorkshire that year won 21 of their 28 matches. It is a total of victories only twice exceeded in the whole history of the competition – by Yorkshire, who won 25 out of 32 in 1923, and by Surrey, who that year pipped Yorkshire to the title with a remarkable 23 wins.

Bob Appleyard, keen to counter Ray Illingworth's view, had me researching the match records of Yorkshire in the '50s and '60s. I looked at the ten years from 1949 to 1958, when they secured just one joint title, and found that Yorkshire won 45% of their matches. Then I looked at the following ten years, when Surrey had faded and seven titles were won, and I found almost the same proportion of victories: 45.5%.

For Bob the internal rivalries were a good thing: "There's nothing like a bit of healthy competition in a team." The arguments were a built-in feature of Yorkshire cricket, part of a distinctive identity that went way back. As Leicestershire's Maurice Hallam said to me: "They were always arguing but, when you tried to argue against them, you came up against a brick wall. They were one clan, Yorkshire for Yorkshiremen."

Brian Close was not one who viewed the internal frictions of the 1950s side as a crippling problem, as he explained in an interview with Peter Walker in the late 1970s:

> When I started there were some very hard-assed men around, and often the real battle on the field would be amongst the Yorkshire players themselves; the opposing batsmen were just blown out of the way as an afterthought! A lot of great sides are like this. Real nigglers. Surrey in the 1950s for example. I don't altogether go along with the view that a happy dressing-room atmosphere gives a side a better chance of success. Like in boxing, you need mean and hungry fighters, ten men jealous of a team-mate's achievements and each wanting to do a little better.

Norman Yardley stood down as captain at the end of 1955, the same year that Len Hutton retired. The obvious choice of successor was Billy Sutcliffe, whose father Herbert, the great pre-war batsman, had done well in business and sent his son to public school, thereby making Billy the only amateur in the side. He had had a good summer, scoring more than 1,250 runs, and was selected for the MCC 'A' tour of Pakistan.

If Yardley with all his experience was not always equal to the challenge of managing the team, then Billy Sutcliffe had little chance, as Brian made clear in *I Don't Bruise Easily*. His critique of Sutcliffe went to the heart of what Brian saw as the essence of good captaincy:

> He was happier having a pint and a natter when a day's work was over than he was cracking the whip on the field. His problem as a captain was that he had fixed, preconceived ideas about the way a day would go. You cannot be as rigid in ideas as Billy was. Every man in the side knew a great deal about cricket. Most of us had something to say about the way things were going in the course of a day.
>
> Billy did not have as much knowledge as his players, but he had a pleasant personality. His trouble was really in handling the bowling and the field-placing. He couldn't think with a bowler's mind – and what made it worse for him was that he had some outstanding bowlers in the side with minds of their own. He could not stand up to them in the practical arguments which develop during a long, hard season. We had two bad seasons, and he retired.

The county, seventh in Sutcliffe's first year in charge, rose to third in his second year, with Bryan Stott and Ken Taylor emerging in mid-season as a young and dynamic partnership at the top of the batting order. But the rumblings of discontent with his captaincy, led by Johnny Wardle, were too much for him. In Bryan Stott's view he would have been a 'superb' captain with a younger team, but the task of managing all the arguments got him down:

> The spirit in the team was terrible. The players didn't give Billy any respect; they didn't support him at all. He had a hard, hard time. When Ken Taylor and I got into the side, it was a breath of fresh air for Billy. He had two people he could communicate with.

His father interfered far too much. We'd be away somewhere, and Herbert would suddenly appear and take Billy to one side. That didn't go well with the team.

What next after Billy Sutcliffe? Brian's view was that it was time to break the mould and appoint a professional. His choice would have been Johnny Wardle:

> In my experience up to that time I (and others) had learned more about cricket from Johnny than all the other senior players put together. He knew his cricket inside out; he knew the opposition; he knew about field-placing; and by God! he knew about bowling.

Who knows? Brian might have been right; it might have brought out the best in Wardle. Brian's judgement, emphasising the importance of Wardle's knowledge of the game, was at the heart of what he saw as the essence of good captaincy.

Bob Appleyard wondered if the quieter Willie Watson, at the time the senior professional, might have been a good choice, but he was lured away by Leicestershire, captaining them for four years. "He was a very fine player," Terry Spencer said. "We enjoyed the time he was with us, but he wasn't a demonstrative captain. I'm not sure how he would have managed at Yorkshire. Everybody seemed to want to be captain in their side."

The shock choice was the captain of the second eleven, Ronnie Burnet. A 39-year-old chemical engineer, he had never appeared in a first-class match, and his playing record in the second team was modest. But he had worked well with the youngsters in his team, and maybe by force of personality he could create a better team spirit.

Social attitudes were slowly changing. Some counties, notably Lancashire, had appointed professional captains. That was still a bridge too far for Yorkshire who, if Burnet had declined the invitation, would have offered the captaincy to an insurance broker Derek Blackburn, who was captain of the Bradford club. Yet, as a harbinger of what was to come, they broke with tradition by asking Ted Lester, a professional, to replace Burnet as second-team captain.

The summer of 1958 started badly for the new man in charge. Batting in a pre-season match he was struck on the ankle by a Trueman yorker and went off to hospital. Then at Cambridge he pulled a calf muscle as soon as he took the field and had to miss the first eight championship matches.

Wardle, inheriting the role of senior professional after Watson's departure, stood in as captain. He relished the responsibility, though he was irritated by Burnet's insistence on accompanying him to the middle for the toss.

On Burnet's return the tension between captain and senior professional grew steadily. Wardle saw it as his role to help the inexperienced captain, while Burnet thought it important to assert his authority.

Memories differ about what happened where and what the final straw was. There is a story about a match in which Wardle was regularly beating the bat and Burnet asked him to bowl a fuller length. Wardle, incensed by someone of so little experience presuming to tell him how to bowl, was said to have sent down an over of long hops in protest.

In another story, concerning a match at Worthing, there was a damp patch at one end. With Trueman and Illingworth away, Burnet insisted that Wardle bowl from the less favourable end, to give the 'lesser mortals' a better chance. Sussex made too many runs, the match was lost and Wardle was furious.

In one game, leaving the field at the end of a session, it seems that Burnet said something to Wardle that implied he was not trying. Brian Close's memory is that it happened on the first morning of the match against Somerset at Sheffield, but that cannot be right because Yorkshire were batting that day.

> He could not have made a more false accusation. Johnny Wardle not trying! He could as soon stop breathing as stop trying like hell to win every match he played in.
>
> The row developed, and Johnny told the captain: "The committee asked me to help you. Most of the things I suggest you won't do, and because you won't listen you are making us professionals look like fools to the public."

Vic Wilson's memory was that the outburst was overheard by Clifford Hesketh, a leading committeeman. The county had already formed the view that it needed to rebuild with a younger team, and with that in mind they had announced they would not be retaining Frank Lowson and Bob Appleyard, two England cricketers whose best days were in the past. Should they now do the unthinkable and move on from Johnny Wardle?

The denouement came on Wednesday 30 July 1958, the first day of the Somerset match while Yorkshire were batting. Bryan Stott, twelfth man that day, has a vivid recall of the scene as it unfolded in the dressing room:

Johnny had been out with one or two of us in the nets. He'd taken his shirt off and put on his sleeveless sweater. He was cooling off. Suddenly the telephone rang: "Johnny Wardle's wanted down in the office." So John put his blazer on and went out.

After a while he came back in. Nobody took any notice. He went up to the table, put this letter on it and said, "I've been sacked." We all said, "Don't be so silly." "There it is." And there was this letter. Two paragraphs. 'Dear Wardle'. Two short paragraphs. And that was Johnny's career finished.

The press were informed straightaway, and all hell was let loose. We heard steps coming up to the dressing room and banging on the door. Reporters, photographers, everybody wanting to speak to Johnny. It was like a bomb had dropped.

One quick to justify the decision, saying the club needed to build a younger team, was Herbert Sutcliffe. His son Billy's experience as captain almost certainly shaped his view.

Any hope of a reconciliation ended when Wardle went into print in the *Daily Mail*, airing all his frustrations. The hallowed role of Yorkshire's slow left-armer passed to the young Don Wilson, a less talented bowler but a breath of cheerful fresh air in the side. The county ended the season down in eleventh place. The dynamics of the team were suddenly different, as Bryan Stott astutely observed:

> Johnny's leaving shook Fred up a bit. It took away the focal point of all the micky-taking and backchat. He was in a different position in the team now.

The next summer, 1959, saw a new Chairman of the Cricket Committee, Brian Sellers. He asked the press not to expect too much too quickly; they were at the beginning of a three-year project, looking to mould a young side into championship winners once more.

Burnet's senior professional was Vic Wilson, at 38 the only player other than the captain to be older than Fred Trueman and Brian Close, both 28. A tall left-handed bat and outstanding close fielder, good enough to be selected for the England tour of Australia in 1954/55, Wilson's form had fallen away in recent summers, and in mid-season he lost his place in the side. As a result Brian Close was promoted to the role of senior professional, relishing the opportunity to influence events on the field. It was his first formal taste of decision-making, the first step on his journey to captaincy.

> Nothing was done ostentatiously. We exchanged views as we crossed between overs. I talked to the close fieldsmen and the wicket-keeper. In this way the whole accumulated experience and knowledge of several senior players was made available to the captain. And he listened – and acted.

At the start of Brian's first game as the captain's right-hand man Yorkshire were eighth in the table. Three games and three victories later, they were top. Brian was making a difference, and he knew it. His bowling had come back, too. In the second of the three games, against Warwickshire at Sheffield, Trueman was late at the ground – surviving unscathed from a serious accident in which his car collided with another vehicle, spun round three times and ploughed into the wall of a pub appropriately called The Cricket Ball Inn. In his absence Brian took the new ball and, in humid conditions, bowled ten overs of seamers and took five wickets for 10 runs.

Later in the summer, at Headingley, Yorkshire reached the end of the second day on 231 for five, still 134 runs behind Kent's total. Overnight Brian persuaded Ronnie Burnet to declare, offered to bowl and, with a mixture of medium-pace and off-breaks, took eight for 41, the best bowling figures of his career. It left Yorkshire 244 to win in just under three hours, and they did it with two wickets and two minutes to spare. Brian was at the heart of the action, and he was loving it.

At some point it seems that Burnet got fed up with the constant advice, forcing Brian to adopt a more surreptitious approach. The players would keep their eye on Brian, not the captain, for the small adjustments in the field. Then for the bigger ones:

> I got the bowlers to ask for field changes. Ronnie could scarcely ignore the specific requests from Freddie and Ray. One way and another, we pestered him into taking advice.

Listening to Brian when he talked about that summer, he could make you believe that all the important decisions were made by him, all the bad ones by others or because the captain ignored him. Yet, when you break down the results, his boasting was not so fanciful. Yorkshire won nine of the 11 matches when he was standing in as senior professional, only five of the other 17.

The two defeats came at Bath, when Brian had them trying to sweep Brian Langford, and in the next match at Bristol, where in strangely murky light they crashed to a humiliating 35 all out.

The county were in the middle of a five-match tour of the south – Lord's, Bath, Bristol, Worcester, Hove – at the end of a long and bakingly hot summer. Their bodies were aching, and several of them took the opportunity provided by the early finish in Bristol to go up to Worcester via the brine baths at Droitwich, soaking the strains of the relentless schedule out of their bodies. Suitably refreshed, Bryan Stott batted almost all the first day at Worcester for what proved to be a match-winning 144.

They travelled to Hove at the top of the table, knowing that, if they won there and Surrey slipped up in either of their last two matches, they would be champions – two years ahead of the schedule set by Brian Sellers.

They were a young team, they were enjoying life, and in later years many of them paid tribute to Ronnie Burnet. Jimmy Binks was one:

> When I first came into the side, we weren't a team. There was a lot of self. Ronnie Burnet had us pulling together. Our abilities were not as good as the previous team, but pulling together made a heck of a difference. Ronnie was the guy. Period.

It should be noted that Surrey were no longer the force they had been. The bowlers were past their peak, and that summer Peter May, their star batsman, was ill and played only a quarter of the games.

*

At lunch on the final day at Hove, Yorkshire's chance of victory seemed to be slipping away. Surrey were not likely to win, but they had another fixture to come. Yorkshire could not depend on them slipping up again; they had to win at Hove. But how?

Sussex, 270 for seven in their second innings, had a lead of 183 runs. With the match scheduled to finish at 4.30, there were only 140 minutes of playing time left. If the Sussex captain Robin Marlar did not declare, ten minutes would be lost between innings; soon there would be no chance of a result for either team.

But would Sussex declare? According to Jim Parks, there was disagreement in their side: "Several of us were saying, 'Come on now, Robin, we've got to declare.' But he wouldn't. No way. I don't think he wanted to give Yorkshire anything. That was his attitude."

Marlar, an Old Harrovian with an air that led some on the circuit to nickname him 'Snarler', was the sort of southern amateur who did not naturally endear himself to the Yorkshire professionals.

'He made it absolutely clear,' wrote Ronnie Burnet, 'that under no circumstances was he going to declare since the championship was at stake. He had the whole Yorkshire team seething.'

Bryan Stott agreed: "We were all willing him to declare, to make a game of it. Mind you, if we'd been in his position, we wouldn't have declared."

The Yorkshire team had their own issues, with a flare-up between Fred Trueman and Brian Close. If ever there was a match when the fast bowler needed to be at his best, it was this. It had been a long summer, and Trueman had already bowled more than 950 overs, but for Brian his lack of extra effort was unforgivable:

> He bowled like a drain. For 19 overs of the first innings and 24 of the second he performed as if it was a game of no importance. Maybe he was tired; he had a right to be. But this was an occasion which demanded everything from everybody and conditions were right for him – slope in his favour, wind behind him and the big occasion which Fred loved.
>
> I suggested to Ronnie: "Give Fred these last overs before lunch and tell him to really let it go." Ronnie gave Fred the ball, and he didn't put a bit of effort into it. During lunch I played hell with Fred – the first time I had ever done so.
>
> As we walked out after lunch I asked Ronnie, "What are you going to do now?" He said, "What can I do? I'll have to give Fred another go." I said, "Wash your hands of Fred. Let Ray bowl downwind and Don into the wind. If they can't do it, then we've had it."

The lead passed 200, the minutes ticked by. Then, with more than a hint of help from batsmen tired of their team's tactics, Ray Illingworth took the remaining three wickets. It left Yorkshire to score 215 in 105 minutes, in perhaps 30 or 31 overs, with Sussex free to set defensive fields. By the standards of that time it was a tall order. 'We were mad and frustrated,' Burnet wrote. 'We had not been given a ghost of a chance.'

What followed has entered the folklore of Yorkshire cricket. Ian Thomson, the most steady of seam bowlers, was hit for 30 off his first two overs, with Brian Close losing valuable time by hitting one ball out of the ground. He fell cheaply, but Bryan Stott and Doug Padgett, left-hand and right-hand, ran the Sussex fielders ragged.

Some criticised Marlar for not instructing his bowlers to focus on one side of the wicket and set his field accordingly, but to his credit he thought that would take too long with the left/right partnership and be unsporting. Stott hit 96, Padgett 79, and the match was won with seven minutes to spare. With Surrey not winning, Yorkshire were champions again.

It was an especial triumph for their unlikely captain, the portly, pipe-smoking Ronnie Burnet. Over the years the members of his side have all sung his praises, with the partial exception of Brian Close. For him successful captaincy was about making things happen in the field, and he knew how much Burnet had depended on him in those thrilling last weeks. His verdict on the captain in *I Don't Bruise Easily* was measured:

> Some people believe – and over the years the belief has strengthened – that his appointment was an inspired one, that the committee in one sublime moment found a man strong enough to stand up to the hard characters in the team and then to lead a side composed partly of experienced men, partly of youngsters, back to greatness. Well, he did it, and you can't take that away – but they were two very complex years.

*

There followed an aftermath that would surprise them all. They went to Scarborough where, to tumultuous acclaim, they beat a strong MCC side in another thrilling run chase. After a week's break, they travelled to The Oval for the summer's last match: Champion County versus The Rest.

Ken Taylor had returned to football and Phil Sharpe was not fit so there was room in the side for a fringe player, either the 18-year-old Jack Birkenshaw or the discarded Vic Wilson. In some accounts it was Brian Sellers who asked that Vic Wilson play, but Brian Close claimed it was his idea. Ronnie Burnet wanted to go with the youngster but Brian, keen to win the match, persuaded him that they did not need Birkenshaw's off-spin and it would be better to play the extra batsman. 'Vic had got to come good at some time,' he wrote. 'With his experience he had a better chance of making runs against that standard of bowling than Jack.'

The match was a triumph for Vic Wilson. He top-scored with 41 in Yorkshire's first innings; then, when they followed on 224 runs behind, he hit a match-turning 105. Brian Close supported him with 86, then took five wickets, as they sealed an extraordinary 66-run victory. To their great satisfaction, against the strongest of opposition, they had proved their championship was no fluke.

The assumption, as they went their separate and joyous ways for the winter, was that Ronnie Burnet would be back in the spring, leading them for one more year. In Brian Sellers' mind, however, there was a problem with this scenario. The chances were that by the end of the next summer Vic Wilson would be out of the reckoning, and the club would be left with no viable alternative to Brian Close. And Sellers did not want that. In his eyes Close was an unpredictable maverick – or, as Vic Wilson put it more simply, "He didn't like Brian Close."

Sellers persuaded Ronnie Burnet to write a letter of resignation: 'It would best serve the interests of Yorkshire cricket if I retired and made way for a younger man.' Given that wording, it seems likely that he was expecting Brian Close to be appointed, not someone who was only two years his junior.

A fortnight later Vic Wilson was attending an open day at his children's school when he was called to the telephone. At the end of August he had half-expected to be told he was no longer needed; now, to his great surprise, he was asked to become Yorkshire's first professional captain of the modern age.

The move was widely welcomed. Wilson, a farmer from the East Riding, was described in *The Times* as 'an even-tempered, dependable man' – and 'dependable' was not an adjective you could apply to Brian Close.

"I think it is a very good move," Len Hutton said. "Vic has a young side, and his appointment will stiffen up the team considerably. I have never played with anybody I like better."

If Yorkshire were to jettison the need for an amateur captain, there was some logic to the decision. Ronnie Burnet had completed the task of rebuilding team spirit; replacing him with Vic Wilson would indeed 'stiffen up' the side. Above all, for Brian Sellers, they could put off the day when they might have to turn to Brian Close.

*

So what was it that made the '60s side more successful than the '50s one? Was it the decline of Surrey? Or the creation of a better team spirit? Or, as I suspect Brian thought deep down, his emergence as the tactical brain of the team, making things happen in the field?

8

GIVE HIM MARKS FOR TRYING

'Never a season goes by without the desire to give Close another outing,' wrote John Woodcock in *The Times* when Brian was recalled to the England team in 1961. Even by the fickle standards of the selectors at that time, his speckled Test career was a remarkable one: one Test at the age of 18 in 1949, one in Australia in 1950/51, one in 1955, two in 1957, one in 1959 and now another chance in 1961.

Had he failed on his last four outings? Not in his view. In 1955, after a handful of matches opening the batting for Yorkshire, he was sent in first against a strong South African attack and his 32 was the highest score in either side's first innings. In 1957, in the First Test against the West Indians, he again opened, hitting 15 and an important 42, then found himself dropped down to number seven in the Second Test, playing more as an off-spinning substitute for the unavailable Jim Laker. He made 32, was not required to bowl and was discarded again. 'He must be wondering if his time is up,' wrote John Woodcock.

But Brian's time, it seems, was never up. In the summer of 1959, still only 28 years old, he scored 1,879 runs, took 88 wickets and held 37 catches. With England trying a range of options against a weak Indian team, he forced his way back into the side, playing in the Third Test at Headingley. Again he had a decent game. He came in at 375 for four and hit a brisk 27; he took five wickets and held four catches. Yet it was not enough to keep him in the side, leaving some observers, notably John Arlott, bemused:

> He batted better than was necessary, bowled better than anyone had a right to expect, and fielded well enough; since then he has made a century against the Gentlemen at Lord's. It is very perplexing.

In our filmed interview I asked him if he felt there was any southern bias in Test selection in those years. He answered not with a tirade as Fred Trueman would have done but with a thoughtful yet firm certainty:

I'm sure there was. The amateurs ran the game. You had to be quite a bit better to get selection over somebody who was from counties like Middlesex, Sussex and Kent.

Across the summers of 1957 and 1958, of the fifteen men who batted in England's top six, nine were amateurs. The only Northern professionals among these batsmen were Willie Watson (two Tests) and Brian. There were some great batsmen among the amateurs – Peter May, Colin Cowdrey, a young Ted Dexter – but it is easy to understand how a Yorkshire professional might have felt as Brian did.

The summer of 1960 passed with no further recognition. Then came 1961 and the arrival of the Australians. Captained by Richie Benaud, they were looking to retain the Ashes they had regained in 1958/59, and they got off to a good start. They had much the better of a draw at Edgbaston; then they won at Lord's, a victory which Benaud sat out with an injured shoulder. Next up was Headingley.

Once more Brian, now turned thirty, was in great form with the bat, finishing the summer only 15 runs short of 2,000. Even after being so many times discarded, it was not a great surprise when he was named in the twelve. John Woodcock took the opportunity to summarise his career to this point, inevitably referring to his ill-fated shot at Melbourne:

> Close is one of the enigmas of cricket since the war. He has played half a dozen times for England in five different series. The last was against India at Leeds two years ago when he made 27 and took five wickets in the match for 53, only to be omitted from the side at Manchester. His one appearance against Australia was at Melbourne ten years ago when, at a critical time, he played a lamentable stroke which he has carried around ever since like a lead weight. His ability is a by-word and, if he had the temperament to match it, he might have played not six but 60 times for England.

Jim Laker, a Yorkshireman himself though he had played for Surrey, saw the fault in selecting Close too young:

> If in his early days he had been allowed to mature in every-day county cricket, this extremely capable and at times brilliant cricketer would surely have made himself a permanent niche in Test cricket by the middle fifties.

Jim Swanton in the *Daily Telegraph*, one whom northerners did suspect of having a southern bias, made it clear that he would have preferred the selection of a Middlesex man:

> Close at his best is a first-rate bat, unpredictable as in all his cricket but brilliant on his day. Titmus's all-round credentials would on the whole have appealed more to many people.

Replacing the injured Brian Statham in the England side was the 40-year-old Les Jackson, who was playing his second and last Test. His first, by the richest of ironies, had been at Old Trafford in 1949, alongside the 18-year-old Brian Close. His slingy action and Derbyshire vowels might not have been to the liking of Lord's, but in those intervening years he had taken more than 1,350 wickets at an astonishing average of 16.3.

On Thursday morning it was Close who was omitted from the England twelve. Thus it was that on Saturday, when he was at Chesterfield, helping Yorkshire to beat a Jackson-less Derbyshire, he missed the drama at Headingley. On a pitch that was breaking up Trueman tore through the Australian second innings, at one stage taking five wickets in 24 balls without conceding a run. By close of play England had won by eight wickets, squaring the series at one game each. There was all to play for at Old Trafford.

*

Tuesday 1 August 1961. The final day of the Fourth Test at Old Trafford. A day that would go down as one of the most dramatic in Ashes history, sealing Richie Benaud's reputation as one of the great captains. But, alas, another day that Brian would never be allowed to forget, another 'lead weight' for him to carry through life.

At start of play Australia, batting for the second time, were six wickets down with a lead of 154 runs. 'Stand By For Photo-Finish,' ran the headline in the *Daily Mirror*, 'Thrilling Finish in Prospect' in *The Times*.

England's position would have been much stronger if three crucial catches had not been dropped on the previous day. Neil Harvey, who made 35, was put down twice, once by Brian in the gully, but the most expensive miss was of the opener Bill Lawry, who should have been caught at slip by Subba Row for 25 and went on to hit a century.

However, none of these mistakes looked important when, within half an hour of the start, Australia were nine wickets down, with a lead of only 157. The game, it seemed, had tilted decisively England's way.

All three wickets fell to David Allen. With the last Australian pair, Alan Davidson and Garth McKenzie, looking just to survive, the Gloucestershire off-spinner's first nine overs of the morning, relentlessly accurate, conceded only two runs. His figures at this stage were 37 overs, four wickets for 38 runs.

If he had taken that last wicket David Allen would have had five in the innings. Furthermore, he would have gone down in the history books as the man who spun England to an Ashes triumph. Instead, when he sat with me 48 years later, reflecting on the day, he could only shake his head and wonder about the might-have-beens.

"Decisions were made," he said in his warm West Country voice, "and I do question them in hindsight. But that's being clever. At the time I didn't question them."

Brian Statham's pace, though it had kept the batsmen quiet, was not posing a threat at the other end nor was Statham able to prevent Davidson, the much better batsman, from being on strike whenever Allen began a new over. According to reports, his first nine overs contained only three or four balls to the number eleven.

"If only Tony Lock had been playing. He was a super bloke to bowl with. If he ever had the good batsman down his end for the fifth and sixth balls, he'd make sure you'd have the tail-ender next over."

The frustration was beginning to build. The lead was gradually creeping up, the time left to bat slipping away.

"Then Fred Trueman decided to have his say. 'Why don't you try Closey?' he said to Peter May. 'He's got a knack of getting wickets when you want them.'"

'While McKenzie appeared confident enough against the pace stuff,' wrote Ron Roberts in his book about the series, 'it was very likely that spin would confound him. So Close was tried. This, I felt, would have been a shrewd move with a bowler of more control. Close could bowl an unplayable one, but was equally likely to ease the pressure.'

Alas, Brian did the latter, sending down five full tosses in two ragged overs, and the total leapt by 15. "That released it a bit," David Allen said with a sigh.

There followed, at the start of Allen's next over to Davidson, an even more ill-fated piece of captaincy. "Peter May came up to me. 'Let's encourage him to play a shot or two at your end,' he said. He was the captain, I admired him a lot, and I was still young. I said, 'Yes, right.'"

No longer bowling a tight line, Allen varied the deliveries, and Davidson – perhaps loosened up by the easy runs off Close – swung his bat. Four times the ball flew in the arc between extra cover and mid-off, twice for four and twice for six, the last one landing near the top of the terraced crowd. 'They were not wild slogger's swings,' John Arlott wrote, 'but superbly made, measured strokes of immense power and perfect timing.'

Immediately May summoned Trueman to take over from Allen.

"I walked away, and I thought, 'A pity, that,' as you do. In hindsight I think we got it wrong. If he was going to go after the ball, let him do it when you're bowling tightly."

'Such is the lot of the spin bowler!' Jim Laker wrote acerbically. 'I might be a little biased, but I felt certain Allen should have been allowed at least another over.'

'Hindsight is not difficult,' Benaud later wrote, 'but there was no hindsight about the relief felt in the Australian dressing-room when Allen disappeared from the attack.'

Trueman was not at his best, and the runs continued to flow. By the time the last wicket fell the target had risen from 158 in five and a half hours to 256 in less than four. Only once in England, in 1902, had England scored that many in a fourth innings to win. The game, and the Ashes, were slipping away.

Yet at 3.55 pm the English gloom had dispersed. Dexter, on 76 not out, was at his imperious best, taking the total to 150 for one. "Ted played magnificently," David Allen said. "One of his great innings. He'd already taken Benaud apart at Edgbaston, and he was doing it again."

The Australian captain was at rock bottom: three runs in his last four innings in the series and two wickets for 295 runs in his last five bowls. He was still feeling the effect of his shoulder injury, and none of the other main bowlers was fully fit either.

As a final throw of the dice Benaud took to bowling his leg-breaks from round the wicket. Afterwards he told the gathered journalists that he had discussed the idea the previous night with Ray Lindwall, the former Australian fast bowler. It was not a common ploy at that time, but he had seen the opportunity presented by the rough created by Trueman's follow-through.

"Richie was the greatest captain I played under," David said, experiencing him later on a private tour of Pakistan. "He was such a great public relations man. He was a press man; he had a smell of that world,

94

and he worked it out wonderfully well. He'd come straight off the field, and he'd be talking to the press in the corridor outside the dressing room. Why he'd bowled when he did, why he went round the wicket. And I'm not sure, I'm really not sure. I personally believed at the time that it was a desperate, negative move. He'd tried everything else, and he was being hammered around. But he said it was his last attacking move."

How would history have judged Benaud if he had failed, if he had surrendered the Ashes that afternoon? The South African writer Charles Fortune recalled his thoughts at the time: "Poor chap. He's been a fine cricketer and captain, but this time it's gone. No wickets, no runs. Sad this should happen when he's captain, but that's the way it goes."

Dexter, attempting to cut Benaud, edged the ball into Grout's gloves. Worse followed when Peter May attempted to sweep his second ball and was bowled behind his legs. "Like all the university boys he didn't lap," David Allen said. "He didn't even get down on one knee."

Now it was 150 for three. At the other end, playing the support role, was Raman Subba Row, a stolid left-hander with a limited range of shots.

Enter D.B. Close. Tea was approaching, and the match was in the balance. If ever there was a chance for him to press his claim to a regular place in the side, to show what England had been missing, this was it.

With the left-handed Subba Row still at the wicket and the right-handed Ken Barrington next in, it created a situation Brian claimed to have warned his captain against. "As soon as Richie went round the wicket, I said to Peter May, 'For heaven's sake, don't get two left-handers in together.' But he took no notice."

What followed was, in the words of Jim Laker, 'the most extraordinary innings I can ever recall from an accredited batsman in a Test match'. In *The Times* John Woodcock wrote that Close's effort was 'best talked about in whispers ... He swung wildly at his first ball and continued to play as if he was out of his cricketing senses.' In the *Daily Telegraph* Jim Swanton wrote that the task of describing it 'taxes charity beyond endurance, as indeed it taxed credibility to behold.'

There was worse in the popular press, with Brian Chapman in the *Daily Mirror* calling it an 'outstanding example of folly run riot, of Russian roulette on the cricket field, of unforgivable *felo de se*, of unconscionable lunacy'.

The first ball pitched outside the off stump, Brian got his foot across and with a horizontal bat went to swing it hard to the leg side. It flew off the top edge of the bat, over leg slip's head, and ran away for two runs. 'Some people described it as a sweep,' Ray Lindwall wrote. 'It looked more like a swipe to me.' For Jim Laker it was simply 'a dreadful cow shot'.

If he had fallen to that shot, as he did to the one false stroke he played at Melbourne, perhaps the criticism would have been less severe. But he attempted to repeat the ugly shot five times, 'swinging his bat' in the words of one reporter 'through strange arcs that bore relation more to hammer throwing than to batting.'

Only with the last of these five attempts did he make proper contact, sending the ball – inevitably in the eyes of most observers – into the hands of Norman O'Neill at backward square-leg. To make matters worse, in the midst of this sequence of sweeps and swipes, he had executed perfectly one orthodox shot, stepping forward and lofting the ball cleanly over long-on for six.

D.B. Close caught O'Neill bowled Benaud, 8.

The reporters shook their heads in bewilderment. 'It was quite impossible,' wrote Jim Laker, 'to understand what was passing through Brian Close's mind.'

Most hurtful of all, for Brian, was the response of his old Yorkshire captain Norman Yardley, at the time on air with *Test Match Special*. Appalled by what he had witnessed, he declared emphatically that Close should never play for England again.

Yet, if you listened to Brian, even after half a century to reflect, he could make the innings seem perfectly logical, almost to the point of convincing you that he had no alternative. As ever he could not be wrong.

There were only three wickets down, they were still trying to win, and Subba Row was "not the greatest stroke player in the business". It was Brian's job to take it on, to knock Benaud out of the attack or, at least, force him to go back over the wicket. Yes, he had connected perfectly with a straight six, but the wind was against the shot. If he hit the next one only three-quarters cleanly, it would hold up in the air and be caught by long-on. It was a risk he could not afford to take.

No, his only option was the sweep. He noted the positions of the leg-side fielders – a leg slip, a backward square leg saving a single and a man in the deep in front of square – and he convinced himself the shot carried little danger. The sweep was the horse that he would back.

"If I was going to hit it properly, it was going to go behind square, carry over Norman O'Neill. But if I got a top edge, it would go finer. So I was fairly safe ... or at least I thought I was."

Young and innocent
The 18-year-old England Test cricketer, 1949

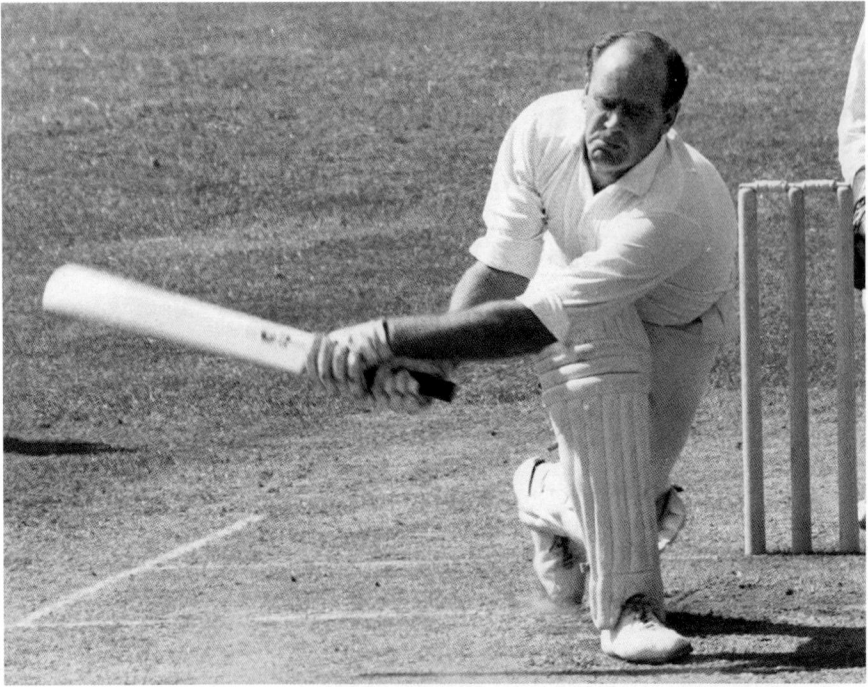

All-rounder

34,994 first-class runs and 1,171 wickets

He batted left-handed, as he wrote, but he bowled right-handed.

Left-handed golfer, right-handed golfer, snooker player and footballer

Motor Racing Champion, Brands Hatch, March 1974
Winner of the 10-lap Evening News Celebrity Race,
ahead of show jumper Richard Meade

Entertaining an audience
(top) Diving in the pool on the boat to Australia
(bottom) Picking up the matchbox without spilling the wine

First year of captaincy: Yorkshire, 1963

standing: George Alcock (physio), Doug Padgett, John Hampshire, Don Wilson, Mel Ryan, Tony Nicholson, Bryan Stott, Phil Sharpe, Ted Lester (scorer)
seated: Jimmy Binks, Fred Trueman, Brian Close, Ray Illingworth, Ken Taylor

Last year of captaincy: Somerset, 1977

standing: Phil Slocombe, Dennis Breakwell, Brian Rose, Joel Garner, Colin Dredge, Ian Botham, Keith Jennings
seated: Peter Denning, Mervyn Kitchen, Brian Close, Derek Taylor, Viv Richards

Waiting to bat

Crayon portrait by Ken Taylor

Like David Allen, he was sure Benaud had only gone round the wicket to stop England winning. Under the lbw law at the time the point of contact had to be between wicket and wicket. "If we'd have been playing for a draw I could just have put my leg out there, and Richie Benaud couldn't have done a damn thing about it. If I hadn't had to chase the win, he'd have had to do something different. Unfortunately I all but hit one properly, and I was out. If England were going to win, it was the only way I could see that we were going to do it."

Even O'Neill's catch, in Brian's account of the game, was the most wretched piece of ill fortune. O'Neill had just replaced Mackay, a shorter man, in that position, and he jumped his full height, stretching up with one arm and somehow holding the ball with the tips of two fingers. The surviving film footage does not capture the moment, but newspaper reports do not describe O'Neill's catch as being remarkable in the way it was in Brian's memory.

On the stroke of tea Subba Row played a loose drive and was bowled between bat and pad. Then in the evening the wickets tumbled. Barrington played across the line to Mackay and was lbw, Allen drove airily at Benaud and was caught brilliantly at slip, Trueman after a patient start 'could not resist having a swipe'. All out for 201, England lost their last nine wickets for 51 runs, with Benaud – at one stage nought for 40 – finishing with six for 70 and being feted for the rest of his life as a tactical genius.

Brian's seven-page justification of his innings in *I Don't Bruise Easily* ended by reflecting on the wickets that fell after his:

> Watching our later batsmen play some strange shots and get out I thought, 'No one knows whether we are going for the runs or playing for the draw or what. No one has set any guidelines or laid down any policy.' At least I knew what I was trying to do.

It was a despondent England eleven who left Old Trafford for their county matches the next day, none going further than David Allen who had a five-hour train journey to Pontypridd. "It was a wonderful Test match," he said. "It swayed one way and then the other; that was the beauty of it. But it was a huge disappointment to lose. And I'll tell you what. Sat on that train, going down to Pontypridd on my own, it got worse."

He was not as unkind about Brian's innings as the men of the press. "There was no plan. We all went out and played as individuals. And Brian was going to take Richie apart. Give him marks for trying, I suppose."

Ken Barrington also tried to see it from Brian's point of view: 'I can only assume that Brian felt "having a go" at Benaud was the best thing to do. If so, I feel that he was wrong, but in fairness a few more hefty blows like the six he hit would have put England in clear sight of victory and would also have meant that Benaud would have had to come off.'

Alan Davidson, whose own gamble had paid off so spectacularly in the morning, reckoned Brian had played like an Australian, not like a cautious Englishman. He had not played for himself; he had taken a risk in pursuit of victory: "It took a brave man to do what Closey tried to do."

Benaud agreed: "The slating of Close was one of the most unjust things I have ever experienced. He could have turned the game in minutes if some of his attempted sweeps had come off."

"You can talk about Peter May's shot and Brian Close's innings," David Allen said, "and the bowling changes. I think what lost us the match was our catching. They caught magnificently; we caught badly."

*

It was all over once more for Brian. If Benaud's star soared that day, Brian's fell to earth with another almighty crash. With a gambler's instinct and seemingly little care for the potential damage to his reputation, he had played a 'Russian roulette' innings and finished up shooting himself. As a result he was once more the fall guy, an outcast from Test cricket.

"On the radio they said I should never play for England again," he said defiantly in our filmed interview. "They didn't say anything about Peter May who got bowled behind his legs. And what about the wickets that fell after I got out? They could have played for a draw, but they kept getting out. Silly devils. If I'd have been captain, I'd have had a completely different attitude to it all." He paused for a moment. "Never mind. It put me into sleep again for another two years." Then he burst into a rasping guffaw, as he often did when he related his disasters.

'Poor Close!' John Woodcock wrote when the selectors announced a twelve for the final Test that included neither Brian nor Fred Trueman. 'He is such a splendid, natural cricketer, and yet no one would have thought so to see the innings that he played on that Tuesday afternoon. As it is, the last has probably been seen of Close as an international cricketer – the last and nothing like the best.'

The last of Brian Close? Oh no! There were three more recalls to come, one a full fifteen years later. Again and again he got knocked down, but somehow he kept coming back.

9

THE PRODIGAL IS FORGIVEN

> J.V. Wilson, in his three years as captain, led Yorkshire to the title twice and they were runners-up on the other occasion. His retirement left the county with quite a problem in finding a new captain.

With the benefit of hindsight these words by Bill Bowes, written at the end of 1962 for the *Wisden Almanack*, seem most peculiar. Brian Close was to become one of the greatest captains in the post-war English game. He had enjoyed success when he deputised for Vic Wilson, he was now the senior capped player, and he would have been a shoo-in if there had been a vote in the dressing-room. What was the problem in finding a captain?

Yorkshire had already broken the mould by appointing a professional, but Vic Wilson was a steady, dependable man, someone who could be relied upon to do the right thing, both on the field and off. Brian Close, in the eyes of the committee, could not be relied upon at all. He was an unstable maverick, one who had not fulfilled his great talent, and he always seemed to know best, never wanted to listen to the advice of his elders.

Jim Kilburn, that most headmasterly of cricket writers, summed up the common view of Brian that had formed during the early years of his career:

> Close remained an exceptional cricketer but he allowed himself to become a fatalistic one. He treated cricket without due respect and he paid appropriate penalties. His successes he regarded as the natural consequence of his outstanding ability, as they were. His failures he attributed to misfortune and therefore beyond control, which is a philosophy of immaturity.

The Yorkshire committee wrestled with the decision, not announcing it till the end of January after what the *Guardian* described as 'six months of informed debate':

This unhurried, almost judicial process eliminated at least seven other names, several with more impressive social qualifications than a weaver's son.

They certainly considered returning to an amateur, notably Robin Feather, the Old Harrovian who was captain of the second eleven, or Derek Blackburn, who had been the committee's second choice when they appointed Ronnie Burnet. Feather had never played a first-class game, Blackburn one against Cambridge University. Jim Kilburn reflected on the decision some years later:

> Yorkshire did not appoint Close in 1963 because they thought him a heaven-sent leader, appearing in time of need. His appointment was probably viewed with as much anxiety as optimism in the corridors of administrative power.

Eric Todd in the *Guardian*, while observing that Close had not lived up to the promise of his debut season, greeted the decision with enthusiasm:

> Not even his severest critics can deny that Close is a most accomplished cricketer and a keen and very shrewd student of the game. As a player he has made his mistakes and paid for them. As captain of Yorkshire he may start afresh and enlarge the rare image the world had of him 15 years ago.
> The prodigal has been forgiven.

"I was very surprised," Vic Wilson told me. "Brian Sellers disliked Brian Close so much, I never thought he'd appoint him."

The old order was giving way to the new, and there was more than a little trepidation. In 1962 Yorkshire had been one of only four counties with a professional captain. For 1963 Close's appointment took the total to nine, which the following day went up to 17 when MCC took the momentous decision to abolish the distinction between amateurs and professionals. The meeting was held with the flag at Lord's at half-mast, mourning the death the previous day of Sir Pelham 'Plum' Warner, the very archetype of the old order.

Meanwhile at Westminster, after the death of the Wykehamist Hugh Gaitskell, the Labour Party was in the process of electing as its leader Harold Wilson, a grammar school boy from Yorkshire. A new world was beckoning.

*

The three years of Vic Wilson's captaincy had been frustrating ones for Brian. The captain, himself a professional, saw no need for a senior professional, and he certainly did not want Brian as his right-hand man, preferring to consult Ray Illingworth. "Raymond was the one I always turned to. His advice was very sound."

Yet it seems that Brian did not hold back, regularly making suggestions to the captain. As when Ronnie Burnet had been captain, he had the team keeping an eye on him so that he could make surreptitious adjustments to the field. On one occasion there was a bust-up in the dressing-room: "Don't you interfere with my field settings," Vic Wilson blasted. "I'm a professional, I'm captain of this side, and I don't need you to be setting fields." On another occasion, when Brian argued too persistently for the bowlers to change ends, Vic snapped: "If you open your mouth just once more, I'll send you home on the train."

Brian's way of thinking was that matches were won by taking wickets, and wickets were taken by posing problems for the batsmen. Never let a game drift, keep playing on a batsman's mind. Don Wilson might not be doing much with the ball, but put in a leg slip and make the batsman wonder. Stand absurdly close at silly mid-off and force him to ask, 'Why is he doing that?' "Don't give the batsman time to compose his thoughts," Brian explained. "That's half the battle of getting somebody out."

That was not Vic Wilson's way. As Brian rather witheringly put it, "He was a farmer. You know what farmers are like. They take three months to know when the grass needs cutting."

An exchange between the two of them, when they took the field at Old Trafford in 1960 with Lancashire needing only 78 to win, was typical:

> "What are you going to do?" I asked as we went out. Vic said, "Well, we can't do any more than try our best", which meant that we were going to go through the normal motions and hope that something might happen.

According to Brian in *I Don't Bruise Easily*, he persuaded Vic Wilson to stifle the batsmen's scoring shots by setting a six-three field and getting the bowlers to stick to an off-side line. The fast bowlers Fred Trueman and especially Mel Ryan bowled magnificently, time started to run short, and Lancashire were reduced to 43 for six. The bowlers, having already run in hard for an hour and a half, started to wilt, and the score crept up. Brian urged a change, offering to bowl himself, but the captain stuck

101

to his Plan A for the full 31 overs of the innings. The match was lost by two wickets on the very last ball, a wayward delivery down leg by a tired Trueman. 'If I had been captain,' was the clear subtext of Brian's account, 'we would have won the game.' It was a familiar refrain, containing in all probability an element of truth.

There was a wide age difference between Vic Wilson and the members of his side, a gap that was the greater for Vic not often staying to drink with them at the end of the day. He was a quiet, introverted man who was happier talking cricket with his father back on the farm than with his young team in a crowded and noisy bar.

I interviewed Vic for one of the Yorkshire films. At 85 years old he was slow of speech, not one to use more words than necessary. It was a different experience from interviewing Brian Close, who with barely a prompt was up and away with the story of his life. Yet Vic was a man of obvious integrity, with Yorkshire cricketing pride running through his veins, and everything he said carried weight.

He was astonished to be offered the captaincy, revealing that his first thought was that now as captain he did not need to worry about being dropped from the side. In his first championship match in charge, back at Hove where they had won the title in Ronnie Burnet's last game, he had boldly declared their first innings on 281 for no wicket (Stott 138, Taylor 130) and lost in an over-optimistic run chase on the last afternoon. "I bloomered," he said simply.

Attending committee soon afterwards, he was assured by Brian Sellers that the club stood by his conduct of the game, only for Herbert Sutcliffe to weigh in: "Mister Chairman, I wish to disassociate from that remark. Myself and one or two others consider Vic made a mistake."

It was an inauspicious start for their first professional captain, with Vic all too aware of the consequences if he made what he called a 'hash-up' of the job: "It could have made trouble for years ahead."

He did not make a hash-up. Far from it. He won the title in his first and last years and felt he should have won in 1961 as well. The death of his father in mid-season distracted him, and he berated himself for being too complacent after the previous year's success. They ended the summer as runners-up, with Brian Sellers telling him bluntly, "It's no good to me finishing second. You may as well finish second last." Essex's Trevor Bailey, arriving at Scarborough for the Festival, was astonished to run into so much disgruntlement. "I don't know what the fuss is about," he told Vic. "If we'd have finished second, we'd have been over the moon." Such were the forces that swirled around the Yorkshire captaincy.

Sellers, with his no-nonsense style, made his mark at the start of the next summer, Vic's last in charge. Yorkshire, unlike other counties, hired their players for one year at a time, and by 1961 they had 14 capped men on the staff. With promising youngsters such as Geoff Boycott and John Hampshire coming through, it was too many. This led to a scene that Bryan Stott has never forgotten:

> On the first day of outdoor practices in April, we had our players' meeting with Brian Sellers. We were all sitting in the old dressing room with a fire going, waiting, and Brian Sellers comes clomping along the corridor. He closes the door behind him and leans back against it. "There's fourteen of you buggers here now," he says. "But there won't be at the end of the season." That was our pre-season pep talk.

With Vic Wilson announcing his retirement, there was an expectation that one batsman and one bowler would be culled. The decision, taken by a full committee of 35 that included all the club's vice-presidents, came at the end of July while the team were playing at Bristol:

> Vic had to go off at three o'clock to take the call. We were in the field, and we could see him through the window of the secretary's office, waiting by the phone. Eventually we saw him talking. Then he came back out. "It's Mike Cowan and Brian Bolus," he said.

Bryan Stott soon discovered how close the vote had been:

> One of the senior vice-presidents, a chap called Furniss, he walked with a limp and had a moustache, came up to me. "Congratulations, Stott," he said, "on still being a Yorkshire player – by one vote." 'Thank you very much, Mr Furniss,' I said.

As if this were not unsettling enough for the team, the match preceding this one at Bristol, against Somerset at Taunton, caused an earthquake in Yorkshire cricket. The majority of the team had travelled down from Leeds, but Fred Trueman was driving from London, where he had been given the special honour of captaining the Players in what would turn out to be the last Gentlemen/Players match at Lord's. In the passenger seat was Phil Sharpe whose kit was still in Trueman's car back at the hotel when it came to the toss at the ground the next morning.

In our filmed interview Vic said how much he enjoyed his three years as captain. He paid tribute to the spirit in the team and the way they accepted his decisions when he had to leave players out, something that was never pleasant.

"I think you left Fred out of the side once," I ventured.

"No, I never left Fred out," he insisted to my surprise.

"At Taunton?"

"I didn't leave him out of the side; I sent him home." He chuckled at the distinction. "I warned him the previous Saturday. He was late at Sheffield. I had to give him a rollocking then. He said, 'Bugger you, bugger the cricket. My daughter's been up all night with toothache.' I had no alternative. You can't have one law for the rich, one for the poor."

"Did it have a good effect?" I asked, perhaps naïvely.

"Not really," he said with a smile. "Fred never forgave me."

Indeed, Trueman was a notable absentee at the end of the summer when it came to donating to Vic's farewell present. In his late-life memoir, *As It Was*, in which he looked to set the record straight about all the controversies in which he had been wrongly accused, he explained that he and Phil Sharpe had arrived late at the hotel, there had been a mix-up with the room numbers and he had not received his early-morning call.

Whether that is the truth or whether, as I have often been told, he was allocated the right room but chose to spend the night in another one, booked by a female opera singer, we will never know.

Brian claimed that when Vic consulted him about dropping Fred he replied, "It's your decision, but you should have done that in your first season as captain, not your last. If you had, all would be well now." Was that quite true? According to Somerset's Graham Atkinson, a Yorkshireman himself, the Yorkshire team at Taunton were to a man urging their captain to leave out Fred.

When he did arrive, Fred needed a lot of calming down, with the commentator Don Mosey working hard to prevent him from doing himself more harm and going the way of Wardle.

Somerset had in their side a frail-looking Guyanese batsman Peter Wight, a stylish player who had made good runs against every bowler in the country except Fred Trueman. He was a sensitive man, and something about the Yorkshireman, whether it was the menace of his bowling or the verbal intimidation that went with it, had got under his skin. His career average at this point was an impressive 35, but against Yorkshire it was a paltry 15. When news of Trueman's absence reached him, he apparently let out a high-pitched whoop of delight, went out and, 'confident from the beginning', hit a sublime 215.

The use of Fred Trueman's bowling was a source of disagreement between Vic and Brian. Vic rated Fred as the best bowler he ever saw, paying tribute to his role in those three years: "We wouldn't have won the championships without Fred. He could produce a ball to get out a good batsman when he was set, and not many bowlers can do that." Yet he also thought Fred should have been thankful to him for the way he would bring him back to bowl out the tail: "In the career records nine, ten and jack count no different to one and two."

In those three summers Trueman bowled nearly 3,400 overs and took 485 wickets. He never seemed to break down, with just the masseur George Alcock on hand to deal with the aches and pains.

> Many times I'd say to Fred if he had a niggle, "Have you been on the table? Has George been attending to you?" "No, I can't get on the table," he'd say. "Bloody Closey's been on it all morning." In my day Brian was always suffering from injuries. When he became captain, he seemed not to have so many niggles.

For those brought up on tales of Close the tough nut who never acknowledged pain, this picture of him constantly on the table is quite an eye-opener, just as it is hard to imagine the extreme reluctance to entrust him with the Yorkshire captaincy.

When it came to managing Fred Trueman's workload as a bowler, Brian had a very different approach from his predecessors:

> Freddie was bowling at three-quarters pace under Ronnie Burnet and Vic. They overbowled him. Sometimes they would have him bowling 30 overs in a day. I bowled him in shorter spells. I kept him going for an extra two years.

Whether Fred Trueman ever appreciated that, or even saw it in that way, is doubtful. The two of them were never kindred spirits.

Another ripple in the team came with the first appearances of Geoffrey Boycott, who had been scoring prodigiously in the second eleven. When I asked Vic about him, all he said was: "He was very polite, even called me sir, which was quite remarkable after what Fred called me."

It was not all politeness between the two of them. Boycott made his championship debut at Northampton in Vic's last season. He had not long been in the middle when he refused the call of a run from Phil Sharpe who, turning in mid-pitch, failed to regain his ground. Vic Wilson was furious, venting his spleen in the dressing room. Sitting on opposite sides of the room, in front of the whole team, he tore into the youngster, telling him it was not his job to think whether or not there was a run, he was there to do as he was told by the senior players. Boycott tried to argue back, refusing to accept that he should just do as he was told without thinking. It was an unpleasant scene, one that several of those present thought Vic would have handled better if he had taken Boycott to one side for a private dressing-down.

Bryan Stott remembers driving Boycott to the next game at Chesterfield.

> It was my first meeting with Geoff. He told me about his home, his dad being injured and his working for the civil service. And I explained to him how, when he was batting with a senior player, he should follow his lead on running. And Geoff was very uptight. "I'll show them," he said. "I'll bloody well show them." His fist was shaking, and he was sobbing – whether it was with anger or disappointment. I left him in the car and told him to come in when he was ready.
>
> Then we started to play the next day, and he did exactly the same thing with Ken Taylor. Ken called, and Geoff was there with his back to him. Ken just ran straight off; there was no point in trying to turn back.

Denys Rowbotham in the *Guardian* had no doubt where the fault lay: 'Boycott's inexperience – he backs up badly and is too prone to follow the course of a shot instead of watching the striker – led to Taylor's being run out.'

In my experience Ken Taylor is the mildest of men but, according to Don Mosey, he was not in a mild mood when he took his pads off: 'He retreated to the rear of the pavilion in Queen's Park, there to give his Volkswagen the most vigorous polishing it had ever had, each application of the duster accompanied by the promise, "I'll kill the bastard, I will.""

In two matches the newcomer had acquired a reputation as not only a bad runner but, worse, a selfish cricketer. It did not help him that he was a loner, not one with whom you could sort out the problems over a beer or two in the bar. He played two more matches later in the summer, at the end of which Vic Wilson recommended that the county let him go, judging that he was 'unlikely to make a first-class cricketer'.

When Close was appointed captain, he was asked his opinion, and perhaps it helped the young Boycott that Brian had missed the two matches and not witnessed the run-outs or the bad feeling he had generated in the team. Perhaps, too, Brian was at heart a softer man than Vic Wilson. "I haven't seen much of him," he said. "Let me have him for a summer and see what I can make of him."

How the history of Yorkshire cricket would have been different if he had endorsed Vic Wilson's judgement of the youngster.

As with all cricket teams forced to spend several months together, there were tensions, and the unique Yorkshire pressure of being expected to win added to the tension. Yet, for all that, there was generally a good spirit in the side, a *joie de vivre* captured best by the hearty singing that Don Wilson and Phil Sharpe led.

The Boycott run-outs, the sending home of Trueman and the anxiety about future contracts were all unsettling, and they sapped morale to the point that at the end of the match at Taunton the side was well off the pace in the County Championship, three wins behind the leaders Worcestershire and Warwickshire. At this point, according to Brian, the team met without their captain present and had a heart-to-heart session:

> We knew we weren't a patch on the team we should be. We were doing nobody any good – not Yorkshire, the captain or ourselves. We resolved to try to put things right and see if we could send Vic off to his retirement with another championship win.
>
> The lethargy of the previous few weeks was replaced, almost overnight, by the old urgency and resolution to win. Freddie missed the next two games, but he soon caught the spirit of the team at its best and we were all united once more.

107

With renewed zest they won six of their next eight matches, getting first-innings points in the other two. But a run of three drawn matches took them to the last fixture at Harrogate needing victory to overtake Worcestershire at the top of the table – victory over not only Glamorgan but also, as it turned out, the September weather.

On the first morning the damp pitch was not to Fred Trueman's liking, causing a bizarre delay when he demanded that it be remeasured. But Don Wilson was at his best, taking six wickets as Glamorgan were skittled out for 65. Yorkshire then struggled, all out for a total of 101 that owed everything to a fighting innings of 67 from Ken Taylor. The next day it rained and rained. 'By mid-afternoon,' Jim Kilburn wrote in the *Yorkshire Post*, 'the pools were spreading like a picture of complete cricketing desolation.' The prospect of any further play was bleak.

Yet this was Yorkshire; their cricket was a way of life. Before dawn on the final day, with car headbeams lighting the scene, an army of volunteers arrived with garden forks, squeegees and all sorts. Aided by a strong wind, the water was cleared, and play began on time. Such was the expectation of glory that the little club ground was bursting with more than 10,000 spectators.

Don Wilson and Ray Illingworth reduced the visitors to 72 for seven, then they ran into an obdurate pair of batsmen who steadily used up vital time. In the words of Kilburn, 'Spinning fingers tired, and the pitch eased beneath the absorbent wind.' Was Vic Wilson's last match to end in disappointment? He recalled the tension of that afternoon in Don Mosey's book *Champion Times*:

> There was the danger that it would rain again. Just one more shower would have killed off any chance we might have had. For some time Brian Close had been dropping hints (in the ponderous way that only he could) about having a bowl, and eventually I gave him the ball. What happened next was, I suppose, typical of the way he played his cricket. The first ball was a long hop and was despatched for four; the next eight produced three wickets and no further runs!

Soon enough Yorkshire had knocked off the required runs and were celebrating another championship. Vic could enjoy his 'story-book ending' while Brian, when he was eventually appointed, would inherit a successful side.

10

PURE, UNALLOYED JOY

At Lord's on Tuesday 25 June 1963, against the West Indies, Brian Close finally rose to the challenge of Test cricket, playing an innings that would last forever in the memory of those who witnessed it, an innings like no other in the history of the game. It was a heroic knock, brimful of crazy courage, at the centre of a day's action that built up to one of the greatest ever finishes in Test cricket, a climax that captured the imagination of the nation. At last, fourteen summers on from his teenage debut for England, Brian Close was a national hero.

To most observers it was a great surprise that he was back in the England team, called up for the First Test at Old Trafford only two years after an innings at the same ground that seemed to have written him out of international cricket forever. "Be careful!" he responded when told the news of his recall. "At my age I can't stand shocks like that."

Batting at number six he scored 30 and 32 at Old Trafford, 9 in the first innings at Lord's, and his bowling yielded no wickets. A low score in the second innings would almost certainly have seen him jettisoned yet again – after nine Tests, spread across seven series: 1949, 50/51, 55, 57, 59, 61, 63.

He was now Yorkshire captain – "officially," as he put it to me. "I'd been captain unofficially, prior to that" – and leadership, as Jim Kilburn observed, was proving the making of him:

> The transformation was psychologically rational. Given responsibility Close became responsible. His authority was firm and acceptable, and his example was inspiring. Not only were Yorkshire the champions of 1963, but Close, in impressive batting form, was taken back into the England fold. He played in all five Tests against West Indies, and at Lord's he epitomised himself in a historic innings.

Yorkshire's championship programme began at Northampton where on the first day they struggled on a lively pitch against the pace of the tall

David Larter. Alone of the top order Close survived, finding an unlikely partner in Fred Trueman who chose the occasion to demonstrate that he could be more than a lower-order slogger. Confident that Larter would not dare to pitch anything short at him, he played a front-foot game with admirable correctness, 'his left elbow a model of righteousness' according to the *Guardian*. He hit his maiden first-class hundred, while at the other end his captain, driving and hooking powerfully, hit 161, towards the end of which 'he was even moving down the wicket to Larter.'

Moving down the wicket to a tall, hostile fast bowler? It would not be the last time that summer he would do that.

He masterminded victories over Northamptonshire, Warwickshire, the West Indian tourists and, in the new 65-over Knockout Cup, Nottinghamshire. By the third week of May, when the first-class averages appeared for the first time, DB Close was in second place in the batting, behind the Australian Ken Grieves, with 508 runs at an average of 63.50.

He was absorbed by the challenge of captaincy, Test cricket not uppermost in his mind when he was named in the team for the First Test:

> I must admit my thoughts fly to the Yorkshire fixtures I shall
> miss. We have four injured players out already. It's like leaving
> a flourishing business when it needs you most.

Ted Dexter, as England captain, may have promoted his cause. Though they came from different stock, they respected each other's spirit of adventure, and Close had a surprisingly good record as a bowler against Dexter, often boasting in later years that Ted was his 'rabbit'. Close was coming into the team in place of Tom Graveney, of whom Dexter was not a fan. "He only scores runs when you don't need them," he once told Sussex team-mate Alan Oakman who, with his engagingly laid-back humour, responded by asking, "When don't you need runs?"

The tour of Australia the previous winter had been a disappointment, an opportunity to reclaim the Ashes lost in part because England's fielding was poor. So, to strengthen this aspect of their game at Old Trafford, in came Keith Andrew as wicket-keeper, Micky Stewart and Brian. Denys Rowbotham in the *Guardian* even wondered if the inclusion of Stewart and Close, both county captains, was 'with half an eye on the need to find a captain for the next tours of South Africa and Australia'.

Another repercussion of the winter tour was MCC's decision to withhold some of the good-conduct bonus from the two Yorkshiremen in the party, Fred Trueman and Ray Illingworth. Neither, in Dexter's end-of-tour report, had contributed positively to team spirit off the field. The manager, the Duke of Norfolk, went further, saying that Trueman's 'general manner off the field left a good deal to be desired.' This was red rag to Trueman who called it a 'filthy insult' and let it be known that he did not intend to play for England again. By the time the First Test team was announced, he had withdrawn the threat.

His conduct on his first tour of the Caribbean had almost certainly cost him a place on the next two tours, to Australia and South Africa, and he was not picked for another tour after this one to Australia. On paper he should have gone to South Africa in 1964/65, but I was reliably told that, at the selectors' meeting, the desire for a harmonious tour counted against him when it came to the crunch. In the 13 years of his Test career, from 1952 to 1965, the great fast bowler went on only four of MCC's nine tours, and he lost good-conduct money on two of them.

He was an outsize personality, often at odds with authority, and at the start of the summer it seems there were rumours that he resented the appointment of the new Yorkshire skipper. In his column in the *Sunday People* he sought to scotch 'whispers going round that our new captain, Brian Close, and myself are at loggerheads':

> I can tell you that's a load of rubbish! I reckon Brian is handling me just fine. And, as you know, that's an outsize job at any time – nuff said!

When the two of them were absent with England, Yorkshire were captained by either Jimmy Binks or Ray Illingworth, both thinking cricketers. At Cardiff, against title contenders Glamorgan, Illingworth surprised everybody by throwing the ball to the young John Hampshire, a batsman who had one first-class wicket to his name, and his improbable leg-breaks claimed a match-winning seven victims.

In a season when injuries and Test call-ups depleted Yorkshire's resources, Geoffrey Boycott repaid his captain's trust in him. He was batting at number five when he hit his maiden century, in the high-pressure environment of a Roses match at Sheffield, but Brian Close turned him into an opener and he finished the season with 1,628 runs, second in the national averages. Tony Nicholson, a swing bowler who had come into the game late, also established himself in the side, and the championship was won again – for the fourth time in five years.

Whatever friction did or did not exist with Fred Trueman, Brian was in his element from his first day as captain, as he made abundantly clear in *I Don't Bruise Easily*:

> Captaincy came to me as a joyous relief, rather than a strain. I had spent something like six or seven seasons watching successive captains dabbling with a job I regarded as highly specialised and vitally important. For five of those seasons I had been in a position where I urged, coaxed, pleaded with first the senior professional, then the captain himself, to take action which seemed to me at the time to be necessary, even essential. Sometimes my advice had been taken, sometimes it had been ignored. It had been a highly frustrating time and now, at last, I was free of all those frustrations. I could follow my own instincts, put my own ideas in operation. To back me up I had a team of superb professionals who were not only great, or very good, players but who all thought about their cricket day and night.
>
> There was a pure, unalloyed joy in playing cricket in 1963.

'Unalloyed joy' is not the first phrase that springs to mind when looking at the state of Brian's upper body after his Lord's innings, but without doubt he loved every minute of the challenge.

At Lord's he came to the middle on the afternoon of the fourth day, with the sky dark and the tall and very fast Wes Hall running in from a Pavilion End that had no sight-screen. There was an awkward patch just short of a length, from which the ball was lifting nastily, and Close's arrival came as a result of Colin Cowdrey being hit by a rearing delivery and retiring hurt. The score was 72 for three which, with an x-ray revealing a broken bone in Cowdrey's forearm, was effectively 72 for four, 162 runs away from victory. Close, the last of the specialist batsmen, joined Ken Barrington – who, as a selector in 13 years' time, would be persuaded by Tony Greig's appeal to have 'Closey' in his side to face another generation of West Indian fast bowlers.

With the light worsening, rain in the air and the tea interval, they were on and off three times before play was abandoned early in the final session. Barrington, battered by Hall, had opened up against the off-spinner Lance Gibbs, pulling two great sixes and taking his score to 55. Close played watchfully for 7. The total was 116 for three.

Play did not begin till 2.20 the next day. With a 20-minute tea interval at 4.15 and close of play at 6, it left England three hours 20 minutes to score 118 runs. By modern standards it was not a difficult chase, but the West Indian bowlers and fielders gave nothing away. Hall and his partner Charlie Griffith, freshened from their rest, bowled from the start, while Barrington, in the words of Alan Ross of *The Observer*, was 'a pallid ghost of his yesterday's self', taking 45 minutes to score his first run, a single that flew off his glove from a Hall delivery:

> He batted like a man suffering from battle fatigue – as maybe he was. His back-foot defence was as nervous as that of an old lady trying to get across Piccadilly in the rush-hour. His forward defensive was as indecisive as the same old lady half-way across. It was no surprise when he edged Griffith to Murray at 130.

A target of 118 runs in 200 minutes had now become 104 in 150, with Close having advanced his score in those 50 minutes from 9 to 18. Amid Barrington's struggles, he was taking almost all of Wes Hall's bowling. His strategy for dealing with the awkward lift was extraordinary, though it had a logic, as he explained to me:

> At that time fast bowlers looked forward to playing at Lord's. And Wes was the fastest bowler in the world. He was a magnificent human specimen, with tremendous shoulders, powerful. And Charlie wasn't all that slow when he let it go. I won't tell you how he let it go. *(followed by a guffaw)*
> Every time the ball lifted, I got my hands and bat out of the way. That way he couldn't get me out. I let the ball thump me on the chest. I must have been hit twenty times. No messing. A fast bowler's weapon, when he's got something lively to bowl on, is short of a length, isn't it?

There was much criticism in the newspapers of the slow pace at which the West Indians bowled their overs, managing only 48 in the three hours 20 minutes. Notably, in light of the events that later lost Brian the England captaincy, he never complained of this when he described that afternoon. For him it was all part of the game, two fast bowlers making life hard for the batsmen. Unlike the public school cricket that had nurtured Dexter and Cowdrey, it was the cricket he had grown up playing.

Life in the north in the 1930s was a grim fight for survival. The cricket I grew up in was played fair, played tough and without any kid-glove approach. But it was *cricket*. The sort of cricket that produced Herbert Sutcliffe and Len Hutton. The sort of cricket I was to encounter when I played against Australians and West Indies, where you give nothing away and you play to win.

Wes Hall bowled unchanged for a marathon spell of 24 overs, with his partner Charlie Griffith bowling 19 at the other end. In all, Hall bowled 40 overs in the innings, an exhausting workload from which, he reckons, he did not fully recover during the rest of the series. Mike Procter, the great all-rounder of later years, was in the crowd that afternoon, a wide-eyed 16-year-old on a South African Schools tour of England, amazed at the sight of white people sweeping the streets. He said emphatically that there was no falling off of Hall's pace as the game drew towards its evening climax.

Jim Swanton in the *Daily Telegraph* searched hard for a precedent for such a herculean labour by an out-and-out fast bowler:

> For a physical feat comparable to that of Hall, who, apart from the tea interval, bowled non-stop fast and furiously from 2.20 to six o'clock, cricket history shows no parallel, so far as I know, since Tom Richardson slaved away for much the same sort of stretch at Old Trafford in 1896.

Barrington's departure brought in Jim Parks who drove Griffith for two fours. Close battled on at the other end, as JS Barker described in his book *Summer Spectacular*:

> He took Hall's thunder on thigh, hip, chest and shoulder, unflinchingly and impassively. His judgement was unfailing, backward and forward in defence, commandingly upright, taking Hall, the greater menace, for his own and leaving Parks for the most part to attend to Griffith.

Parks fell lbw to Griffith for 17, playing across a ball that kept low. Next in was Fred Titmus, who injected a fresh urgency into the running between the wickets. At tea England were 171 for five (effectively six), needing 63 runs in 85 minutes. Close on 37. After a brief flicker of sunshine, the light was almost as bad as it had been when they came off the previous day.

After tea Close and Titmus pressed on. Close hooked Hall to bring up his fifty, he swept Gibbs for four, and the target came down to 31 runs in 45 minutes. Victory was now within reach. But Hall, in his 19th over of the day, was not letting up. He sent down a brute of a delivery that Titmus could only fend into the hands of short leg, and next ball Trueman, showing none of the skill that brought him a century at Northampton, pushed indecisively at his first ball, wide of off stump, and was caught behind. Suddenly it was 203 for seven and, though Cowdrey was changed and ready to bat if required, nothing could be expected of him. If they were to win, it was down to Brian Close, with off-spinner David Allen and the ageing medium-pacer Derek Shackleton for support.

It was a moment of truth for the badly bruised Yorkshireman, with what Ian Wooldridge called 'an awful decision to make':

> Did he see the game out and risk the accusation of losing a great chance to square the series? Or did he go for runs and risk losing the match?

The decision was made. As Brian put it:

> Something had to be done. I decided to try to upset Wes.

As Hall ran in again from the dark background of the pavilion, his cross bobbing around his neck, reaching the last strides of his run-up, he saw in front of him the near-incredible sight of a batsman shuffling several paces down the wicket, bat raised, before the ball was bowled. In his astonishment he pulled up, seeming to rick his back and having to be calmed down by his skipper Frank Worrell. He ran in again, Close once more came down and swung across the line, the ball catching a bottom edge and dribbling towards the slips. It happened several times more, bringing two boundaries to leg. It was theatre of the highest order.

Now 15 runs were needed in 20 minutes. The battle was almost won, with many in the press box thinking it was time to revert to orthodox methods. Brian was 70 not out; his eye was in, the runs would surely come. But that was not the Close way. Noticing a gap wide of Rohan Kanhai at midwicket, he came down the track to Charlie Griffith and heaved at a ball slanting across him.

"I thought I had my body behind it," he said. "It went up the hill from the Nursery end, just grazed the bottom of my bat and carried through twenty yards to Deryck Murray."

Charles Bray in the *Daily Herald* shuddered with dismay: 'This was tragic. It was also stupid. Having created the winning position, Close had thrown it away. Those last 15 runs could have been got in singles.'

Frank Worrell was of the same view: 'I thought he threw the match away. Perhaps he was carried away by the crowd.'

Close came back to the pavilion to great applause, which made in Jim Swanton's words 'the sweetest music in his ears', but to his great disappointment he had left the job unfinished.

Brian stuck firmly to the belief that he had done the right thing, putting his dismissal down to Griffith bowling the ball faster than normal by bending his arm. Otherwise how could it have gone up the slope? It is hard to see any of that in the film footage, but then Brian always looked for something beyond his control when things went wrong. In truth he had been playing a gambler's innings, and he had almost pulled it off. Almost. The story of so much of his life.

In the words of Denys Rowbotham in the *Guardian*, 'Close had aimed at a million and missed by a unit.'

John Woodcock gave a balanced verdict on the dismissal:

> Perhaps if Close had been prepared quietly to glean the remaining runs, England would have won. It is a reasonable line of argument. Had he done so the misdemeanours of his career, if you can call them that, would have vanished in the evening air. As it was they mostly had, for without him there would not have been the climax there was.

Allen and Shackleton continued to press for victory, reaching the last over from Hall in need of eight runs. BBC television had ended their coverage at 5.50, giving way to the early evening news, only to be flooded with complaints and to return four minutes later in the middle of an item about a typhoid outbreak.

It was six to win off three balls when Shackleton swooshed and missed, Allen called for him to run the bye, and Shackleton took forever to set off, failing to keep pace with Worrell, two 38-year-olds in a dash for the stumps at the bowler's end.

Amid great tension Colin Cowdrey, arm in plaster, walked to the non-striker's end where he watched calmly as his partner blocked the final two deliveries. It was a draw, perhaps the most thrilling draw in the history of Test cricket.

"If I could have stayed for another five minutes," Brian told me, "we could have won. We were a bit unlucky with the weather. But no messing. It was a great game of cricket."

Micky Stewart, brought up in the hard school of the 1950s Surrey dressing-room, was not impressed by the marks on Close's upper body. "There was no short leg," he ribbed him. "Instead of taking all those balls on the body, you could have got a run round there every time. We'd have won the match but for your bloody bruises."

Fred Trueman, writing in his *Sunday People* column, recalled the scene next morning in the Sheffield dressing-room, when the Yorkshire captain proudly displayed his battle scars to one and all:

> I counted 16 bruises on Brian Close's body as we were stripping on Wednesday morning for the game against Glamorgan. The bruises hadn't come out the night before at Lord's. They were just hurting then. But at Bramall Lane he looked like he'd been out for a quick fight in the Yemen. Those bruises I counted included patches where one or two were joined up. I reckon he must have been hit about twenty times. You could see the impression of the seam on some of them.
>
> The worst moment came when Brian went onto the table for a massage. He's tough is Brian. But he had a real ripe time as some of the stiffness was eased out.

That day at Sheffield, on a pitch made for seam bowling, he ignored the pain, running in for 25 overs and taking six wickets for 55 runs. The following day he hit the only fifty of the match, then followed up with four more wickets, securing a vital ten-wicket victory on the road to the championship title.

In the world of Brian Close, the glory and the bruises were all part of the fun – the 'pure, unalloyed joy' of that summer.

Jim Kilburn, writing nine years later, thought much of Brian's career in cricket was epitomised by the match at Lord's:

> The innings was a success without a successful conclusion, a romance without an ending of happily-ever-after. Close carried England to the doorstep of victory and stumbled at the threshold. That was the story of his cricketing life. He touched the top but could not hold his footing there.

Brian stayed in the England team for the rest of the series, hitting two more fifties and finishing with 315 runs, second only to Ted Dexter among the England batsmen. His bowling was little used, but in the final Test at The Oval, when Jim Parks left the ground for an x-ray on a bruised foot, he kept wicket for a whole morning, conceding no byes and drawing favourable reviews from the press box. Jim Swanton thought he did 'as adequately as could be expected from one unaccustomed to the job'; John Woodcock called him a 'natural athlete'; Denys Rowbotham went further, saying he 'had no difficulty in looking a thoroughly practised wicket-keeper.' It was a performance of which Brian was proud, certainly one that he never forgot, as his Somerset team learned to their cost ten years later.

His success in that most special of summers brought him one of cricket's greatest accolades: selection as one of the *Wisden Almanack*'s Five Cricketers of the Year, the only Englishman alongside four West Indians. The profile of him was written by the former England bowler Bill Bowes, a veteran of Brian Sellers' great Yorkshire side of the 1930s:

> Yorkshire in 1963 offered the captaincy to their all-rounder Brian Close who hitherto had never quite accomplished what was expected of him. It was a trial appointment. Nobody quite knew how it would work out.
>
> The result was astonishing. Almost overnight it seemed that Brian Close matured. He showed a knowledge of his own team and the play of opponents which immediately stamped him as a thinker and tactician. His field placings were as intelligent and antagonistic as any seen in the county for twenty-five years and, like Brian Sellers before him, if a fieldsman was required in a "suicide" position, the captain himself was first for the job.
>
> He kept the fiery and volatile Trueman happy, used him in effective short bursts, and balanced those occasions when he asked for long and sustained effort with opportunities to bowl at tail-enders. Determination and purpose came into his own cricket. He regained his place in the England team and won national approval for the unflinching way he played the West Indies fast bowlers, Hall and Griffith. To his own great delight he saw Yorkshire, in their centenary year, to outright Championship success.

11

AN ARTIST'S EYE

> Brian was a great leader, the best captain I ever played under. Without doubt. You admired him so much because he had so much natural ability. Anything that he asked you to do, you always felt that he could do it better.

Ken Taylor was a quieter man than most of his Yorkshire team-mates. In the photographs you will usually find him at the back, sometimes partly obscured, never craving the limelight as others did. Yet what an intriguing man! What joy I had working with him on a book!

Ken played cricket for Yorkshire and three times for England. He played football for Huddersfield Town in the old First Division and was tipped at one stage for an England cap. And, as if that were not enough, he spent several winters as a full-time art student, winning a place at the prestigious Slade School of Fine Art in London.

The son of a Huddersfield millworker, he grew up in a cramped terrace house, sharing a bed with his older brother Jeff till he was eleven. Jeff also had prodigious talent, playing football for Huddersfield and Fulham, gaining a Geography degree from the University of London, then becoming an opera singer and a much-respected teacher of singing.

As a footballer Ken played alongside the young Denis Law and was managed by Bill Shankly, later to become a legend at Liverpool. In cricket his team-mates included Fred Trueman, Brian Close and a young Geoffrey Boycott. The book interwove his memories of them with his artwork.

Ken loved his years with Bill Shankly, an outsized personality with a passion for football that had more than a streak of madness.

> He knew what he wanted, and he had this great ability to inspire people and to create enthusiasm. He was by far the best manager I played under.
>
> One day he told us that it was his wedding anniversary and he was taking his wife out. So the next morning we asked him if

they'd had a good time. "Very nice, thank you," he said. So we asked him, "Where did you take her, Bill?" And he said, "I took her to watch Accrington Stanley Reserves."

The training sessions run by Shankly's predecessor at Huddersfield were dull affairs, involving repeated laps of the field, little serious ball work and, when they did play, only gentle tackling. Shankly, by contrast, had them playing robust five-a-side matches in the car park, no-holds-barred contests between England and Scotland, always with Shankly himself at the heart of the Scottish team.

> At half past twelve, when we should be finished, if he was on the losing side, we played on and on. In the end we used to let him score, just to get the game over with.

There was a similar streak of madness in Brian Close, and Ken loved that, too. As a stroke-playing batsman and a superb cover fielder, Ken – with his artistic temperament – did not want to spend his days playing cricket that was dull, accumulating runs for a better average, drifting through time in the field.

> You always knew that something was going to happen when Brian went in to bat – or came on to bowl. When he was captain, there was never a time when we went onto the field and just went through the motions for two hours.
>
> As a batsman he could give it a slog or he could play defensively, whatever the situation required. His technique was excellent. If he'd played for himself and not the team, his average could have been far higher.
>
> He'd sometimes have these pre-conceived ideas of what he was going to do: coming down the wicket to a quick bowler, or pretending to move before the bowler released the ball, to put him off. He'd get an idea, and he'd have to try it. Sometimes his ideas would come off, but they'd be his downfall on a few occasions each season.
>
> With Closey as captain, you played to win. There was always something happening. His theory was that you declared on how long it was going to take you to get the other side out, not on how long they needed to get the runs. It was a different approach from most counties. He sent Phil Sharpe and me out

one time to score some quick runs before a declaration. "I want 100 runs in 40 minutes," he told us. "Don't get out, and don't make it look easy." Well, we got the 100 runs in 40 minutes, but I think we lost six wickets.

He'd get frustrated if people started to play for themselves. He'd strut up and down in front of the window, making his presence felt. "Get on with it, or get out." That sort of thing. And of course it affected all our averages. But we won the championship with that system.

It was an unselfish side. Everybody was happy for everybody else to do well, and Closey was the most unselfish of players.

The feeling started to fall away towards the end; people came in who had a different attitude.

I could name one or two counties who would have been pushing us for the championship if their star players had played more for their teams. But they played to get a nice average at the end of the season and to be picked for England.

The great thing about Closey is that he loved a physical challenge. He always liked facing the quick bowlers, and of course he was fearless when he fielded at short leg. He stood closer than anybody does today and without a helmet. There was a game at Bristol when the batsman lapped the ball, and it hit Closey so hard on the forehead that it flew all the way to Phil Sharpe at slip. And he hardly flinched. It was as though it had hit a lump of wood.

Phil Sharpe confirmed the story: "It came like a rocket off him. And, after we'd persuaded him to go off, he came back on with this minute bit of sticking plaster in the middle of his forehead."

Closey was a tough cricketer, but he had this childish, giggling side to him as well. He would act the fool. I remember him batting at Bristol with about a quarter of an hour to lunch. I was next in, on a pair, and I was quite anxious.

It was a dusty wicket, and the wind was blowing the dust into the eyes of short leg. And Closey thought this was a great challenge. He kept rubbing his feet into the ground and laughing, 'Ha ha ha', as the dust got up. And I was waiting there, on a pair, getting more and more agitated. I could see he

Brian Close
felt pen drawing
by Ken Taylor

wasn't concentrating, wasn't thinking about me. 'Ha ha ha,' he was going. He got out. I had to go out to bat just before lunch, and I think I did bag them.

Wisden confirmed the story: 'Taylor bowled Brown 0, lbw Mortimore 0'

Closey was always up for a challenge. If you said, "Brian, I bet you can't ..." he'd say "What?" And off he'd go.

We were in the bar at the Diglis Hotel at Worcester. We'd had an evening meal, and the river was very full. Somebody said, "Jesus, Closey, I bet you can't swim that river." "What?" And straightaway he was throwing his coat and his shirt off and running down the lawn. We looked at each other. It was a silly thing to do, the river was running quite fast, but he swam there and back.

Of course they collected up his clothes and took them into the bar. I can still see him, knocking on the french window, trying to get back in, dripping wet, just in his underpants.

Another time we were playing Hampshire at Portsmouth, and we were invited to a cocktail party on the HMS Victory. Closey was having a few and someone said, "I bet you daren't go up to the crow's nest, Brian." "What?" So again everybody put their glasses down and went up on deck to watch him climb this rigging. And, instead of going through the trap door in the middle, as you're supposed to do, he clambered up the outside of the rigging and over the top. It was really very dangerous, but he always managed these things. He was so strong.

He did this walking on beer bottles in the bar. You had to stand with your feet behind a line and walk the bottles with your hands, without touching the floor in front of the line, see how far forward you could walk them. Nobody ever beat him.

Another trick he had was putting a wine glass on his forehead. He'd stand up, then go down, then he'd lay on the floor and get back up. With the wine still in the glass. He was always good value.

Ken was no raconteur, but when it came to Brian Close he flowed more freely than he did with any other subject. The memories of his old captain animated him like nothing else.

Ken was teaching art in a Norfolk school, barely aware of what was now going on in the world of cricket. He was not one to attend the dinners at which retired cricketers recycled and embellished old stories, and he did not boast about his own achievements. He simply chatted away cheerfully, revisiting his own memories, and the little nuggets emerged. On one occasion, when he was recalling the soccer matches the Yorkshire team used to play, I asked him what sort of footballer Fred Trueman was:

He wasn't a bad player in a rugged kind of way. He liked to play centre-forward, but then so did Closey. And neither of them had any idea of passing the ball. We needed three footballs – one for Fred, one for Closey and one for the other twenty of us.

Ken's brother Jeff gave me a recording of a radio talk he had once given, exploring the similarities between singing and football. It began with a snatch of Maria Callas singing a Bellini aria, followed by commentary of a Bobby Charlton goal. Then Jeff's mellifluous voice came in, talking about rhythm, poise, balance and self-discipline.

It fitted neatly onto one of our large pages so I came up with the idea of placing Ken's thoughts on sport and art opposite it. I put the idea to him, and he agreed to think about it. When I rang back three days later, he told me he could not think of a single thing to say. Yet within minutes he was coming up with the most thought-provoking material. It was so typical of Ken; he never comprehended how much he had to offer.

He talked about concentration, about letting go and becoming totally absorbed in what you are doing. First he related this to art:

> You have to know your strengths and your limitations, but you're at your best when you get beyond thinking, when your concentration is so great that the line just flows. You feel as if you're in another dimension.
>
> A lot of people lose it halfway. With my art scholars at school now, you can tell the ones with a bit extra – because of their concentration. The ones who are fiddling about, dropping their pencils, talking, they may have talent, but they won't get to that point where their work flows.

Then he talked about sport, going on to illustrate his central point by referring to sportsmen he had known:

> The great footballers, people like George Best and Denis Law, all had it. When Denis came to Huddersfield, he was just a little lad in glasses but give him a ball and you could see straightaway that he'd got it. Garry Sobers had it. He was a completely natural player, and he so obviously enjoyed everything he did.
>
> You would think that Brian Close had it. He had so much ability. But he never achieved what his potential was, and that was probably because he lacked something in concentration. He could be distracted.
>
> Geoff Boycott was different. He had a great ability to concentrate, and he had a lot of talent. But I feel that he didn't let himself go into that other dimension; he was conscious all the time.

All this and much more – and he thought he had nothing worth saying!

Ken had long left behind the world of cricket and football, but at the time of our book he still enjoyed a round of golf. Inevitably he had tales of Close the golfer:

He went to Australia when he was 19, and he was playing golf left-handed. The team had a lot of good golfers, people like Reg Simpson and Len Hutton, and they said to him, "You don't want to play left-handed. It'll interfere with your batting, it's a different swing altogether." He was playing to a handicap of about four at that time. So he switched to right-handed and got down to about two. He was an amazing chap.

The first time I played with him was at Cambridge. He said, "Does anybody want to play golf?"

I said, "I'd like to come, but I haven't played much, I haven't got any clubs."

"That's all right," he said. "You can use mine." And off we went to the Gog Magog Club. "You haven't played much," he said. "I'll give you a stroke a hole."

After nine I was one up. So he said – because he likes to win – "I'll only give you a stroke on the long holes."

We got to the 17th, and I was one up still. I could see he was worried. His brows were meeting, and he was thinking. Then suddenly his face lit up. It was a long hole and he said, "You can't use me woods."

He won the hole. We halved the game. And everything was all right. That was Closey.

Another time we played at The Belfry, and he wasn't hitting the ball too well. He played his shot, it was a duff one, and he swung the club again in annoyance. Only he let it go. It went miles up in the air, as far as you could see, and landed right in the middle of a pond, sticking up amid all these reeds. I've still got the image in my mind. Closey taking off his shoes and socks and wading out into the pond.

There was a sort of childish innocence about him. He couldn't be nasty if he tried.

12

THERE TO WIN THE GAME

Monday 22 August 1966. 11.35 in the morning at The Oval. The high peak of Brian Close's long career. The moment that encapsulated everything that was best about him as a cricketer: the tactical acumen, the unwavering self-belief, the fearless physical courage.

All summer England had come off second best against the West Indians, having no answer to their brilliant captain Garry Sobers. He had scored 722 runs at an average of 120, taken 20 wickets in three different bowling styles, held 10 catches and led his team to an unassailable 3-0 lead in the series, in the process seeing off two England captains, Mike Smith and Colin Cowdrey. Even at this moment, when his team were facing defeat in the final match, there was expectation in the air as Sobers loped distinctively towards the middle, expectation that he would again thwart England. All summer, when it mattered most, he had risen to the challenge.

Yet this was not the England team Sobers had been playing in the previous four matches; it was Brian Close's England, a tougher eleven, one that at all times looked alert and purposeful in the field. Close was seeing to that, not only by exhortation and example but by demanding from the selectors a different team.

Mike Smith had been a popular captain with his players, but as a specialist batsman his lack of runs was a serious handicap. In 14 Tests across the previous summer and winter he had managed just two fifties, both against a weak New Zealand side at Christchurch. When he was out for 5 and 6 in the innings defeat at Old Trafford, the selectors gave his batting place to the long-discarded Tom Graveney and the captaincy to Colin Cowdrey, who in nine previous Tests in charge had neither failed nor especially enthused the selectors. His genial diffidence, at home in the gentler pastures of Kent, was not thought to be what England needed in the heat of battle against Australians and West Indians.

The 38-year-old Tom Graveney's return was a great success, with 96 at Lord's and 109 at Trent Bridge. Two newcomers also enjoyed success, though they came from very different soil: the roly-poly Colin Milburn and the exiled South African Basil D'Oliveira. Other batsmen struggled, notably Ken Barrington who, unable to cope with the fast bowler Charlie Griffith and his suspect bowling action, became such a nervous wreck that he withdrew from all cricket after the second Test. The selectors chopped and changed the bowling attack but, apart from the steady medium-pace of Lancashire's Ken Higgs, the figures at the end of the fourth Test made grim reading: Snow seven wickets for 345 runs, Titmus five for 190, the newcomer Underwood one for 172, Jones one for 259, Brown nought for 84, Illingworth nought for 103.

The nadir came in the fourth Test at Headingley, where West Indies – with centuries from Sobers and Seymour Nurse – hit 500 against an uninspired display of bowling and fielding, then bowled out England twice to win by an innings. Coming in the week after the nation's World Cup football triumph at Wembley, it was a dispiriting performance, as John Woodcock in *The Times* expressed:

> I have reported well over 100 Test matches in these columns, but never one in which England were more thoroughly outplayed or in which they played so poorly. Any of the other Test match sides, including New Zealand, India and Pakistan, could have expected to make a better showing.

The angry Headingley crowd made their feelings plain, and Cowdrey returned to his car to find it had been badly scratched. It seemed inevitable that the selectors would make a change, and where else could they go than to the skipper of the county top of the championship, the man recognised as the best in the country? It was certainly what the Headingley spectators were vociferously demanding. "Cowdrey go home, we want Close," they chanted.

The decision was not lightly taken, the selectors meeting for four hours before taking the plunge with Close. Among their concerns was the prospect of the Yorkshireman making a success of the job and being in post when it came to leading the team to the Caribbean the winter after next. John Woodcock, knowing the thinking at Lord's, put his finger on this:

> On tour, as distinct from at home, separate qualities are needed to lead an MCC side, which might rule Close out for the visit to West Indies in 1967/68; but his appointment now is understandable. An uncompromising character has been set to trap an uncompromising side.

The *Times* writer also reflected on Cowdrey's lacklustre captaincy:

> If he is disenchanted by his experiences of the last two Test matches, perhaps it is not surprising. He has disliked asking his side to put their physical safety at stake against the methods which Griffith has occasionally employed. For the time being Cowdrey may be glad to be relieved of his burden; but he will be back for sure.

Close ruled out as captain in the West Indies? Cowdrey back for sure? It seems the die was already being cast.

*

Back in 1963 Brian had played all five Tests against West Indies, with some success, but he did not feature in the team the following year against Australia. At the start of that summer Richie Benaud wrote provocatively in the *News of the World* that England's best hope of winning back the Ashes lay in giving the captaincy to Close, not Dexter. In *I Don't Bruise Easily* Brian reported being told by a friend of Benaud that the Australian had advocated this in order to stop it from happening: 'He knew there was no way the England selectors were ever going to do what an Australian had told them they should.' It sounds fanciful, but who knows?

Brian had an unremarkable summer in 1964, and Yorkshire surrendered the championship pennant to Worcestershire. The event that changed Brian's life came after the season was over, when the Yorkshire team embarked on an extraordinary tour of North America. Brian, along with Fred Trueman and Geoff Boycott, ended his season on Friday 16 September, playing at Lord's for an England XI against Sir Frank Worrell's XI. The next day they flew to New York where on the Sunday they had a day of acclimatisation, including a trip to the top of the Empire State Building. On Monday the cricket began, with the eleven of them (no reserves) scheduled to play 13 matches in 18 days. They flew 220 miles to Washington for the game on Monday, back to New York on Tuesday, then again to Washington on Wednesday. After a day's rest they were booked for six successive days of cricket, which incredibly took in Toronto in eastern Canada, Calgary, then Vancouver in the far west and Los Angeles in southern California. The tour organiser, the journalist Ron Roberts, was hoping to sell cricket to the Americans; sadly they showed less enthusiasm for the eleven Yorkshiremen than they had earlier in the year for four mop-haired lads from Liverpool.

Their hosts were not strong, allowing them to win games even when they were in a state of sleep-deprived exhaustion, but a jolly time was had off the field, including some horse riding in Los Angeles where, according to Geoff Boycott, Brian who had never sat on a horse was 'soon in the saddle and galloping around the ground.'

This mad itinerary, involving 15,000 miles of flying, ended with four games in six days in Bermuda. Looking to strengthen the opposition, they invited Garry Sobers to play against them, but he refused. "I'll not be playing on matting wickets against you lot," he said and finished up on their side, hitting a century and opening the bowling with Fred Trueman.

The first overseas player to represent Yorkshire, Sobers could have been their signing when the qualification rules were altered in 1968. I have heard that Brian argued the case for that, and Garry was keen. But it would be another 25 years before the proud county would bend on their 'Yorkshire for the Yorkshire-born' principle. With Sobers in his side, who knows what further success Brian would have enjoyed as Yorkshire captain?

On a beach in Bermuda, on a rare day off, Brian set eyes on Vivien Lance, an air hostess with BOAC. She had already been propositioned by Fred Trueman but gave him short shrift when he admitted to being married. She herself was engaged but agreed to accompany Brian to a reception that evening. At the end of the function, as impulsive in love as in cricket, he told her, "I'm sorry, but I'm going to marry you."

"Don't be so stupid," she told him firmly. "You're not my cup of tea at all, and anyway I'm engaged to a pilot."

In *I Don't Bruise Easily* Brian gave his account of what happened next:

> She wouldn't give me her phone number when she left the island a couple of days later, and that was it. We had had a very pleasant and perfectly innocent acquaintance for a few days in Bermuda, but now we each went back to get on with our lives.
>
> Not me. When we reached London I ferreted out Viv's phone number from BOAC. I rang her and eventually she agreed to see me. We went to a performance of the Black and White Minstrel Show. After the show we went for a chat with Tony Mercer and Leslie Crowther and then to dinner. After the meal she said, "Let's be clear about this. It's the last time you see me." I suppose that was clear enough for anyone. Not

me. I sent her an Andy Williams record, *Can't Get Used to Losing You*, and I kept on phoning her.

We were married at Viv's home in Ottery St Mary, Devon, in March 1965. That was the best thing that ever happened to me.

Vivien became the rock of his life, saving him from a few disasters, but it was far from a conventional courtship, as she revealed in a delightfully honest interview with David Warner in *Just A Few Lines*:

He wore me down, didn't he? He kept asking, again and again and again, and I would say 'Don't write to me', but he used to send me records through the post whenever I came back to England from wherever I had been in the world. He just didn't give in, and this went on from October until the New Year and I had come up to Yorkshire and was beginning to quite like him but he was nothing like anything I had mixed with before.

I didn't know anything about Northerners, and I didn't understand bloody this and bloody that, but I agreed to come up here to a New Year's party with him at the Craiglands Hotel in Ilkley and at midnight he said, 'I am asking you to marry me for the last time.' And he got this diamond solitaire out which was exactly like the one I had on anyway, and I had had far too much to drink and I said 'Yes'.

I didn't really know who he was or anything. I didn't realise, I hadn't a clue who he was until I read the papers the next day. All the time I had known him I was really unaware as to what he was. Why should I? I had never followed cricket, my parents had never heard of him and of course it was winter – and you don't play cricket in winter in England.

So he just ran his paint business or whatever it was. It makes me seem ridiculous but I was busy working and I had my fiancé, so why should I know about him?

I felt really sorry for my other fiancé, it was a bit cruel really, but he was called Brian as well so that helped. They used to phone me and say 'Hi, darling' and I wouldn't have a clue which it was, but eventually this Brian would put a 'bloody' in or 'bloody hell' and I would think 'Right, I've got that one on the line.'

That's not good, is it? And I had fixed the wedding up to the original Brian, my pilot, so I didn't change the date, I just went and saw the vicar who I knew well – obviously, in a small town in Devon – and I said I am still getting married on that day but it is a different surname. When you see it in print it sounds awful, doesn't it? My poor parents!

We did 50 years together, and I wouldn't say I never regretted it. I did regret it at times. When we came back off honeymoon I still didn't fully comprehend that he was well known, and he said 'I am off to play cricket' and then he buggered off for about six weeks and left me in complete isolation because I knew nobody up here in Yorkshire at all, so it was a bit hard initially; it wasn't much fun.

But I supported him fully throughout our married life. He was easily led and even for all his travelling he was still quite gullible. He never saw bad in people ever and unfortunately I do. I always look for the bad and unfortunately 50 per cent of the time you find it but he never bad-mouthed anybody, ever. But I could see him doing the wrong things and heading for trouble and I thought, 'Don't do that, Brian.' So I am just glad that I was there for him because we were like chalk and cheese really.

He was far cleverer than I was, far cleverer, but whereas he was clever and a mathematician I was well read and into literature and also artistic, so together we made a good combination. But I am glad I married him because I think he would have gone under. I am sure he would have gone under.

Pregnant during the summer of 1966, Vivien was not allowed to go down to Devon to visit her parents. "I'm not having a son of mine who can't play for Yorkshire," Brian insisted.

On the day in September when a girl, Lynn, emerged, Brian was playing cricket in the annual match of the Pateley Bridge Show; he arrived late in the day, bearing much of the contents of the flower tent.

*

The summer of 1965 brought no England call-up for Brian and no championship title for Yorkshire, but in the third year of the Gillette Cup they won a stunning victory in the final at Lord's. Torrential rain the previous day delayed the start of the 60-over game by 90 minutes, and Surrey, captained by Micky Stewart, asked Yorkshire to bat first in the unfavourable conditions. In the twelfth over, when Ken Taylor was caught, he and Geoff Boycott had taken the total to just 22.

In came the captain, promoting himself up the order to inject some urgency into proceedings. Quite what he said to his young opener has no doubt been embellished over the years, but the result was extraordinary. A new Boycott was revealed. The running became sharp, the shots gained power, and to the amazement of all Boycott lofted sixes over midwicket and long on. Close, heaving to leg, was out finally for 79 while Boycott went on to 146, a record that stood for a Lord's final for 52 years. Yorkshire, by the emphatic margin of 175 runs, were one-day champions, and Boycott could never again insist that he could not play that way.

The summer of 1966 saw Yorkshire crowned champions again, with Brian's captaincy at its most urgent and unconventional in the early August Roses match at Old Trafford. At the start of the final day, as a result of rain, the game had got no further than Yorkshire scoring 65 for three in their first innings. Led by Brian's 'fine' 54 on an awkward surface, they declared at lunch on 146 for seven. Lancashire declared after two balls and Brian responded by being the first captain, following a change in the law the previous winter, to forfeit a whole innings. With what turned out to be 66 overs, and with fielders clustered eagerly around the bat, Lancashire's final wicket fell on the last possible ball. It was a triumph for Close's captaincy, though not everybody in the cricket world saw it that way, some questioning the ethics of it in the championship race. One who was in favour was John Kay in the *Manchester Evening News*:

> Close controlled matters magnificently. I counted five bowling changes in half an hour and fielding positions were altered almost ball by ball. With their captain setting the example Yorkshire fielded like the champions they are sure to become in a few weeks. This was cricket with a purpose. It upset the theorists and traditionalists. There will be squealing from the South and some muttering in the North, but for me cricket came to life again – for three brief hours.

Rain was everywhere. At Portsmouth, on the last day of the next match, Close had his team mopping up the standing water in a vain attempt to make time for a near-certain victory. Then, at Leyton, Essex's Trevor Bailey persuaded the umpires to take them off when Yorkshire were 26 runs from winning. "I'm absolutely livid," Ray Illingworth fumed. "It seems to me that other counties don't want us to win the title."

"I don't know what the game's coming to," blasted Fred Trueman in a style he would later perfect on *Test Match Special*. "Nowadays they're more interested in having a good time off the field. It's disgusting."

"It was odd that they didn't come off earlier when it was raining heavier," Brian Close told the journalists, showing a more diplomatic side. "Now, lads, don't get quoting me for all sorts of things. The umpires were quite within their rights."

Three days later Brian got the call from Doug Insole, the Chairman of Selectors, to captain England. In an upbeat television interview Brian described the English cricket professional as "the best in the world". As they had done once before, when they appointed Len Hutton, the cricket authorities had turned to the professional cricketer – indeed, the Northern professional cricketer – in pursuit of victory.

On the Sunday before the Test the England selectors drove to Leicester to sit down with their new captain and choose the team for the final match of the series. Doug Insole, perhaps with more than a little poetic licence, recalled the drift of the discussion when interviewed by Richard Whitehead for Brian's obituary in the *Wisden Almanack*:

> We quickly picked nine players, and I said, "Let's stop for a minute and see what we've got and where the gaps are. What about openers?" Closey said, "Well, at Yorkshire we have Boycott and Ken Taylor, but if we need quick runs I go in first because I can see the ball better than either of them." I said, "OK, do we need a second spinner?" Closey said, "Well, we have Don Wilson and Ray Illingworth, but if the ball is really turning I go on because I turn it more than those two." I said, "OK then, what about seam bowlers?" Closey said, "At Yorkshire we have Fred and Tony Nicholson, but if it's really swinging I bowl because I can swing it more than either of them." So I said, "Well, then, it doesn't look like we need to bother with the other two players."

I have heard another version of this in which Brian, recalling his stint behind the stumps in 1963, offered to keep wicket.

From Headingley five survived: Ken Higgs, the only man to play in all five Tests, Tom Graveney, Basil D'Oliveira and the openers Geoff

Boycott and Bob Barber. In came John Edrich and Dennis Amiss in place of Colin Cowdrey and Colin Milburn, John Murray as keeper instead of Jim Parks, John Price for John Snow, Ray Illingworth and Close himself instead of Fred Titmus and Derek Underwood.

The two most contentious decisions, both ones in which the new captain fought to have his way, were the dropping of Colin Milburn, because of his lack of agility in the field, and the return of Ray Illingworth. "No, Ray's had his chance and failed," the Chairman argued, provoking the reply, "He's failed because he's never been captained properly." It was three-quarters of an hour before the captain won that battle.

In our filmed interview he spoke passionately about this:

> I knew how good Illy was. On a good wicket he was very difficult
> to score off; his variations were slight. And on a turning wicket
> he was a cracking bowler, top class. International class.

It is another of history's what ifs. If Brian had not been in post to argue for the inclusion of his right-hand man at Yorkshire, would Ray Illingworth have stayed in the discard pile, not considered when they needed a stand-in captain at the start of 1969?

The selected team would not only field better but also contain more grit. There was only one with a public school/Oxbridge education, Bob Barber, and he was far from an MCC type: a physically tough Northerner who went his own way in life. He had been a success on Mike Smith's tour of Australia the previous winter but, pursuing a business career, he was now playing part-time for Warwickshire. His first Test appearance that summer came in the fourth match at Headingley where he was shocked by what he encountered: "The team were really down. People were saying, 'We'll be home by the weekend.' The attitude was pathetic." He liked Colin Cowdrey as a man – "but he couldn't captain a team of boy scouts."

Traditionally, for Tests in England, there was an eve-of-match dinner attended by the selectors and the team, with the selectors withdrawing after the meal to allow the players to discuss the game ahead of them. In Bob's memory such conversation had rarely amounted to much – but it did at The Oval:

> Suddenly we'd got somebody in charge who'd come to win a
> game of cricket. Brian stood up: "You boogers probably don't
> think I should be here, but I bloody am." Then he turned to the
> bowlers: "What are you lads going to do about Sobers? What do

you think?" He was a positive cricketer, there to win the game. When we went onto the field the next day, the atmosphere was quite different from at Headingley.

"It's a question of believing in yourself," Brian told an ITN interviewer. "From the brief glimpses I had on television, and from what I read about the previous Tests, it appeared that the lads in the earlier Tests were mentally beaten before they got out there."

'He treated the job,' the Glamorgan captain Tony Lewis wrote of Brian's new role at the helm of the England team, 'as if it had always been rightfully his. Others had just kept the captaincy warm.'

On the first morning John Price pulled out with a tender hamstring, bringing back into the fold John Snow. The England captain went out to toss with a Bermuda coin given to him on his honeymoon the previous year, but it brought him no luck. Sobers, as much of a gambler on the horses as Close, called correctly for the fifth time, and Close led England into the field. Strangely, for a man who so much relished captaincy, he confessed to feeling awkward whenever he had to go out first, another sign that he was not quite as straightforward a character as people paint him.

Snow bowled the first over, and Close crouched down at short leg – in the words of Brian Scovell, 'back bent and hands touching the ground as though feeling for unseen mines'. He was there not only for the catches but to unsettle the batsman, as Glamorgan's Peter Walker knew only too well:

> My own recollections of playing against Brian Close are vivid. Memories of the balding pate, the huge forehead and beetle eyebrows underneath, with two intense light blue eyes glaring at me when batting, still make me sit up in bed with a start during a restless night!

There were no catches for Brian, but his bowling did take a wicket when a trademark full-toss was walloped by Basil Butcher – double-centurion at Trent Bridge – into the hands of Ray Illingworth at square leg. He was not frightened to bowl Bob Barber's leg-spin, bringing him on early on the first morning, and it was Barber who dismissed Sobers for 81. 'Unbelievable!' wrote Brian Scovell. 'It was his favourite clip to midwicket off the back foot, the Sobers patented shot that had been a winner every time he tried it in the previous Tests. Perhaps that was because England didn't have a fielder in the right place. This time Graveney was in the right spot. He didn't have to move.'

Tom Graveney was not as impressed as Brian Scovell. 'For some of us older players,' he wrote, 'he was too consciously the leader for comfort. When you were fielding away from the bat he never left you alone. Every few minutes he would be adjusting your position a foot or two either way. It was unnecessary and irritating. We had been playing against some of these batsmen for years. We knew exactly where they were going to hit it. We had the intelligence to take up the position accordingly.' Ken Barrington felt the same the next summer, complaining that he was being moved not three yards or three feet but three inches, sometimes as often as twice in an over.

With West Indies all out for 268 and England 20 for the loss of Boycott, John Woodcock reckoned 'Close could reflect happily upon his first day as England's captain. His bowling had served him well; he had shown an eye for the attacking chance, and England still had everything to play for.'

Whether the West Indians were tired after a long summer, or unsettled by the umpires in the previous two Tests making an issue of Charlie Griffith's bowling action, or whether England were given fresh belief by their new captain is open to speculation. Whatever the reason, England staged an astonishing comeback on the second and third days. After collapsing to 166 for seven (Close run out unluckily for 4), they added a further 361 runs. Tom Graveney was at his graceful best in an innings of 165, John Murray – introduced not for his batting but for his superior keeping – hit an almost equally elegant 112, and to universal disbelief Snow and Higgs broke records galore with a last-wicket stand of 128. By close West Indies were four down, needing a further 124 to make England bat again.

The reason for England's transformation? Len Hutton in his *Observer* column saw one crucial factor:

> A very pleasing feature of this game has been to see a much brighter, more alert England team in the field. Brian Close so far has skippered England very well. He gave a life to his team which previously in the series has been sadly lacking. To take over a team which was in the doldrums and bring new keenness, new life and endeavour is a fine performance.

At 11.35 on Monday morning came the defining moment of the match. Sobers approached the wicket, and Close hatched his plan. Knowing that the great man was a compulsive hooker and puller, he asked Snow to fire the ball short, getting it up into Sobers' ribs, while he would stand as close as he could at forward short-leg.

The ball was bowled, its speed caught Sobers a little by surprise, and his great swish of the bat brought only an under-edge that bounced off his box into the hands of Close. Sobers out first ball! I was there that day, sitting among West Indian supporters on the seats in front of the gasometers, and none of us could quite believe what we had seen.

Sobers himself, while reflecting that the ball might not have carried if it had hit a fleshy part, paid tribute to Close in his autobiography:

> That was good captaincy. A batsman may have a reputation but when he walks to the crease for the first time it's a new day. He's vulnerable; that's the time to attack. Get them in the first 15 or 20 minutes, or you are going to pay the penalty. That is something Colin Cowdrey did not do as captain; he often let me off the hook. I would face a couple of overs, play a few shots and Colin would back the fielders off – but not Closey.

It was a dolly of a catch, but that was not the point, as Brian Scovell knew:

> Ninety-nine out of a hundred cricketers would have turned their backs when Sobers shaped for that hook. Not Close. He looked it straight in the eye. And when it misfired, he was there, upright and waiting, to take the catch that virtually ended the match. It takes courage to do that, the kind of courage that inspires the troops under you. All ten players knew then, if they didn't know before, that Close would never ask them to do something he wouldn't do himself.

John Woodcock made the same point:

> Nine fielders out of ten would have been ducking for cover when Sobers made his fatal stroke. And when, just before the end, Griffith crashed a long hop from Barber perilously close to Close at silly point, Close's reaction was to come a foot or two closer to the bat.

Brian had many great achievements in cricket but, with West Indies going on to lose the Test by an innings and 34 runs, this was his finest moment, capturing all that was best about him: the physical courage, the tactical genius, the ability to motivate a team and, above all, the love of the battle. "A fine bunch of lads," he called the West Indians in a speech that evening. "And a magnificent side to play against."

13

CHANGING TIMES

Britain's recovery from the Second World War was slow, with the last of rationing not ending till 1954. The post-war Labour government, elected in a landslide in the summer of 1945, created the National Health Service, undertook a massive programme of house building and enacted many of the welfare provisions proposed by the 1944 Beveridge Report. Yet they were hard years of austerity, and in a General Election in October 1951 the people, weary of it all, returned the Conservatives to office.

The young Brian was not yet 21, not able to vote, but he had strong opinions, views which were widespread in the proud working-class community in which he grew up. Down in London, on the books of Arsenal, he wrote to his friend John on the day the result of the election became clear:

> What a calamity!! The Conservatives have won. They'll make a mess of it as they always have done so I can expect to be in khaki again soon (short-lived freedom). It's alright for the 'old fellows' voting the Cons in to power – they've no thought for the young fellows.

He returned to the subject in a letter the next week:

> By the way, tell Margery that if she wants a cure for her 'supposedly' Conservatism she should listen to the programme 'Any Questions' each Friday night – I said 'supposedly' because she doesn't know the difference between the parties except that the people of one particular party 'which shall be nameless' usually send their children to private schools etc (!!) and are recognised 'by the fools' as the elite of the community. It's quite a good programme and very funny when you get the questions answered by the different political representatives chosen to answer them. Of course Labour always come out on top as they rightly should when people don't have blinds pulled over their eyes.

They (the Cs) can't satisfy everyone, and their policy (if they have one) doesn't allow them to look after the ordinary people at the expense of their backers, the people who sink their money into their party.

He was not wrong about the social make-up of the leading Conservatives. Almost without exception Winston Churchill's Cabinet were products of the top public schools, most of them graduates of Oxford University (though not, of course, Churchill himself).

It was the same mix around the table at MCC committee meetings, though with a higher proportion of Old Etonians (nine out of 19) and almost as many from Cambridge as Oxford, with the Duke of Edinburgh adding a touch of royal class. Their shared outlook was to uphold the traditions of the game and its amateur leadership, so much so that when in 1956 a serving minister Walter Monckton was invited to be their President he observed that, in comparison with the attitudes of the MCC committee, the Cabinet were 'a bunch of pinkos'.

This 'Establishment' held sway in both government and cricket throughout the 1950s, though the occasional grammar school product made it into the charmed circle: Edward Heath and Enoch Powell to the Cabinet, Doug Insole to the MCC Committee.

Yet, beneath all this, the country was changing. Employment was full, people had more money, and popular culture, shaped by American imports and the new commercial television, was undermining the old-style deference on which the English class system depended.

Nowhere was this more evident than in the north of England, where between 1957 and 1960 a string of working-class writers emerged, producing ground-breaking novels that became box-office successes at the cinema. Alan Sillitoe's *Saturday Night and Sunday Morning* was set in a Nottingham bicycle factory, Keith Waterhouse's brilliantly funny *Billy Liar* in a Leeds undertakers, while John Braine's *Room at the Top* and Stan Barstow's *A Kind of Loving* featured unhappy, young Yorkshiremen in dead-end white-collar jobs. Then there was David Storey from Wakefield, whose *This Sporting Life*, about a rugby league professional, was a masterpiece of unsentimental realism.

Away from fiction two seminal academic works emerged from Yorkshire. In *The Uses of Literacy* (1957) Raymond Hoggart drew on his Leeds childhood to consider the impact of 'mass culture' on the traditional attitudes of Northern working-class communities. One chapter describes the ingrained assumption of a 'Them' and 'Us' in society, some parts of which Brian Close could be said to have retained in his view of the people at Lord's who ran English cricket:

> 'They' are 'the people at the top', 'the higher-ups', the people who give you your dole, call you up, tell you to go to war, fine you ... 'aren't really to be trusted', 'talk posh', 'will do y' down if they can', 'are all in a click together', 'treat y' like muck' ...
>
> There exists a feeling among working-class people that they are often at a disadvantage, that the law is in some ways readier against them than against others ... Towards 'Them' generally the primary attitude is not so much fear as mistrust: mistrust accompanied by a lack of illusions about what 'They' will do for you.

Brian Jackson, a leading figure in the creation of the Open University, spent his teenage years in the same Huddersfield youth club as Ken Taylor. In *Education and the Working Class* (1962) he and Denys Marsden explored the experiences of men and women from working-class families, who like themselves had been to grammar schools. The majority of those interviewed had shed the attitudes of their parents, though often – as with Brian Close – the sense of 'them' and 'us' survived in a strong regional identity:

> Every paper you pick up, it's London, London, London. You come home from work, turn on the news and the announcer says the temperature on the Air Ministry roof is such and such. And there you are! Buses can have been blown over in Newcastle and people killed – but the temperature on the Air Ministry roof is such and such!

Across in Lancashire, in the early 1960s, *Coronation Street* became the most watched programme on television, *Z Cars* brought gritty realism to police drama, and the Beatles transformed popular music. From Newcastle came the BBC sitcom, *The Likely Lads*, which created humour from the contrasting outlooks of two working-class youngsters. It was fashionable to be a Northerner, especially one with humble roots – a counterpart to what was increasingly seen as a stuffy, out-of-touch ruling class. Harold Wilson, with his pipe and HP sauce, was never averse to thickening his Huddersfield accent when it suited him. And, as the decade went on, new celebrities emerged from Yorkshire: Jimmy Savile, Michael Parkinson, Brian Clough and, perhaps greatest of them all, Freddie Trueman, who was in great demand from the advertisers. Not for Fred the acquired vowels of Herbert Sutcliffe and Len Hutton. He was proud to be a raw Yorkshireman, bred among the pits, and to speak like one. Though he was never much of a beer drinker, he was happy to play the part if it brought in good money.

Brian Close was not a Hutton, trying anxiously to speak in a way that would make himself acceptable to the Establishment, but nor was he a Trueman, consciously refusing to do so. He could speak well when required, but there was always Yorkshire in the vowels.

Built into the attitudes of those at the top of the English class system was a distinction between 'old money' and 'new', with those of the highest pedigree looking down on those who had made their money in manufacturing and retail, disparagingly calling them 'nouveau riche'.

John Pretlove told me a story that illustrated this beautifully. A product of Alleyn's (a public school) and Cambridge University, he played for Kent as an amateur, as was expected of someone with his educational background. He was not in a position to do so without any financial recompense, as few of the amateurs were by the 1950s, so the county offered him the nominal position of Assistant Secretary, a common arrangement at that time. He had not long been there when a leading member of the club suggested that he join the Band of Brothers, an ancient cricket club with an exclusive membership. He duly made his application, only for weeks to pass without a reply. "I filled in the form for the BB," he enquired finally, "but I haven't heard a thing." And, with some embarrassment, he was told he had been rejected. "I'm sorry, John, but your father's in trade."

For a time at the start of the 1960s MCC tried to crack down on the bogus arrangements for paying amateurs, but in the winter of 1962/63 the county clubs, to the surprise of many, voted to abolish the distinction, and with considerable reluctance MCC endorsed the decision. Norman Preston, editor of *Wisden*, thought cricket was 'in danger of losing the spirit of freedom and gaiety which the best amateurs brought to the game', while Jim Swanton in the *Daily Telegraph* called the decision 'not only unnecessary but deplorable', attacking the attempt 'to introduce a classless society on the cricket field'.

Though such comments were laced with snobbery, there was also an idealism at work in thinking that sport was healthier if it was played purely for joy, not tainted by money. Yet the extent to which some took this disapproval of the commercial, at a time when cricket was struggling to pay its bills, was – to modern eyes, at least – close to absurd. Progressive counties, notably Warwickshire, brought in huge sums by promoting football-pool schemes, but others found the idea 'vulgar', with MCC's Secretary disapprovingly calling it 'easy money'. Geoffrey Howard told me that at his first meeting as Surrey Secretary in 1965, when the club was close to bankruptcy, a committee member who worked for Guinness offered to replace the broken clock at the Vauxhall end, the clock by which the umpires told the time. It would be at no cost to the county and would carry the words 'It's Guinness time', their slogan. But no, the committee rejected the idea, thinking that commercial advertising would tarnish their image.

Cricket had been unusual in having professionals and amateurs playing alongside each other. Soccer had separate national teams and played in different competitions, with the Amateur Cup Final at Wembley a major event in the sporting calendar. In rugby the two codes were split between Union and League; in tennis those who turned professional were barred from the All-England Championships at Wimbledon. In hockey and athletics there were strictly no professionals.

The top golfers were professionals, but at the clubs where they were employed they did not enjoy the same social status as the members. Derek Ufton, a professional cricketer, told me of a Sunday at Worcester when four of the Kent team, including Cowdrey, played golf at a local club:

> At the end of the round we went to the clubhouse, and only Colin was allowed in. We were professionals in another sport. To be fair to Colin, he stayed with us, but we couldn't have a wash or a beer or anything. And that applied to the club professional as well. Even the top golfers in the country, they couldn't go into their clubs unless one of the members invited them in.

In cricket, though amateurs and professionals played together, they changed in separate rooms, a practice that lasted into the 1960s at many counties. Bob Taylor, the Derbyshire wicket-keeper, told me of a 1961 game at Worthing where the dressing rooms were on opposite sides of the ground. Before taking the field at the start of each session the Derbyshire professionals had to wait by the boundary for their captain Donald Carr to appear on the other side.

It was in the south of England where the amateur ideal was at its strongest. In club cricket there was a marked difference between the north, where leagues predominated, professionals were employed and the matches had a hard-edged quality, and the south, where the governing body, Club Cricket Conference, saw its mission as 'to foster amateur cricket on non-competitive lines', making it a condition of membership that, with very limited exceptions, 'no club shall be connected with any organised cricket league or other competition.' Through the 1960s, among those who ran club cricket in the south, there remained a view that 'pot-hunting' was vulgar.

Inevitably there was much hypocrisy, with the professionals often chuckling at the absurdity of what they witnessed. I love the story Fred Root, the inter-war Worcestershire bowler, told of a batsman lying injured in mid-pitch. Root, with the ball in his hands, was urged by an amateur team-mate to run out the stricken man, an act he considered unsporting. "Here's the ball, you come and do it then," he suggested, getting the reply, "Oh no, I couldn't do that, I'm an amateur."

I was told by a young Derbyshire amateur of a Sunday charity match in which he did not walk when he edged a ball to the keeper. The county's senior professional Cliff Gladwin, a hard man from a mining background, grabbed him by the lapels and shook him. "We do not play our cricket like that in Derbyshire," he said emphatically.

It was moments like that which Brian Close will have had in mind when he said to me: "Among the professionals there were such high moral standards. If anybody tried to cheat, like not walking when they knew they were out, their own players would set about them. The attitude of the professionals in those days was absolutely first-class."

Brian's youthful faith in the Labour Party did not stand the test of time, the last straw coming when the Wilson government set about the abolition of grammar schools. Cricketing success brought Brian into contact with a stratum of society different from the Labour-voting world in which he had grown up. He set up a paint-selling business, he became a freemason (a strong tradition in Yorkshire cricket) and, though he was never at home in the scheming world of party politics, he was happy after his playing days to be taken up as a local celebrity by his Conservative MP, Marcus Fox, a plain-speaking Yorkshireman who like Brian had been to grammar school.

Yet, for all this, he retained his northern class-consciousness to the end. Though he was never one to make things personal, he simply did not respect the MCC men who ran the game, nor were they ever comfortable with him.

Cricket and football were England's two national sports, and their star professionals – Stanley Matthews, Len Hutton, Denis Compton – were idolised. Yet the wages were poor and the terms of employment distinctly feudal. When I worked with Ken Taylor on his book, he produced all his old football contracts. In 1955/56 he was playing regularly for Huddersfield Town in the old First Division on football's maximum wage of £15 a week, reduced to £12 in summer. His annual income was about £750 – or, in today's money, £25,000. A fair few of his modern-day equivalents earn that in a day.

As a representative from Huddersfield Ken attended in Manchester a meeting of the Professional Footballers' Association, chaired by the Fulham footballer Jimmy Hill, at which they voted to press for the abolition of the maximum wage, a campaign which they won in 1961. Two years later the Association successfully challenged in the High Court a regulation allowing clubs to retain players even when they were out of contract. In the case of the Newcastle United forward George Eastham, who asked to move to Arsenal, this resulted in his spending several months out of the game, selling cork in Surrey, before Newcastle relented.

Eastham, who was part of the England World Cup squad in 1966, reflected on this years later:

> Our contract could bind us to a club for life. Most people called it the 'slavery contract'. We had virtually no rights at all. It was often the case that the guy on the terrace not only earned more than us – though there's nothing wrong with that – he had more freedom of movement than us. People in business or teaching were able to hand in their notice and move on. We weren't.

The same issue was present in cricket. In the winter of 1960/61 Gloucestershire objected to Tom Graveney moving to Worcester, and as a result he was forced to spend the following summer playing for the Worcestershire second eleven. Six years later Barry Knight, another England cricketer, chose to move from Essex to Leicestershire and received a two-year ban from County Championship matches.

Players' loyalty to their county clubs was firmed up by a benefit system, by which a capped professional after ten years would have the profits of one match allocated to him. Yet even in the 1960s some of the counties held back this money, insisting that the professionals would spend it unwisely if they received it all at once. The money was often invested without any approval by the player – disastrously in the case of Yorkshire's Harry Halliday, whose Australian shares collapsed. Ken Taylor was still trying to get part of his money after thirty years.

Cricket was slower to change than football, but it could not resist forever. The world was not as it had been fifty years earlier, when many of the professionals were uneducated men, glad to have escaped from jobs in factories and mines, not accustomed to handling income beyond a weekly pay packet. In some tragic cases they became alcoholic paupers as a result of their benefit money.

A pivotal figure in the 1960s was the fast bowler Fred Rumsey, whose autobiography I published. A docker's son from the East End of London, he was doing well in the glove industry, soon to manage a factory in Yeovil on £3,000 a year, when at the age of 24 he gave up his business career to sign a contract with Worcestershire for just £300. The coach was Charlie Hallows, a former England batsman who knew nothing of the technicalities of bowling, and after two years of little progress Fred was released.

He played the following summer as the professional at the Kidderminster club where the previous professional, the England off-spinner Roy Tattersall, was still playing. At the first net Tattersall queried why Fred with his action did not swing the ball. For the first time in his life, despite two years on a county staff, Fred was shown how to do it, with results so spectacular that, when the county in an emergency recalled him, he took eleven wickets in the match. The next summer, with Somerset, he took 102 wickets; the one after, he played for England. Such was the primitive state of coaching in many of the counties.

In the summer of 1966, in a lone initiative, he proposed to form a County Cricketers' Association, to provide a voice for the professional cricketer, as the Professional Footballers' Association was doing in soccer. To further this aim, he arranged to spend half an hour after close of play in each county's dressing-room, explaining the idea.

With the exception of a handful of cricketers for whom anything akin to a trade union was an anathema, the response was overwhelmingly positive. I asked Fred which county was the most receptive to the idea, and without hesitation he replied, "Yorkshire. They were all enthusiastic, from Brian Close downwards."

On Monday 4 September 1967, at the Press Club in London, with Jimmy Hill in attendance, the Cricketers' Association (later renamed the Professional Cricketers' Association) was founded. Each county, bar Worcestershire who were abroad on tour, was represented, with Ken Taylor there for Yorkshire as he had been six years earlier for Huddersfield Town. They succeeded in getting Barry Knight's ban reduced to the one year he had already completed, and the following summer they demanded £400 per capped player for agreeing to appear in the proposed Sunday League. Fred had been in business, he could read an accounts sheet, and he had established the income the Sunday League would be generating from sponsors and television. He knew the demand could be met and, despite resistance from Lord's, the full £400 was reluctantly agreed. The Cricketers' Association was another nail in the coffin of the old order.

The following year, at the insistence of a government unprepared to provide money for a private members' club, control of the English game passed from MCC to a wider body, albeit one in which the same men were in key positions. By the end of the decade, overcoming further opposition, there would be league cricket in Surrey, spreading rapidly across the south of England. The world of cricket was changing.

When it came to negotiations over money Brian Close was not in the same league as Fred Rumsey, and in any case he was up against a formidable opponent in the form of the autocratic Brian Sellers. The owner of a family printing firm, Sellers had a radically different style from the smooth-talking men who ran MCC, a style that in its bluntness of speech was quintessentially Yorkshire.

Geoff Cope recalls an occasion when the team, on the verge of another championship, invited Brian Sellers to the dressing-room to ask him for a bonus in recognition of their success. Before any of them had a chance to speak, the Chairman leant across the big table in the middle of the room and ripped into the performances of every one of them.

> I was a young twelfth man, and I sat in awe, looking at my heroes being torn apart by this man whom I'd never seen in this light before. It was quite frightening.
> "Is there something someone wants to say?"

We all looked to Fred who was our spokesman. Fred was looking at his steel toecap. "Has tha' got something to say, Trueman? Let's be having it?" And Fred said, "The captain wants a few words with you."

Closey stood up, and he invented the word 'erm': "Well, erm, Chairman, erm, it's good of you to ... erm ... come and ... Well, erm, the lads have been thinking ... erm ... if we're successful in this game ... erm ... and there's no reason to think we won't be and ... erm ... we know in your era you were a wonderful side and you won eight championships in ten years, well ... erm ... the lads were wondering if there may be some remuneration."

"Remuneration," bellowed Sellers. "You'll get your remuneration on the day of the sacking meeting. Them that survive, you've done it by the skin of your teeth. Them that goes, well, you've had every opportunity. Now, you lot, listen to me. I'm going over on a boat to France tomorrow, and I want to read in the *Telegraph* that tha's pulled thee socks up, tha's played the cricket that this Yorkshire public demands and that tha's got stuck in."

He went out of the room amidst a stony silence. Six or seven steps. Then he came back and put his head round the door. "And I know what you're all thinking. Bad luck. I can swim."

It was an inflexibility that would cost the county dear in the years ahead, with Ray Illingworth, a pivotal figure in the winning team, the first to depart. Times were changing, and it was neither Sellers nor the MCC but men such as Mike Turner, the young grammar-school-educated Secretary at Leicestershire, a keen supporter of Fred Rumsey's Association and an early recogniser of cricket's commercial potential, who had their fingers on the pulse of that change.

The men of the amateur class, who were still in charge of cricket in 1967, were not at ease with the new professional age, nor were they comfortable with the strong-willed Yorkshireman who was captaining the England side. The gentlemen and players might all be called cricketers now, but there lingered an invisible but real divide between the traditionalists at the head of MCC and the Northern professionals, a sense of 'them' and 'us'.

14

DEFIANT OR DAFT?

"For God's sake, Brian, keep your nose clean," counselled the veteran reporter Crawford White of the *Daily Express* in a phone call. "They're just waiting at Lord's for a chance to prevent you leading the side in the West Indies."

He was not wrong. In the archives at Lord's there is a letter, dated 28 June 1967, to Billy Griffith, the MCC Secretary, from an anonymous 'Old West Indian Cricketer' in Trinidad. It begins:

> The general rumour in Trinidad is that Mr D.B. Close will be appointed Captain of the English side which will come out here later this year. Right here I will tell you that that kind of decision is among the worst mistakes English Cricket has been making in recent years by appointing 3rd or 4th Class Types of men to lead their Cricket Teams both at home and abroad.

The letter goes on to talk of 'the sad day' when the 'very ordinary' Hobbs stood in as England captain during a Test, followed by the 'still worst' Hammond (a professional who turned amateur) and Hutton:

> Gone were the days when an Empire was made and cemented by such men as Lord Hawke, Lord Harris, Lord Tennyson, the Hon F.S.G. Calthorpe (later Lord Something), A.P.F. Chapman, D.R. Jardine to mention a few. Badly behaved and ill-mannered men like Lock, Trueman and some others would have shivered in their shoes before displaying their true side had they been under those mentioned above.

The letter finishes with an appeal to MCC to 'go back to your old policy of appointing University Graduates ... instead of the very ordinary bunch of Professionals now leading your counties'. At the foot of the typed sheet of paper, written in red pen, are the words 'We must keep this letter as it clearly represents my views', signed 'DBC' – Donald Carr, Assistant Secretary of MCC.

India and Pakistan toured England in 1967. Neither was considered a strong opponent, and in the first half of the summer Brian Close's England won decisive victories in all three matches against India. In cricketing terms, with four wins out of four under his belt, Brian should have been an automatic choice to lead the side in the winter. Yet this was not the outcome when the tour selection committee sat down for the first time during the First Test against Pakistan at Lord's.

The committee consisted of seven men: the four selectors (chairman Doug Insole, Alec Bedser, Peter May and Don Kenyon), the MCC President (former Conservative Prime Minister Alec Douglas-Home who sent his apologies to the meeting), the all-powerful MCC Treasurer (Gubby Allen) and the man appointed to manage the tour (the Kent Secretary/Manager Les Ames). In attendance, but not voting, were the MCC Secretary and Assistant Secretary (Billy Griffith and Donald Carr).

The minutes only record the decisions of the meeting, but clearly unease was expressed by some about the choice of Brian Close. Although it was minuted 'that the choice of captain lay between Mr D.B. Close and Mr M.J.K. Smith, with the former as the most likely selection', they deferred the decision for three weeks, till after the Second Test. In the meantime Doug Insole undertook to telephone individual members of the MCC Committee to establish 'if there were any serious doubts to the selection of Mr D.B. Close'.

Brian's winning run as England captain came to an end when Pakistan held on for a draw at Lord's, but true to character he laid the blame for his failure on the selectors. They had insisted, against his wishes, on picking Colin Milburn whose slowness in the field led to his dropping Hanif Mohammad on 51. The Pakistan captain went on to 187, a nine-hour marathon that shut out England's chance of victory.

For the Second Test at Trent Bridge England gave a first cap to the 21-year-old Kent wicket-keeper Alan Knott. Prone to pre-match nerves, which he eased with a kaolin-and-morphine mixture, he was made to feel at home immediately by his captain: 'Brian Close was a very warm man. He spoke to you as if you were part of the scenery, confirming what I had felt when playing against him on the county circuit, that he was a very friendly person.'

Colin Cowdrey was brought back to open the innings in place of Milburn. In a low-scoring match on a difficult pitch he was out cheaply, and England's total of 252 owed much to a laboured 109 in 6¾ hours by Ken Barrington. It was tedious cricket at a time when the authorities, conscious of a declining audience, were trying to promote 'Brighter Cricket', and it created another controversy for the press to work up.

Twice in the recent past batsmen had been dropped for slow scoring: Barrington himself in 1965, for taking 7¼ hours to score 137 against New Zealand, and Boycott earlier that summer against India, for crawling to 106 in the six-hour first day. The next day he batted with greater freedom, going on to 246, the highest score in England that year, but, against the wishes of Brian Close, the selectors cracked the whip.

An incensed Boycott responded by spending the first day of the next Test hitting 220 against Northamptonshire, and he has never forgiven Doug Insole. 'He put a stain on my character and my cricket that I could never get rid of,' he wrote in a recent book. 'Wherever I went and whatever I did, that disciplinary measure would follow me.'

The decision enraged Michael Parkinson, who gave his *Sunday Times* column to a full-on attack on cricket's establishment and its culture, an attack that led the selectors to issue a writ for libel:

> The simple fact of the matter is that if England is to win Test matches against the best opposition in the world, it will do so only because of people like Boycott, Barrington and Close. It will be their dedication, application and bloody-mindedness that will be decisive when the chips are down, not the half-hearted efforts of some character who enters the game uncertain as to whether he's a cricketer, a stockbroker or a chicken farmer.
>
> What happened to Geoffrey Boycott last week was an unnecessary, hurtful and shaming insult to someone whose only fault was that he tried too hard. It will prove nothing except that the England selectors are a bunch of palsied twits, which fact we already know. One day in the future, Geoffrey Boycott might find it in his heart to forgive and forget. I doubt if I will, ever.

The 'bunch of palsied twits' – Insole, May, Bedser and Kenyon – were all former England cricketers, three of them educated at state schools. Three had captained their counties, with Kenyon still playing for Worcestershire. None of them were hard-bitten Northerners, it is true, but as a quartet they were hardly the out-of-touch fools that Parkinson's article implied.

Nevertheless, in a time of crisis for the English game, there was a faultline between the game's rulers at Lord's and an emerging professional class. It would be at the heart of the crisis that unfolded at the end of that summer.

Appalling weather at Trent Bridge nearly produced a second draw, but on the final day a purposeful England took ten wickets in less than four hours, with *Wisden* lauding Close as a tactician: 'three times a wicket fell immediately he changed the bowling.' With the Test ending on Tuesday 15 August, the tour selection committee agreed to meet on Saturday.

Memories of Hutton's tour of the Caribbean in 1953/54 still haunted the men at Lord's. They saw the West Indies as difficult territory, throwing up unexpected and awkward incidents, and they did not trust their single-minded Yorkshireman, with his focus on winning, to handle such situations with traditional MCC diplomacy. Yet at this point they did not have the ammunition to press their case.

As in British politics, English cricket emerged from years of little change to a period of rapid reform in the mid-to-late 1960s: the abolition of the amateur/professional distinction, the introduction of the one-day game, the breaking of the taboo on Sunday play and in 1968 the acceptance of overseas players into county sides.

The regulations for the County Championship were changed almost every year, rarely with beneficial consequences. In 1966 a scheme to limit first innings to 65 overs in many games produced a surfeit of negative medium-pace bowling and was abandoned after one year. In 1967 a new point-scoring system put greater emphasis on the first innings – eight for a win, two for a draw, four for first-innings lead – and this led to a record number of drawn matches, some of them exceedingly tedious. At Lord's in July the Hampshire captain Roy Marshall hit a brilliant 153 in under 3½ hours, then let his side bat well into the second day, so annoying his Middlesex counterpart Fred Titmus that the match concluded in the dullest of stalemates, with three full days of cricket not even producing a result on first innings. By contrast Brian Close's Yorkshire brought more games to a positive conclusion, win or lose, than any other county in 1966 and 1967.

A further concern for those promoting Brighter Cricket was the decline in the rate at which teams bowled their overs, the average across the season dropping below 19 an hour. A crackdown on deliberate time-wasting was agreed, and in May Leicestershire were formally censured for preventing a Sussex victory by bowling only 33 overs in 2¼ hours.

In mid-August, with the championship programme into its home straight, Brian Close's Yorkshire were in a four-way race for the title, vying with Colin Cowdrey's Kent, Tony Lock's Leicestershire and Micky Stewart's Surrey. Every point looked like being crucial.

In the round of matches starting on Wednesday 16 August Yorkshire were at Edgbaston, where on the second day Mike Smith's Warwickshire, with nine wickets down, pipped Yorkshire to the four first-innings points. It was tense, keen cricket, the sort that Brian Close revelled in, but it was not to the taste of John Woodcock, covering the match for *The Times*. He felt Yorkshire were pushing the boundaries of what was acceptable:

> One pondered on the rights and wrongs of sending Boycott in to open Yorkshire's innings. Boycott had spent all day in the pavilion with a "bruised" toe while Taylor, one of the game's best fielders, saved countless runs and held one good catch in the covers. Come the evening and out came Boycott for the last 50 minutes – without a runner, fresh and fit enough to run a four with Sharpe, and with the experience to counter the new ball. A less easy-going character than Warwickshire's captain might have had something to say about this.

Those boundaries were tested further still on Friday, with consequences that went far beyond the County Championship. At the close of play Brian was due to drive to Northampton to select the team for the final Test, facing the thorny question of whether to drop Barrington for his slow scoring at Trent Bridge. Little can he have imagined when he took the field that morning that this would be the least of his concerns and that his world would be falling apart by the time he got to Northampton.

Yorkshire started the day on 42 for one, 38 runs ahead, and that became 93 for six. All they could reasonably hope at this stage was to use up time, prevent a Warwickshire victory and hold on to the two points for a draw. With the ever-accurate Tom Cartwright taking four wickets for 26 runs in 25 overs, they were all out finally for 145 in 77 overs, attritional cricket that left the home side 100 minutes to score 142 runs.

The outcome was that Warwickshire, losing five wickets, finished nine runs short, and Yorkshire left the ground with the two points that put them joint top of the championship table with Kent. Yet the way Yorkshire prevented Warwickshire from completing victory was not to the liking of the Warwickshire supporters nor the men in the press box.

In 100 minutes, employing only their three quicker bowlers Fred Trueman, Tony Nicholson and Richard Hutton, Yorkshire bowled just 24 overs. In the last 15 minutes, four of which were lost to a shower, they bowled two overs. The first of these two, by Trueman, included three bouncers and two no-balls, thereby reducing the likelihood of a third over. Fred later went into print admitting that the no-balls were deliberate (his idea, not his captain's); he said he bowled a third which the umpire, rumbling what he was up to, chose to ignore. The second over by Hutton started with a practice run-up. Furthermore, they were slow to reappear after the shower, and there was much drying of the ball and changing of the field. They came off to a rowdy reception from the Warwickshire supporters whose mood had grown increasingly ugly. Close claimed that someone tried to trip him up when he came out after the rain break, and Trueman was struck by an umbrella. It was not cricket's finest hour.

'Yorkshire had got their two points,' Crawford White wrote in the *Daily Express*, 'and lost a good many friends.' John Woodcock, calling the two points 'dishonourable', raised the issue of the England captaincy:

> Without exception, Yorkshire's performance was, of its kind, the least attractive I have seen on the cricket field, and the blame lies squarely at the door of England's captain. Yorkshire employed all the known methods of wasting time.
>
> After the match Close left for Northampton to help choose the England side for the next Test. I wished it had been Mike Smith instead. A man capable of condoning and conducting such an operation as Yorkshire's last evening would seem a peculiar choice to take an MCC side to the West Indies on an expedition that demands from its leader a strong sense of sportsmanship and responsibility.

The newspapers had a story, Close's critics had their ammunition, and the wheels of the crisis turned rapidly. In Saturday's *London Evening Standard* John Thicknesse advocated that not only should Yorkshire be stripped of the two points but also MCC, in the event of Yorkshire finishing top of the table, should award the title to the runners-up – 'as is their right'.

Against this new backdrop the tour selection committee met on Saturday. Don Kenyon, playing at Worcester, and Peter May were absent, and MCC were represented this time by David Clark, a former Kent captain. 'Doubts were raised as to the suitability of Mr D.B. Close,' the minutes record, with Les Ames arguing that the team should be chosen ahead of the captain: 'He was not convinced that on these grounds Mr D.B. Close would be selected.' However, Doug Insole reported the selectors' view that 'Mr D.B. Close was the best man for the job. Other candidates had been considered; and, taking everything into consideration, his Committee felt bound to recommend Mr D.B. Close.'

The decision was deferred till after the umpires' report of the Edgbaston match had been considered. Further, Doug Insole and Billy Griffith would meet Brian Close 'to get an undertaking that he would be guided by the Manager on all aspects appertaining to behaviour on the field – if he were selected.' Finally, approval of the choice of captain would need to be sought from the MCC committee.

The decision not to drop Barrington was now a minor sideshow, though John Woodcock saw it as further evidence of the England captain's unsuitability for office:

> Barrington was fortunate on two counts. In the first place, only one selector was there to see it; in the second, he had Close's blessing. As we have seen again since then, Close believes, to a greater extent than most, that the end justifies the means.

Jim Swanton in the *Daily Telegraph* took the opportunity to lament once more the passing of the amateur from the county game:

> In these days, when almost every first-class player plays for his livelihood, the temptation is becoming the greater to overstep the line that separates the utmost keenness – which is the essence of all good cricket – from sharp practice, which is a different thing altogether. As always there is a tiny "lunatic fringe" supporting the win-at-all-costs philosophy.

Almost certainly in this last remark he was having a dig at Michael Parkinson, whose regular attacks on MCC irked him greatly.

MCC set up a meeting for Wednesday morning at 11.30 to hear the case against Yorkshire. In attendance were four members of the Advisory Committee – all former county captains: Arthur Gilligan (Sussex), Cecil Paris (Hampshire), Eddie Gothard (Derbyshire) and David Clark (Kent) – plus, in a non-voting capacity, Brian Sellers and Doug Insole. Cyril Goodway represented Warwickshire, and the two umpires Laurie Gray and Charlie Elliott gave their report.

Brian Close, who had been in Scarborough on Tuesday, left his home in Baildon at seven o'clock on that Wednesday morning for a 220-mile drive to St John's Wood. From there he would go on to The Oval for the eve-of-Test practice session. Should he have gone down the previous night, as Geoff Boycott believes, made sure he arrived in good time and in a calm, prepared state of mind? Whether he was at fault or was just unlucky is not clear. The known facts are that he broke down on the M1 near Leicester, had to hitch a lift with a Surrey supporter and turned up 55 minutes late. It was not a start designed to get the panel on his side.

Brian was completely clear in his mind that he was not guilty of any wrongdoing. He played the game hard and he stretched things to the limit at times, but he had been brought up with a strong moral code, walking when he was out, respecting the opposition, never challenging the umpire. It clearly offended him that he was being accused of a crime that in his view was within the bounds of what was permitted.

Tom Cartwright did not think Yorkshire's time-wasting was that extreme:

> The ball was taking an age to get back to the bowler, but it was the sort of thing that was going on in other games at that time. They probably carried it a bit further – but not that much. There was a game the next week against Somerset, and I remember sitting in the dressing room, thinking it wasn't that dissimilar.

By my calculation, excluding the rain break, Yorkshire bowled 24 overs in 96 minutes, a rate of 15 overs an hour. Somerset the next week bowled 43 overs in 170 minutes, a rate of 15 overs 1 ball.

Even Trueman's deliberate no-balls had a precedent at Yeovil in late July, when Essex's Tony Jorden bowled four no balls in an over to use up the remaining time, leaving the field to loud boos from the home crowd. Such gamesmanship was becoming common, and the following summer a new regulation required a minimum of 20 overs in the last hour.

At the hearing at Lord's, Brian was defiant. He would not accept that he had done any wrong, not one jot. He had a host of reasons why they took so long to bowl the two overs: the wet ball wanted constant wiping; the noise of the crowd made it hard for him to be heard; he had to go for a pee when it was time to return to the field; Richard Hutton was new to bowling at that end and needed a practice run-up; two wickets fell in the two overs; and so on. He even suggested they had helpfully saved time by not returning the cloth to the umpire, as required, after each wipe.

He could not be wrong, and he would not back down, would not show a glimmer of the contrition that would have allowed the panel to reach a fudged conclusion. Defiant to the end or just daft? Take your pick.

Nor did it help his cause that he had got on the wrong side of at least two of the panel. He had publicly pooh-poohed the findings of a committee, chaired by David Clark, on the future of county cricket, and he had had an unfortunate confrontation that summer with Eddie Gothard in a hotel during the Lord's Test:

> He came into a room where someone had got me going a bit on the subject of that overworked cliché 'brighter cricket'. A crowd of us were there, and Mr Gothard – a stranger to me – joined in. I asked him, "Who do you support?" and he replied, "Derbyshire." So I told him, "You're the worst team in the country for defensive attitudes." He got up and walked out, and it was then that I was told he was the President of Derbyshire.

The Derbyshire man, in fact the Treasurer, was not impressed.

To Brian's astonishment the Yorkshire team were unanimously found guilty of tactics that 'constituted unfair play' and the captain was held 'entirely responsible for these tactics'. He was so angry at the verdict – 'boiling' – he was in a mind to drive to The Oval and tell them to find a new captain, but Brian Sellers caught up with him on the staircase and told him, "Forget about this, Brian. You've got a job to do."

"As far as I am concerned," Brian told the waiting pressmen, "the matter is finished. It is history now. Tomorrow is another day." For those at Lord's, however, the 'matter' was far from closed.

That afternoon the tour selectors met at The Oval. This time the four regular selectors and Les Ames were joined by Arthur Gilligan, who was due to succeed Alec Douglas-Home as President. Their task, already difficult, was made more complicated by the announcement two days earlier by Mike Smith, their other candidate, that he had accepted a business appointment and was retiring from cricket.

Was it fair that Close was being punished twice for the same offence? Would Close really pose a risk in the West Indies? The argument was protracted. It is clear that Gilligan and Ames were resolutely opposed to Close and that the majority of the selectors remained in favour of him. What is not quite clear is how the voting went. The minutes of this meeting state that three of those present 'considered that it would be most undesirable to appoint Close.' The remaining members stuck by their original decision, believing him to be 'the best candidate'. They also 'found it difficult to find a suitable alternative.' When pressed to say who should be captain if Brian Close was unacceptable, three opted for Colin Cowdrey, one each for Jim Parks and Fred Titmus.

Doug Insole undertook to report to the MCC Committee that they were 'evenly divided regarding the appointment of Close', yet at the meeting the next afternoon he 'indicated that, by a 4 to 2 majority, the Sub-Committee had decided to confirm their nomination of Mr D.B. Close as Captain for the tour.' So had the fourth selector, the one who had initially thought Close's appointment undesirable, decided to stick with his fellow selectors after all, or had Doug Insole, resolutely standing by his captain, bent the truth a little? We will never know. In any case it made no difference. By 14 votes to four the full Committee of MCC, chaired by Alec Douglas-Home, appointed Colin Cowdrey.

Doug Insole has taken much flak over the years for events during his time as Chairman of Selectors, notably the dropping of Boycott for slow play and the non-selection of Basil D'Oliveira for the tour of South Africa, the fallout from which left him on valium. And here he was at the centre of another headline-catching row.

The son of a local government officer in East London, he went from grammar school via war service at Bletchley Park to Cambridge University. Through the 1950s he captained a happy Essex side that regularly won the *News Chronicle*'s award for Brighter Cricket, and he somehow became a protégé of 'Gubby' Allen, the most powerful man in English cricket in those years. "He nominated me for the MCC Committee when I was only 29," Doug told me. "I was the first non-public school bloke on it. 'Come and put a bit of life in the place,' he said."

Perhaps all chairmen of selectors, making and breaking careers, will divide opinion. Some, notably Geoff Boycott who has never 'found it in his heart to forgive and forget', paint a picture of Doug Insole as an untrustworthy, devious man; others are adamant that he was as straight as they come. "Boycs wouldn't have a clue about Doug," says Micky Stewart, whose friendship with Insole went back to footballing days with Corinthian Casuals. "Devious was the last thing he was. He loved the game of cricket, and he would never do anything that he felt would damage it."

Insole was sensitive to the importance of team spirit. His Essex side were notable for having a happy camaraderie, and as an England selector he was keen to discourage what he saw as excessively selfish behaviour. For a captain he looked for someone who would create a dynamic environment and inspire his men. In all this he was at one with the

Lord's traditionalists. Yet, in my experience of him, he was more straight-talking, less class-conscious, than many of those at the heart of MCC.

He knew the England team were a happier, more purposeful team than under Colin Cowdrey. So he was an unwavering supporter of the captain. Brian was never going to be at ease in the rarefied world of MCC, but he was not going to fall out with the West Indian cricketers or behave badly at social functions. As the journalist John Thicknesse put it, 'He may be an obstinate man, but he is not my idea of an irresponsible fool.'

On the day of the MCC meeting at Lord's *The Times* and *Guardian* carried editorials on the matter. Taking a slightly different line from its cricket correspondent, *The Times* was in forgiving mood:

> Cricket thrives upon hard conflict and the urge to win. These are much nearer the true spirit of the game than a nonchalant indifference to victory and phoney attempts at brighter play. Close has erred, but this one episode should not be enough to deprive him of the England captaincy.

The *Guardian*, agreeing that the censure of Close should end the incident, included a fascinating paragraph on the outdatedness of cricket's attitudes:

> A class-conscious observer might think that only games of proletarian origin have ever dealt effectively in their rules with the undoubted fact that people play to win. Sports where the law-makers have traditionally been of the leisured classes, notably Rugby and cricket, have not. To say that "it is not cricket" is no longer enough in a world where other countries, and other counties than Yorkshire, want to win. The umpires should have powers to deal with flagrant delays by extending the playing time, as referees have in soccer.

The opening day of the Oval Test was a tough one for Close, but he came through it triumphant. He took the brave decision, not common at the time, to ask Pakistan to bat first and reduced them to 214 for nine at close. He took a superb catch in the gully, the best of the summer in some eyes, and when Boycott pulled out of the team first thing with an 'infected throat' he opted to open the batting in his place. He would go out first with Colin Cowdrey, the two men between whom the MCC Committee were choosing that afternoon. Neither would know their fate till the end of the Test.

One thing was clear in all this. The England eleven were happy to play for him. 'Never did a captain have such loyal, almost fierce, backing,' wrote Brian Chapman in the *Mirror*. 'Close can be proud of his men, and England should be proud of Close. I say no more.'

A fresh bombshell hit on Sunday morning, with a splash across the front page of *The People*: 'BRIAN CLOSE SENSATION – He attacked a man in the crowd'. With two eye-witnesses, one a British Legion officer with an MBE, it alleged that on the second day of the match at Edgbaston the Yorkshire captain had assaulted a Warwickshire member as he left the field for lunch. Then, going out to field, he advanced towards another heckler before thinking better of it. Of the first incident, a case as it turned out of confronting the wrong man, the British Legion witness said: "I could hardly believe my eyes when I saw Close wheel five or six yards into the enclosure, grab the man next to me and begin shaking him like a rag doll." Of the second a 'keen club cricketer' said: "If ever I saw a man looking for a punch-up, it was Close. He got as far as the members' fence, then he suddenly seemed to think better of it and turned on his heels."

In the end nothing came of any of it. Journalists on the ground had chosen to draw a veil over it, no complaint was made to Warwickshire, and in any case the MCC's choice of tour captain had already been made. Brian was adamant that he had simply approached the man, put his hand on his shoulder and asked if he had been the one to call out, accepting his assurance that he had not. But Brian was a powerful man who could look threatening so maybe he was under-estimating the effect of his actions.

That Sunday morning, when the story of the 'attack' was raging, he played a round of golf, then he and Vivien went to Ken Barrington's house, where their host threw the press off his scent. There he resolved to pack up and emigrate to Australia, maybe play for a state side and start a new life. As he confided to the *Sunday Mirror* a week later: "The whole turmoil affected me deeply. I couldn't think straight. I had a feeling of overwhelming despair. Without the tremendous support and understanding of my wife, I don't know what I might have done." Returning late in the evening to the hotel, he hid among packing cases at the back till a night porter opened a door for him.

The next day England won the Test, bringing his record as England captain to six wins and a draw. He had still heard nothing when Hanif said quietly to him, "I've heard rumours that they haven't picked you for the West Indies. I sincerely hope you get it." Whatever problems Brian had in the game, they were not with his fellow players.

Shortly afterwards Doug Insole took him aside, told him the news, and he broke down in tears. "I thought it was the end of my world," he said a few days later, "because cricket has been my life since I was a kid." Insole waited for him to compose himself and, revealing nothing, Brian went out to receive the congratulations and to make the required speeches. In the most telling line in his autobiography, he admitted his vulnerability: 'I may not bruise easily, but I do bleed. It was all so horribly unfair.' And he could not resist having a last word at the end of the chapter:

> So Colin Cowdrey was recalled as captain and, in the West Indies, slowed down the bowling rate so ostentatiously that it is the only time I have ever seen Garry Sobers really angry! One law for Close ...

The offending passage of play, on the final morning of the Trinidad Test, saw Cowdrey's England bowl just 24 overs in two hours – a rate of 12 an hour, a full three overs an hour fewer than Yorkshire at Edgbaston.

Brian had been warned by Crawford White to keep his nose clean, but it was not in Brian's nature to adapt his behaviour in that way. At his best that was his strength, but tragically it was also the cause of his downfall.

The press, spotting the movements of Close and Cowdrey, worked it out, but there was a shock at Wednesday's press conference when Doug Insole, questioned insistently, revealed that the vote had been very tight and that he as Chairman had cast his for Close. Denying that he had considered resigning, he said his term of office was now over, adding "If I were re-elected next March, I would certainly consider Close again as captain."

All this caused outrage in Kent, not helped by the leaked news that Mike Smith, if available, would have been chosen. "I feel as if I have come third in an egg-and-spoon race at school," Colin Cowdrey said, "and been awarded the prize because the first two had been disqualified."

While all this was going on, Brian was up in Middlesbrough, playing the return game against Warwickshire. Receiving a standing ovation from the 4,000-strong crowd, an ovation that was still going strong when the Yorkshire captain was playing his first balls, he hit what turned out to be a match-winning innings of 98. 'Quick of eye, strong of arm and excellent in judgement,' was the *Guardian*'s description of his batting. 'An outstanding performance for a man who has just suffered the greatest disappointment of his life.' "My only ambition now is to lead Yorkshire to the championship again," he told the pressmen.

The daytime diet
A cup of tea and a cigarette, 1965

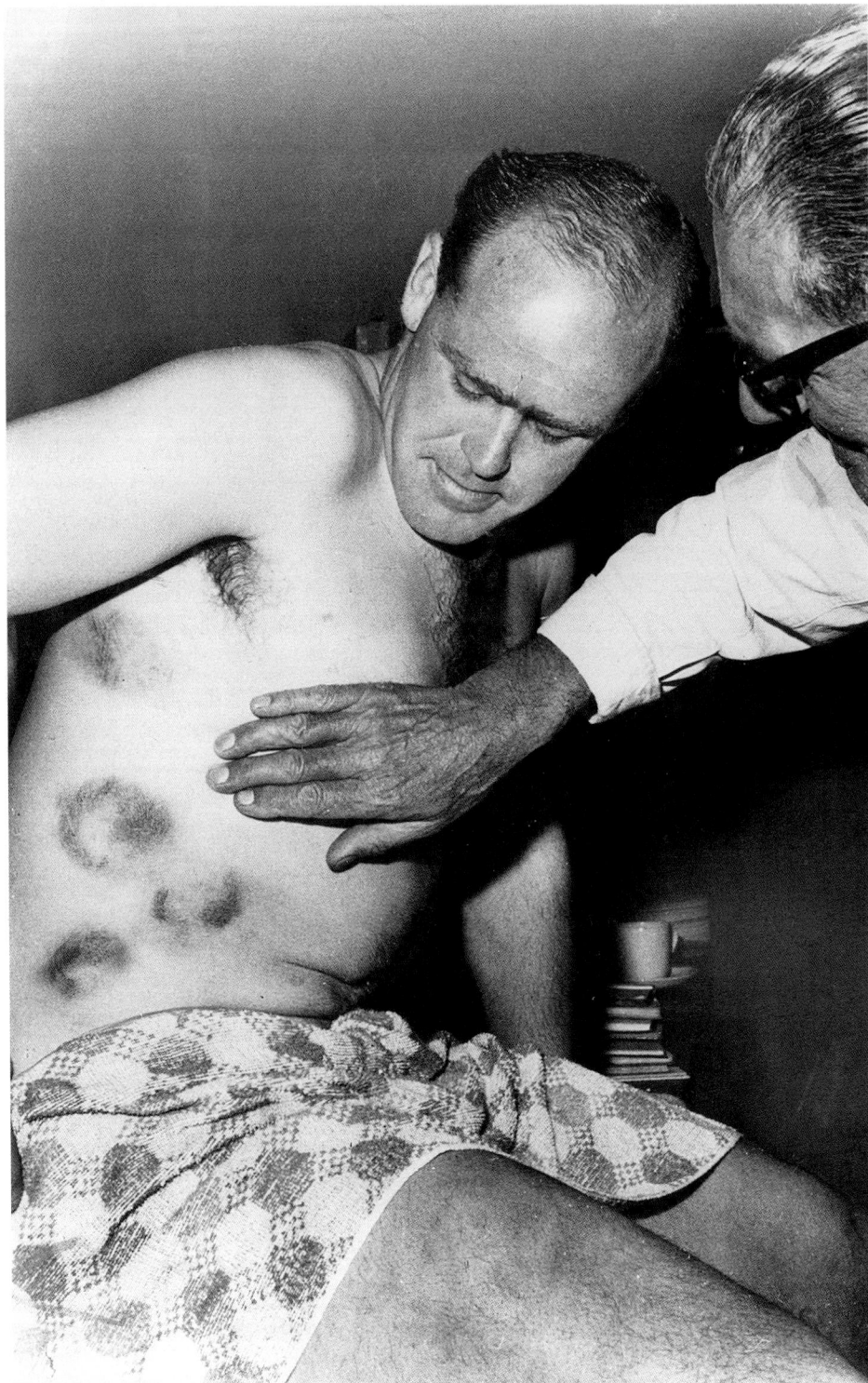

The morning after the Lord's Test in 1963
There were twenty bruises in all.

With Garry Sobers on the Oval balcony, August 1966
Both happy to take a chance as cricketers
and as followers of horse racing.

Captain of England, Headingley, 1967

John Edrich, Robin Hobbs, John Snow, Ken Higgs, Basil D'Oliveira, Geoff Boycott
John Murray, Ken Barrington, Brian Close, Tom Graveney, Ray Illingworth

Another wound, another championship title, Harrogate 1967
(from left) Don Wilson, Brian Close, Ray Illingworth, Phil Sharpe

Fred Trueman and Brian

Team-mates for twenty years but never quite kindred spirits

Receiving the Prudential Trophy, August 1972
Despite his dislike of limited-over cricket, he captained England
to victory in the first ever series of international one-day matches.

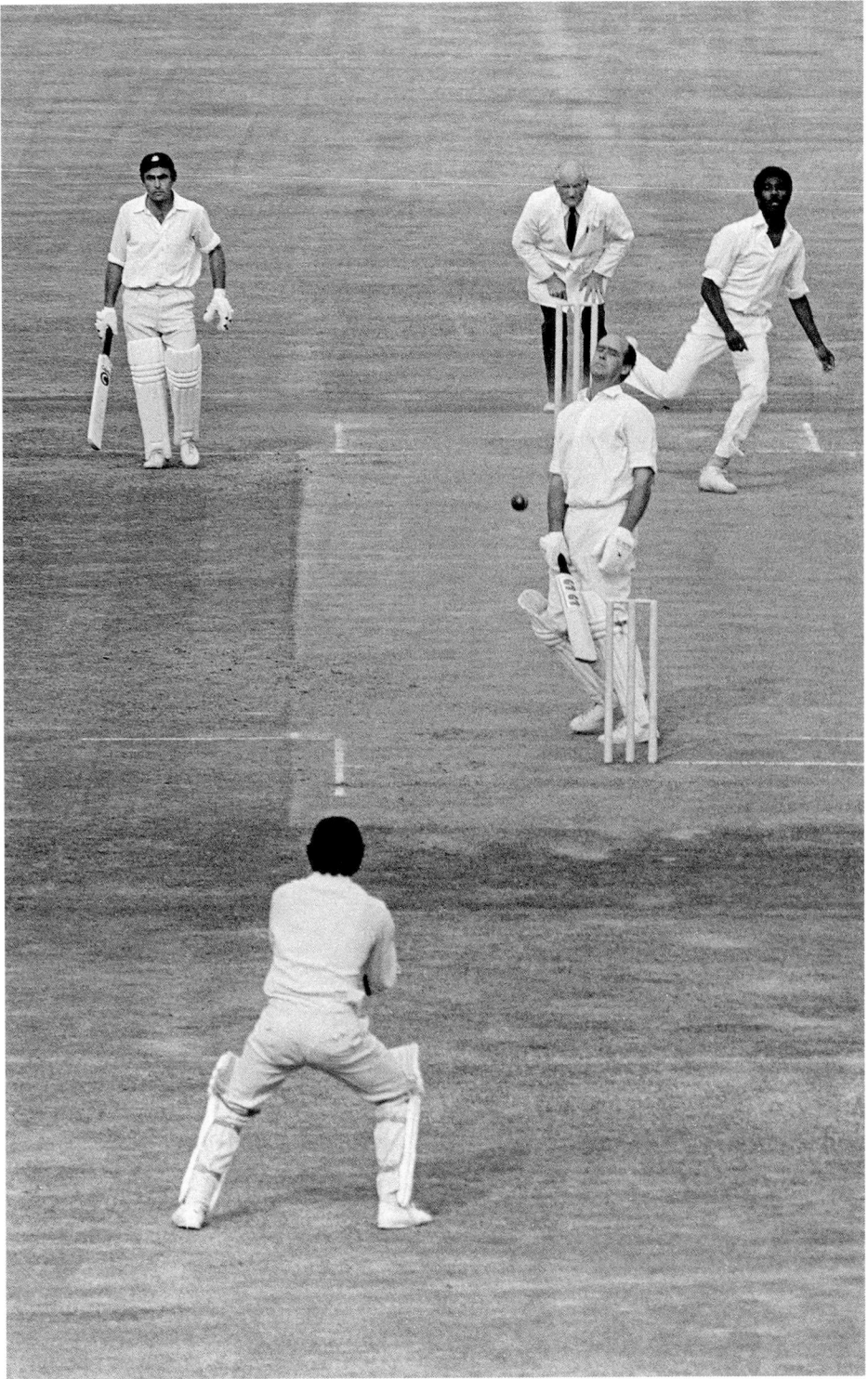

Test cricket at the age of 45, Old Trafford, 1976
John Edrich looks on as Michael Holding sends down another short ball.

(top) County Champions Yorkshire at Buckingham Palace, 2001,
with David Byas (left) and Prince Philip

(bottom) Lynn (left) and Vivien, with former Yorkshire Chairman
Robin Smith at the unveiling of Brian Close Walk in Baildon

Though Jim Kilburn had censured his time-wasting in the *Yorkshire Post*, there were plenty who saw his sacking as an attack on the North, notably the *Bradford Telegraph & Argus* whose thundering verdict was bordered in black:

> This was war, not a game: a war of North v South, Yorkshire v The Rest, professionalism versus the establishment. England has chosen to do without his qualities because he is not one of the 'magic circle', does not have a double-barrelled name, went to the wrong school, speaks the wrong language. But above all he comes from Yorkshire, and that is offence enough for some.

Brian himself stayed clear of such talk. He sent a telegram of congratulation to Colin Cowdrey and wished him well in a public statement. He also sent telegrams to all those who had been selected. On Saturday Cowdrey had the joy of leading Kent to victory in the Gillette Cup final, and the following week Brian was toasting another championship title at Harrogate. He had put aside the plan to emigrate, cheered up by the words of Doug Insole at the press conference, by the ovation at Middlesbrough and the 500 or so letters of support, many of which he kept till his dying day, and by the offer from the *Sunday Mirror* to fly him to the Caribbean to report on the tour. In a week that had seen his second business venture – Brian Close Building Supplies Ltd – go into liquidation, it gave him financial security for the winter.

So much of the fuel for the furore had been supplied by the newspapers, and the aftermath rumbled on. 'The guillotine has fallen,' Crawford White wrote on the front page of the *Daily Express*. 'The decision has the look of the hanging law being brought back for a parking offence.'

The *Daily Mail*'s bumper post bag was ten-to-one in favour of Close, with Alan Wharton, the former Lancashire and England batsman, leading the way: 'Close is, by record, the best captain since the war. He is dour and refuses to treat cricket as a game for playboys. As long as a bunch of "old school tie" administrators run our game, so long shall we be the underdogs in international sport. They are too full of good manners and gentlemanly instincts to realise that games are played to be won and, if not, fought to the death.'

MCC's files bulge with hundreds of angry letters: from a retired naval commander seeing in Close 'qualities of leadership all too rare these days' to a man in Billericay quoting from Shakespeare's *Julius Caesar*: 'You blocks, you stones, you worse than senseless things.' 'Are you lot out of your toffee-nosed minds?' wrote one; another that MCC was 'a closed shop for snobs'. The redoubtable Wilf Wooller, Glamorgan Secretary, resigned from MCC's Cricket Sub-Committee in protest.

The Australians joined in. Keith Miller in the *Daily Express* tore into the 'old boy brigade' at Lord's, calling the sacking of Close 'the most outrageous piece of small-minded priggishness ever to come out of the MCC establishment'. 'In no other country,' wrote Richie Benaud, 'would the captain of the national side lose his job because of something that happened in a relatively unimportant match – and it is unimportant when put alongside the coming Tests against West Indies and Australia.'

Ted Dexter offered a witty comparison with the prime minister:

> CRASH! Close is only too familiar with the word. As if two business liquidations were not enough, he has just had to endure the biggest clatter of all, the sound of his own cricket career subsiding like rubble around him. No doubt Close believes that these things just happen, but the unusual and unlikely have followed him so often that we must be allowed to wonder whether he brings them on himself.
>
> I can't help feeling that his countryman Harold Wilson would have talked his way out of the mess instead of talking his way in deeper as Close is reported to have done.

And, of course, Michael Parkinson could not resist another go:

> They've won. There was never much doubt in my mind about the outcome. Close was kicked out of the Test captaincy and cricket moved backwards into the nineteenth century, returning to the dear departed days when a professional knew his place. Departed, that is, except in the minds of those members of MCC (whom God preserve) who sat in judgement on Brian Close.
>
> But it wasn't only MCC who judged Close and sentenced him so severely. Let us not forget the excellent ground work done by several cricket writers in Fleet Street. Now that Close is to all intents and purposes ruined they can, no doubt, feel proud about their role in this affair. If there is an exclusive club that runs cricket – and many people would find in the events of this week proof that it does exist – then it is nourished by

the pompous drivel that oozes from the minds of a few middle-aged cricket correspondents.

What a storm it had been but, as Parkinson in his closing paragraph foresaw, it was nothing compared with the one that would hit the world of English cricket in a year's time:

> The Close issue was one which demanded that the people stand up and be counted. They will have ample opportunity to prove the consistency or otherwise of their arguments in the very near future when faced with the problem of Basil D'Oliveira and the tour of South Africa. It will be interesting then to see how some people live up to their present fine phrases about fair play and decency.

Parkinson's reference to the professional knowing his place appeared in the *Sunday Times* the day before the inaugural meeting of Fred Rumsey's Cricketers' Association, a seismic event that received little attention in the various cricket publications. From now on, the professional cricketers would be making their views heard.

The England captaincy became an issue again in May 1969. Colin Cowdrey, after 18 months in charge, was appointed for the whole summer. An hour after receiving the news, while batting for Kent in a Sunday League match, he set off for a run and snapped an Achilles tendon. It was a serious injury, carrying the possibility that he would not play again – so, with six Tests that summer and a tour of Australia only eighteen months away, the selectors had once more to assess the merits of several candidates.

If Doug Insole had still been Chairman of Selectors, perhaps he would have argued the case for bringing back Brian Close, who in the year since his sacking had led Yorkshire to another championship title. Brian had his advocates in the press, notably Crawford White in the *Daily Express*:

> If we are honest about this, the best man to take over this injury-ravaged England side could still be Yorkshire's Brian Close. I am well aware that he was 'fired' from the job after that time-wasting 'trial' 18 months ago. He is still not everybody's favourite at Lord's. But old scores cannot be held against him forever. If we are to have the ablest man available for this job, the selectors can't leave Close out of consideration altogether.

John Woodcock in *The Times* took a different view:

> He has reiterated more than once that he would, in similar
> circumstances, adopt similar tactics. That, to my mind, is
> enough to rule him out.

The press thought the likely choice lay between Tom Graveney, Cowdrey's
vice-captain, educated at Bristol Grammar School, and Roger Prideaux of
Tonbridge and Cambridge. Though they were all players now, there was
still something of the professional/amateur divide about the choice.

To the surprise of many, the selectors opted for Ray Illingworth,
who was in his first month as captain of Leicestershire. It was certainly
a surprise to the man himself. He was playing at Headingley, where a
washout on the last day meant that he had left the ground by the time
Alec Bedser rang at one o'clock. Driving down to Hove, he stopped at a
hospital in Northampton to visit Colin Milburn, who had lost an eye in a
car accident four days earlier, then took a wrong turning on the outskirts
of London, only arriving at his hotel at eight o'clock. There, to his great
bewilderment, he found his car surrounded by photographers.

John Woodcock smelt in the choice of Illingworth a strong whiff of
the emerging power of the players:

> Man management means more than ever these days, with
> cricketers forming, as it were, a union among themselves.
> With the amateurs now extinct it is the foreman who is in his
> element, so that when Cowdrey fell out it was to the shop floor
> that the selectors went. Alec Bedser was an advocate of doing
> so long before he ever became chairman of the selectors.

For the third time England had appointed a professional captain. All
three – Hutton, Close and Illingworth – were Yorkshiremen, and in their
different ways they were the three outstanding captains of the first thirty
years after the Second World War.

*

It is easy in all this to over-simplify the issues and the personalities. In
one version Colin Cowdrey is the archetypal establishment man – "yes,
sir, no, sir, three bags full, sir," was Brian's caricature of him in a much
later interview – but Cowdrey himself had his own issues with the
administrators. In a revealing interview during the summer of 1967, when
Brian was still captain, he told John Reason in *The Cricketer* that, since

Peter May's day, England captains had not had the authority they should have had, suffering from demands for 'Brighter Cricket' and the like:

> At about the time I took over, I had the feeling that the official view, the view of the executive, was that the players had become too strong; that they were too independent; that they were not disposed to take advice; that they tended to ignore selectors and tour managers. Accordingly, the executive set out to break the power of the players and, of course, they succeeded.

He reflected on the success of Bradman, Worrell and Benaud as captains:

> They had their own way. This helps so much. It helps the players. I'm not bitter about this. I don't say I should have been the one. But one person should have done it. This constant concern with cricket politics is bound to affect the captain. I think Brian Close may be in the position to reassert this dominance. I hope he does.

Colin Cowdrey won the series in the West Indies, albeit thanks to a reckless declaration by Garry Sobers and the last-wicket pair hanging on for a draw in the final Test. The next summer he acquitted himself well enough in a drawn series with Australia. Tom Graveney, though in a minority, thought him the best England captain he played under. But Brian was so distraught by the unjust way the captaincy had been taken from him that he could not acknowledge this, as was clear in his closing words on the subject in our filmed interview:

> No messing. It was a cooked-up, bloody job. They brought their own man, Cowdrey, back in, and it didn't take him long to jigger it all up again. I tell you what. If I'd have stayed as captain, knowing the players as I knew them, we could have gone years and beaten any of them. We had artists; we had skilled bowlers, batsmen, the lot. And plenty of youngsters. English cricket was in a good state at that time.

He could not be beaten.

> Anyway, that was it. That was over and done with. So I was back to Yorkshire again.

15

THE END OF AN ERA

County cricket in 1968 welcomed star overseas players without any residential qualification. Garry Sobers, every county's first choice, inspired Nottinghamshire, winless in 1967, to fourth place in the championship; the stylish Majid Khan lifted Glamorgan from fourteenth to third. Runners-up Kent had both Asif Iqbal and the already qualified Barbadian John Shepherd. Barry Richards and Mike Procter, Rohan Kanhai and Lance Gibbs, Farokh Engineer and Greg Chappell, they all added glamour and skill to England's domestic game.

In the face of this Yorkshire stayed faithful to their proud tradition of selecting only from those born in the county. Yet, even with that major handicap and with their star batsman Geoff Boycott missing for most of the matches, they retained their championship crown – their third in three years, seventh in ten. In the circumstances it was arguably the greatest of those seven successes.

As Michael Parkinson wrote many years later of Brian, 'He was the last Yorkshireman to captain a team of fellow Yorkshiremen to beat all-comers. You don't have to be born in Barnsley to recognise the importance of that. But it helps.'

What a time it was to be a sport-loving Yorkshireman! Yorkshire were County Champions yet again, and the following winter Leeds teams won the Rugby League Championship and, for the first time, the Football League. At a celebratory dinner for the three teams Brian Sellers chided the footballers for keeping them waiting so long for the party.

Although not a mathematical certainty at that point, the County Championship was effectively won in the closing minutes of Yorkshire's last match, against Surrey at Hull – and, as ever, captain Brian Close was in the thick of the action. He had declared, setting Surrey to score 251 at the reasonable rate of 60 an hour. When the seventh wicket fell at 121, there remained almost two hours of playing time – plenty, it seemed, for Yorkshire to snap up the wickets of the Surrey tail: keeper Arnold Long and the bowlers Robin Jackman and a young Mike Selvey.

Yet, with the Pakistani Younis Ahmed still at the crease, wickets did not fall, and time ticked by. At one point Younis swept hard at a ball from Don Wilson, and it cannoned into the Yorkshire captain stationed at forward short leg. Ken Taylor described the incident to me:

> John Hampshire was fielding at backward short leg, and the ball rebounded off Closey and hit him, too. And it hit him so hard that he was writhing about in agony with the pain. Closey told him to get on with it and not make such a fuss.
>
> Then somebody said, 'Brian, look at your flannels', and we all looked down and saw all this blood coming out of his leg.

"There was blood everywhere," Don Wilson said. "But Closey wouldn't go off. 'It's all in the mind, this pain,' he used to say."

Younis and Arnold Long batted on with no thought of chasing the target. As Jim Kilburn wrote in the *Yorkshire Post*, 'Overs passed into extended bowling spells, minutes came to be measured as hours. Close began to pace anxiously around like an expectant father.'

It was time to turn to Fred Trueman for one last burst to break the stand. He was 37 years old, no longer a bowler of great pace, and he had taken just three wickets in the last 25 days. But he retained a great aura, and the crowd grew excited as he once more stood at the end of his run-up, as Don Wilson recalled:

> Somebody in the crowd shouted, "Come on, Fred, Yorkshire expects." But he couldn't do it. He just had the one over, and we took him off. It was quite the saddest thing I've ever seen.

'Spin left the sturdy batsmen undisturbed,' wrote Kilburn. 'The speed Trueman could raise brought no alarm.'

Only three overs were left, the first to be bowled by Don Wilson. His second ball was a leg-stump half-volley which Younis swept with force, and again the ball thudded into the formidable figure of Brian Close, who was much too near the bat to evade the impact. The ball crashed into his forearm, leaving an egg-sized lump, and looped in the air to Jimmy Binks behind the stumps. Eight wickets were down.

The two umpires, as it happened, were both Yorkshiremen: Ron Aspinall and Albert Gaskell. It was Gaskell whose finger went up when Younis, unsure what had happened, looked towards him, and two balls later his finger went up again when a ball from Don Wilson thudded into the pads of Robin Jackman. Gaskell was unusual at that time in not having played the first-class game. According to Don, "He was a great big man. He drank an enormous amount, and he had this great purple nose. He was from Northallerton, and he was Yorkshire through and through. Everybody seemed to like him so they gave him a couple of seasons on the first-class list."

"He was a lovely, happy character, always with a smile," remembers Micky Stewart, who still shakes his head at the lbw Gaskell gave against him earlier in the innings. "The game at Hull was his finest match."

With one wicket remaining Close turned to Tony Nicholson for the next over, and off his final delivery Arnold Long edged a catch to the keeper. With one over to spare Yorkshire were champions again and, according to Mike Carey in the *Guardian*, 'they leapt and bounded their way from the field like a team of Morris dancers.'

The champagne corks popped, though there was no fizz for the captain. "When he got in the dressing room and unlaced his boot," Phil Sharpe said, "there was blood everywhere." A doctor appeared from the crowd, Brian was driven to hospital in a spectator's car – and "You know what hospitals are like. I missed all of the champagne and most of the party."

Mike Carey's report concluded:

> In the end it was that remarkable rebound that broke the partnership. One left the ground thinking that blood, champagne and guts was an accurate description of Yorkshire's cricket in this match.

*

The Yorkshire team at Hull contained eight of the men who had been at the heart of their championship triumph in 1959. Ronnie Burnet's young side had been growing old together, with only Richard Hutton (26 the next week) and John Hampshire (27) of this Hull eleven under the age of thirty. Brian had demonstrated great loyalty to his established players and did an outstanding job in maintaining their zest and their desire for victory through the years, but it was becoming a problem that they were mostly in the latter part of their careers.

Though Fred Trueman was the official vice-captain, it was Ray Illingworth on whom Brian relied most for advice. Their personalities were radically different, yet there was a mutual respect that made the combination work so much better than a Close/Trueman partnership would have done. Brian was the great motivator, a leader from the front whose instinct was to attack. He needed a quieter man to calm him down when outright attack was not the best option, to steer him towards a subtler approach. Even he admitted as much in his autobiography, in a passage that reveals a surprising recognition of his own limitations:

> No one would ever suggest that Raymond and I were in the least bit alike, either in character, temperament or approach to cricket. But in a marvellous way we seemed to complement each other.
>
> A man who knows us both well was once asked which of us he would rather have as an officer in war, if an attack 'over the top' was due to be made. He replied without hesitation: "Illy, every time. He would ask for three intelligence reports on the strength and disposition of the enemy, six Met reports for the next twenty-four hours, an expert soil analysis on No Man's Land, plus a detailed breakdown of our own forces, then he'd decide the attack was not feasible at all. Closey would pick up a crowbar, or anything which was lying handy, shout 'Come on, then' and chase off without checking whether we had any cover or support."

In the summer of 1967, when the pair were away with England, Yorkshire brought in the young off-spinner Geoff Cope. He had immediate success, taking 24 wickets in his first four matches at an average of 9.50, figures which the newspapers were quick to point out were considerably better than those of the man he was standing in for. 'Colt leads Test Ace in Wicket Race' and 'Young Cope spins a problem for Yorkshire' were two of the headlines. Cope was 20, Illingworth 35 – how long would it be before the county looked to the future by changing the pecking order?

Such was the background when Ray Illingworth, an England Test cricketer in the summer of 1968, reflected on his future prospects and made what he regarded as a reasonable request for a three-year contract, to run from 1969. His idea of reasonable, however, was not that of the Chairman Brian Sellers. Yorkshire gave one-year contracts, nothing more, and he had no interest in conceding any power to the players. His reply, reported third hand to Illingworth, was: "He can go, and he can take any bugger with him who feels the same way."

He went to Leicestershire. Their offer was not the best financially, but it included the captaincy, which, together with the warmth of the welcome when he and his wife visited, appealed to him. Apart from four games as stand-in Yorkshire captain in 1963, he told me that the only team he had ever captained had been the Farsley Under-16s – "and they banned me from playing because I was in the first team."

From 1969 Brian would be left to captain Yorkshire without his chief lieutenant. He would also be without Ken Taylor, retiring from the game to coach in South Africa, and Fred Trueman, who announced his retirement in November.

Trueman launched himself into a new life as stand-up comedian, television presenter and newspaper columnist, creating a stir in May when his column in *The People*, under the headline 'WHY I QUIT', gave the 'full, fiery story' of his departure:

> I told a little white lie last winter about why I retired from first-class cricket. It wasn't only that I wanted to go out still at the top with a world record of 307 Test wickets and as deputy captain of the champions. Nor even that I could see myself earning a bomb by writing for The People and snapping up all the offers from Yorkshire TV, publishers, radio and night clubs.
>
> No, there was something else that I left out of my resignation letter to Yorkshire. Something I've told no one about until now. I QUIT BECAUSE I COULDN'T STAND ANOTHER SEASON UNDER BRIAN CLOSE.

Trueman and Close had made their debuts together as 18-year-olds in 1949, but they had never quite been on the same wavelength. Gloucestershire's 'Bomber' Wells worked with me on a book in which we recreated a 1957 match at Cheltenham. In it he painted the scene in the bar at the end of the first day's play:

> It was lovely playing against Yorkshire when Fred and Closey were young. You'd split up into two parties. Fred would be at one end of the bar, Closey up the other. You could have half an hour of Closey lambasting Fred, then when you got fed up with that you could go and hear Fred lambasting Closey.

Intriguingly this quote has undergone a kind of Chinese Whispers through several publications, eventually appearing in Brian's own voice with a completely different meaning:

> Bomber Wells always said how much he liked playing against Yorkshire. Why? Because at the end of the day's play the opposition's young players could go into the bar, spend half an hour with Fred, another half hour with me and learn more in that hour than they would in a whole week.

Managing Fred Trueman was not always easy. Vic Wilson had struggled, but Brian had the advantage of a heavyweight boxer's build. "Fred didn't have the physical presence of Closey," Geoff Cope told me. "He had his broad shoulders and his big beam, but Closey was frightening. If you wanted to have a go at Closey, you always made sure you were between him and the door."

Their biggest public bust-up came in August 1965, an incident recounted (not entirely accurately) in Fred's 'Why I Quit' article. One of Fred's resentments was that, when Brian took on the captaincy, he had to yield his fielding position at short leg to Brian and run around in the deep. This came to a head in a Roses match at Sheffield when, after a lengthy bowling spell, he found himself at mid-on, with nobody else in front of the wicket on the leg side.

> "Bloody hell, Brian," I protested. "You can't expect me to cover half of Bramall Lane on my own." But he did nothing to assist me in the field. So I didn't run for the next ball on my side. I just walked towards it. Very slowly. Unfortunately Brian Sellers saw me ... and he's the Chairman of Yorkshire!

Although he does not mention it in the article, press reports at the time suggest that he made a finger sign towards the captain. He claimed in the *Daily Mail* that he was 'gesticulating in a friendly way' for a second fielder, yet this was not how it was interpreted by Sellers. The committee had already admonished him earlier in the year for going into print without first clearing his copy with them, and he was suspended without pay for one match. 'Banned Trueman may quit cricket,' was the headline in the *Daily Mail*.

That blew over, but the problems flared again in 1968. By this time Fred was a shadow of the fast bowler he had once been, and Yorkshire were looking to give playing time to the 19-year-old Chris Old from Middlesbrough, an exciting prospect.

In May at Headingley, as Fred pointed out in his 'I Quit' tirade, he bowled Garry Sobers for a duck. Yet, for all this, the match report in the *Guardian* put a finger on the dilemma of the Yorkshire captain's problem with his ageing star:

> Close, who obviously prefers Trueman to give three overs at speed rather than eight overs at fast-medium pace, will have to realise he cannot have it. Trueman's successes did not lift him to the riproaring bundle of viciousness Close desires or what Trueman would have been a few years ago.

They travelled to Middlesbrough for the next match, and Trueman found himself dropped, not for disciplinary reasons but because the captain thought he was 'not fit enough' to bowl the overs required on the soft pitch. If Fred is to be believed, Brian made a mess of telling him to his face, with Fred finding out first from the opposition captain. It was a humiliating moment for a man who carried such an aura, and it set off thoughts of retirement.

The following week, with Brian out of action, Fred assumed the captaincy, leading the team for eight matches. In his 'I Quit' article he boasted that he had only twice lost as Yorkshire captain, at Northampton in 1966 and Bath in 1967, but he also lost twice in 1968. However, he did have what he regarded as his finest hour as a Yorkshire cricketer, perhaps finer in his proud Yorkshire mind than any he enjoyed as an England cricketer. He led the county to an innings victory over a near-full-strength Australian side at Sheffield. "He talked about it till his dying day," Dickie Bird told me.

Fred enjoyed the captaincy, and he was undoubtedly good at it, drawing warm praise from Brian Sellers. It unsettled Brian, who at one point felt it necessary to appear in the dressing-room and announce: "I would like to remind you all that I'm still the Yorkshire captain."

There was an unpleasant episode involving a cheque from a supporter to the team, which got mislaid in the post. Brian, to his astonishment, found himself accused by the committee of having taken it for himself. The committee had also been told that 'senior players' were concerned by the amount of time the captain was spending on his horse-racing bets.

At the Melbourne Cup on his tour of Australia the young, wide-eyed Brian had experienced the thrill of betting, and gradually it had become an addiction, one that he never gave up though in later life he suffered for it financially. Geoff Cope talked to me about it:

> He knew so many people in racing. If you were twelfth man Closey would have you ringing numbers, with coded messages being given down the phone. "This one's going steadily downstream ... Clodderhops is working hard to get upstream." You never got a conversation, just "Tell him so-and-so" and that was the end of the message. It put me right off betting. If you said some horse was upstream, he'd get the paper out and start marking it.

The accusations about the missing cheque and the obsession with the horses had, in the eyes of some, the fingerprints of Fred on them. Their relationship had reached its lowest ebb.

Among the films I made for Yorkshire was one about Trueman, in which a number of people paid tribute to him. The years had passed, Fred was dead, and Brian arrived, happy to speak fondly of his old team-mate.

> We had so many tremendous occasions; you have so many wonderful memories. We were colleagues for so long, winning matches, winning championships. I can see him now in my mind. He had such a wonderful action, running up to the wicket, turning sideways on, his left arm giving him the direction and the balance. Even in his thirties he was as good a fast bowler as there was in first-class cricket.
>
> No messing, the years of service he did for Yorkshire and England were magnificent.

Moving on to the victory over Australia, I asked him: "Do you think he'd like to have been captain of Yorkshire?"

"I'm sure he would," he replied. He gave a long, awkward laugh, then added: "I'd rather not answer that." After a moment he went on:

> Doing the captaincy in one particular match is not like captaining the side in the whole season. You spend an awful lot of mental energy sorting your own side out. As a captain the game comes first, then the team, then individuals, and

you come last. And whether Fred could have done that over a period of time ...

He left the question hanging. At the time I was captaining a club side, and I often found myself thinking about his four-point order: the game, the team, the individuals and, last, yourself. I repeated it some years later to Mike Brearley. "Did Brian really say that?" he asked, as if he was surprised that Brian would think in that way about captaincy.

Brian as a captain exuded toughness and self-belief, but there was another side to him that he did not so readily let people see, as he revealed in an interview soon after he finished playing:

> Few people, even those closely connected with cricket, fully appreciate the strain in leading a county side seven days a week in the various competitions we play in these days. It really tells. Many cricketers, and in particular captains, find the whole thing building up off the field, putting enormous pressure on personal and family life. It affected me, too. I can't begin to think of how many cups of 3 a.m. tea I've made when I haven't been able to sleep because of an aspect of a game which is worrying me: either the way it's going or perhaps an emotional concern about one of the players. Yorkshire in the Sixties were a team full of strong personalities; they weren't easy to weld together.

One of Fred's gripes in the article was that Brian was a selfish captain, doing too much himself: batting up the order, bowling seam and spin, fielding close. Ken Taylor complained to me that he never bowled much after Brian became captain: "Whenever Illy said to him, 'Why don't you put Ken on?', he'd say, 'I'll have a go.'" But Ken loved playing under Brian. He was a great motivator, he made it fun, and he was never selfish in the way some thought Ray Illingworth was at Leicester, putting himself on to bowl when it suited him. Brian volunteered himself when the going was tough.

Geoff Cope, playing as a youngster when Brian was away with England, has positive memories of Fred's captaincy. He liked his warm encouragement and was touched when, summoned to Bath from a second-team game at Harrogate, he arrived at the hotel at half past two in the morning to find Fred asleep on a settee.

The night porter said, "Mr Trueman's been waiting up for you. I'm to wake him when you come."

He woke him up. "Where am I? ... Oh, you're here ... It's stupid they didn't let you go earlier." A few expletives as well. "Now you get yourself to bed. You're supposed to be at the ground for ten o'clock. You be there for a quarter to eleven."

The next morning it was: "How do you feel? Are you tired?" "I'm OK. I want to play if you want me." "I want you, sunshine." And I played. I thought, "Who else would have waited up?" They're the little things you don't see on the outside.

All this was in contrast to the time the previous year when, with Ray Illingworth out injured, Geoff joined the team at Hove:

I had a letter from the committee that I had to give to Closey before play. He read it and said, "Put that back in your pocket. Tell them you gave it to me at lunchtime. Oh, and you're twelfth man today." I was intrigued by this so I read the letter. It said, 'The committee request you play Geoff Cope in this game to give him experience.'

This was not the only time Brian disobeyed his committee over the inclusion of young players, something that remained in the debit column whenever they reviewed his captaincy. One promising player used up a fortnight of annual holiday, only to find himself twelfth man in all the games. He made himself available one more time on the firm understanding that he would be playing, and still he was twelfth man. Was Brian part of the problem that was stopping the team from developing the next generation? Geoff Cope could see how they might think that:

Closey always referred to 'his' team, and he would support them to the hilt. If somebody was in a bad run, he didn't leave them out for quite a while.

Geoff saw the two of them, Fred and Brian, in action at a formative time in his life so his comparison of them as captains is worth hearing:

Fred was probably more understanding and was closer to you. Half the time Closey would be saying, "Come on, you should be taking wickets. You're bowling it like a pansy. Bowl it a bit quicker, and don't let them get to you." It wasn't a rollocking, but he'd do it in a more abrasive way. Fred was an arm around you: "Now, sunshine, come on, we've got to ..." I responded to that. But don't get me wrong. Closey was the best captain I played under.

For my second book, when I toured the country asking county cricketers of the 1960s to tell me about their most memorable matches, Roy Booth of Worcestershire chose a game against Yorkshire in August 1968. He had been the Yorkshire keeper in the early 1950s, displaced by Jimmy Binks, and in the game in 1968 he was standing in as Worcestershire captain.

It was a week before the dramatic last game at Hull so Yorkshire, pressing for the championship, were desperate for the points. It was a superb contest, which Worcestershire won by one run when at the death Fred Trueman was given lbw by umpire George Pope. In hot weather an injury to his fellow umpire had left Pope umpiring at the bowler's end for most of the match, trying to keep the calm when the game got tense and the appeals grew more and more frequent. He had arranged to get a lift home to Chesterfield in Fred's car so, when Fred remained at the crease, staring disbelievingly at his pads while they all streamed off, he shook his head. "It looks as though my lift's gone," he said – though it hadn't. It was perfect for my purposes, a game rich with incident and character, with the relationship between Fred and Brian a lovely thread in the weave.

Worcestershire were at Chelmsford the next day, and Roy had a memory of stopping for a drink at the London hotel where the England team were staying. His team-mate Basil D'Oliveira had just hit the century that would shake up the cricket world, but Ray Illingworth was more concerned to hear about the game at Worcester:

"All I've heard is that we've lost by one, and it was an lbw on the last one. Who was it?" "It was Fred." "Fred," he laughs. "It couldn't have happened to a better bloke." They'd lost by one, but Ray was only interested in knowing who the last man was. That was the humour they had.

He recalled the earlier game between the two sides at Sheffield, when Fred was not in the Yorkshire side. "He spent most of the time in our dressing room, chatting away. 'A right prat is Close', that sort of thing."

Fred had a habit before each match of visiting the opposition dressing-room, looking round and counting the wickets he expected to take.

It was all part of his psychological menace. By this time, however, his presence among the opposition was lasting longer. According to Bob Carter, another exiled Yorkshireman, he was there among them before play on the third morning at Worcester.

> All of a sudden the door burst open. Closey's there. He hurls a great big leather bag in. "You've been in there for two bloody days," he says. "You can change with the buggers today."

Roy had a memory of Yorkshire in the field. Fred had hardly bowled in the match, yet Tony Nicholson was regularly called into action:

> Fred was fielding down at third man, and he was signalling that he'd like to come back on. In his heart he still thought he could bowl them out, but he'd lost that nip and movement and he wasn't effective. I can still remember him waving to Closey, to say "I'm ready to come back", and Closey was walking backwards, not even looking at him.

'Walking backwards, not even looking at him.' How that image sums up their relationship in those last matches of 1968.

Fred was not one to take such treatment quietly, as Geoff Cope recalls:

> In the dressing room at the end of the day Fred said, "Have you got a spare sweater, young 'un?" "What for?" "Don't worry, have you got a spare sweater?" He walked round, and he got this heap of sweaters in his hands. Closey said, "What's going on, Fred?" He said, "I've just been thinking. I'm going to sleep under the covers tonight so, when new ball's due in morning, you don't miss me." The whole dressing room collapsed.

Yet, despite the unease between them and the plethora of overseas stars in the other counties, Brian Close's Yorkshire completed a hat-trick of championship successes in 1968. It was their fourth outright title under his leadership, a number not equalled by any county captain in the years since.

*

According to Fred Trueman, in his last book *As It Was*, there was an extraordinary aftermath to the season. In November, after he had given the news of his retirement to *The People*, he visited the Yorkshire President, Sir William Worsley, to make sure he heard the news first from him.

He said, "Oh no, Fred, don't do that. We're holding a meeting next week, and there is every likelihood you will be offered the captaincy."

It was too late. The presses were already rolling at *The People*. When he met up with Brian Sellers that week, the Chairman suggested that his retirement had helped them out of an awkward situation. It is hard to guess how it would have played out if Brian, after so much success, had been asked to play under Fred. Would he have stayed, or would he have done as Ray Illingworth did and move to another county?

The big issue at that stage was Brian's loyalty to his old team, his insistence that the young players had to be good enough before they were blooded. The consequences of his approach became clear in 1969 when, with the team breaking up, they fell to 13th in the championship, the lowest position in their history. Brian was out injured for more than a third of the games, with Jimmy Binks standing in as captain, and the season's only consolation was a second victory in a Gillette Cup final, Brian's sixth trophy in his seven years as captain.

Binks fell out with the committee, was offered promotion by his engineering firm and retired. With neither Illingworth nor Binks at his side, with Trueman and Taylor gone, and with the Yorkshire committee expecting success every year, Brian was starting to feel isolated. It was something that Geoff Cope observed with typical perceptiveness:

> You'd run through trenches for Closey, and he'd run through them for you. But I do think he'd lost his rudder with the lads who'd gone. They weren't just people in the dressing room who'd got experience and knowledge; they were friends. When he looked round the dressing room, there wasn't a lot left of what he had, and I think that as much as anything drove Closey down. I'm not sure who he knew to turn to, to talk to. He respected Fred, Illy and Binksy, and I don't know if he had the same respect for those who were left.

For all his belief in cricket as a game that demanded an intense focus, Brian was, as Ken Taylor observed, capable of lapses of concentration. "T' rudder's gone," Binks and Illingworth would sometimes say to each other, and now they were no longer there to jolt the captain's mind back to the game. Despite this, Yorkshire had a better season in the championship in 1970. For any other county, fourth place would have been an encouraging outcome for a team in transition, but Brian was not happy. He reckoned they would have won if England had not taken away Chris Old and Don Wilson for the final two Tests. But then he was always a master of excuses.

One of Brian's great strengths was his refusal to admit defeat, to back off, to give up, but that quality also made him rather fixed in his views, unable to adapt readily to change. In 1969 the Sunday League, a 40-over competition, was introduced, and Lancashire, for so long Yorkshire's under-achieving neighbours across the Pennines, rejuvenated themselves by becoming masters of the shorter game, winning the first two Sunday League titles and three successive Gillette Cups from 1970. Great crowds filled Old Trafford, bringing a major improvement to the balance sheets.

Meanwhile at Yorkshire Brian, an adamant traditionalist, despised the new format. "Throw down some sawdust," he said witheringly. "Put on some party hats and red noses, and you've got the Sunday League." In his view it was coarsening the game, turning the art of bowling and fielding into a negative exercise, preventing the batsman from scoring, not trying to take his wicket. He never changed his view, calling it a harmful 'gimmick' in an interview ten years later:

> Limited-over cricket has had a lot to do with the decline in English standards in the 1970s. When I skippered Yorkshire I used to hate running the game on Sundays. After all week trying to get our players thinking positively, on the seventh day I then had to ask them to do almost everything against the cricketing commonsense I'd been preaching for the previous six!

Another ten years later he bent the ear of Ted Dexter, the newly appointed Chairman of Selectors:

> I used a racing analogy because I know he likes the horses. If you took a racehorse, could be the best in the world, and you put it over a two-mile hurdle one day, a six-furlong sprint the next, a three-mile chase the next, then a mile-and-a-half middle-distance run the next, it'll wonder if it's stood on its arse or its elbow.

"This will never last," he told Geoff Cope at an early fixture. There were even games he missed, saying "I'll have a rest today."

Yorkshire's last Sunday match of 1970 took them to Old Trafford. For the first time for more than twenty years the gates were closed, with nearly 33,000 excited spectators inside, and they spilled onto the pitch and celebrated long after the game's conclusion when Lancashire were crowned Sunday champions again. At the other end of the table only Sussex had fewer wins than Yorkshire.

Worse for Close, he was accused of extreme rudeness to a man who, in the aftermath of the game, was gloating over Lancashire's success and who turned out to be their President and former captain Lionel Lister. Not only did the committee have that to consider, but they also received a consultant's report that Close's shoulder would stand only one more year. He would be 40 in February, and he did not appear to have much more cricket left in him.

Brian's record for Somerset over the next seven years made a nonsense of the medical report. But that was Brian; he did not give up easily. I was told a story by Martin Veal, a cricketer at the Lansdown Club who play on the field next to the Royal United Hospital in Bath. During a match one day in the mid-1970s he went to A&E, only to find himself in the next cubicle to Close, whose Somerset team were playing in the city. He overheard a houseman reporting the findings of an x-ray on Brian's knee, the one he had damaged twice: at football and in a car accident.

"Mr Close, you have no cartilage, and bone is rubbing on bone. It is surprising you can still walk or even stand, let alone play cricket."

"Nothing I don't know, then," came the reply.

The medical report, the reluctance to promote youngsters, the dislike of the one-day game, the rudeness to Lionel Lister. It all added up, and the Yorkshire committee returned to the thought they had entertained two years earlier: a change of captain. It was thinking that Geoff Cope could see the logic of:

> Closey had taken a lot on his own without talking about it to people. He was never one to sit in the dressing room, moping about what had happened in the committee room. I think it was right probably for him to go at that time. You believe a consultant. I can see the reasons.
>
> It's never easy when you get rid of somebody. He'd had the utmost pressure for a long time – 22 years at the highest level,

all the time in a cauldron of expectancy, with highs and lows – and all of a sudden this rug had been taken out from under him. It hurt him a lot, and he took that hurt to the grave with him.

It was brutally done: a call to report to the office, ten minutes to decide whether to resign or be sacked. In a state of confusion Brian opted to resign, a decision he rang and changed later that morning.

> All I wanted to do was get out of that room, away from Headingley, and to talk to Vivien. I drove away with my mind still in a whirl. I wanted to cry. As I drove along Kirkstall Road my vision misted up so much I had to stop. And then I was sick, there at the side of the road.
>
> When I got home Vivien was out, collecting Lynn from play school, so I sat there thinking over all my memories of my days with Yorkshire: the moments of success, the laughs, the men I had played with and against, and gradually realising it was all over.

In *I Don't Bruise Easily* the chapter was entitled 'The Worst Day Of My Life'. In our filmed interview we had to stop the camera. "I'd given 22 years of my life to Yorkshire," he said, fighting back the tears. "There was nothing else in my life that I wanted to do."

Looking back now, at a distance of more than half a century, I am struck how he never had an inkling that his position was in danger, but then Brian never did seem to see danger on the horizon. He always had that naïvety, that tendency to think the best of people.

He was planning to go on for two or three more years. He saw Geoff Boycott as his successor and wanted to work with him, then play one season under the younger man's captaincy, helping him into the role.

Back in the summer of 1968, before Ray Illingworth's departure, he had been rung by Crawford White of the *Daily Express*, who had heard that Close was in bother with the committee. He wanted him to know that, if it came to the worst, Leicestershire would offer him the captaincy there for twice what he was earning at Yorkshire. But Brian gave it no thought; money was never going to trump his loyalty to Yorkshire.

For the summer of 1971 the committee, in a tight decision, chose Boycott ahead of Don Wilson, but with Close's departure the team he inherited was weaker still. Further, the regulations allowed counties to recruit a second overseas player three years after the first one so Yorkshire were at an even greater disadvantage than before. Warwickshire, champions in 1972, managed through various exemptions to field four West Indian Test cricketers: Kanhai, Kallicharran, Gibbs and Murray.

Yorkshire's years of glory were soon a distant memory. Boycott scored his runs, averaging 100 in the 1971 season, but not everybody in his team thought he observed Brian Close's four-point order – the game, the team, the individuals, yourself – and tensions grew. Their next trophy would not come till 1983 when the 51-year-old Ray Illingworth, back as cricket manager, took the field once more and led them to the Sunday League title.

Brian Sellers, a man as reluctant to admit fault as Brian Close, confessed to Micky Stewart in either 1971 or 1972 that he had made a bad mistake. Some years later, when Somerset were playing in Yorkshire, he even apologised to the man he had sacked, as Brian revealed in our film interview:

> I was walking along, and Brian Sellers was coming towards me. He couldn't dodge me if he'd wanted to. He came up and he said, "Brian, you've done a great job at Somerset. I can honestly say that was the worst mistake I've made in my life."

Brian never got over it. Yet I can't help feeling that it all worked out so much better for him than if he had stayed at Yorkshire. Away from the pressure-cooker of the Northern county his career had a glorious renaissance in which he answered his critics. His body stood up to another seven summers of cricket, his batting yielded much improved results, he nurtured a generation of talented youngsters, and – for all his reservations about over-limit cricket – he was the selectors' choice in 1972 to lead England in the first official one-day internationals against Australia.

With Ray Illingworth winning trophies at little-fancied Leicestershire, Yorkshire's dramatic decline was largely self-inflicted.

16

JUST WHAT SOMERSET NEEDED

Brian's first reunion with his old Yorkshire team came in June 1971 in a championship match at Taunton, an occasion he marked with a century. Gerald Pawle in the *Daily Telegraph* called it 'a display of unremitting concentration and superb technical skill which showed Yorkshire that he is no spent force'. His hundredth run was 'applauded by the fielding side as warmly as by the crowd.'

His century set up an emphatic ten-wicket victory, which he reflected upon in an interview the next year with Norman Harris in *The Observer*:

> I knew them better than they knew themselves. I defeated a team that had no rudder. It was like defeating something that you belong to – a cause that I'd fought and lived and nearly died for, for 20-odd years. It didn't seem right, really.

Two weeks later, when Somerset were without a match, he popped into Headingley for the first time since the day of his sacking, to watch a day of the Test against Pakistan. The hurt of his departure was still intense, as he recalled when interviewed by Peter Walker a few years later:

> I stood in the crowd at the back of the public bank and felt terrible. I was so embarrassed. I didn't feel at all at home until after the game when I went into the bar the players use and spoke to the lads there. That wasn't too bad, but I don't want to go through another day like that, thank you.

In his last four years with Yorkshire he had made only two hundreds, but in his first year at Somerset, now past his 40th birthday, he hit five. His batting average, barely 30 in his latter years at Yorkshire, was 43 in 1971, 51 in 1972, the highest of his career – and he scored heavily in the one-day game, too.

"When we played against him in his later years at Yorkshire," Somerset's Peter Robinson recalls, "we felt he was just a slogger. But when he came down to us, we realised what a good player he was."

"Closey's personal figures suffered at Yorkshire," Tom Cartwright said. "At Somerset he batted at three; he could just go in and play. Had he been a number three all his life, I think you'd have seen a lot more runs behind his name and a lot more outstanding innings."

Norman Harris, in his interview, put it to Brian that many thought he could have been a fixture in the England side for twenty years. Did he think he should have scored more runs?

> Well I do, yes. I realise I should have done much better. I'm sure the reason I haven't is that I've not been selfish enough to put myself first in certain situations. I can compare myself with other individualists that I've seen succeed and compare the sort of mental structure that they've built their success on. I just never had that. I don't know, I had to be riled ... and I was always filling in, doing this and that for the team – quite happily – and never developed a definite way of playing.

His hundreds that first summer at Somerset included one on his debut, against Ray Illingworth's Leicestershire, and an unbeaten one against the touring Indians. But the century which his team-mates all talked about was the one he scored against Surrey, that summer's champion county. Brian Langford, Somerset's captain that year, told me the story:

> We were playing on the Sunday at Torquay, and he top-edged a ball into his mouth. He lost a few teeth and went off. He went back to the Crown and Sceptre that evening, got some scotch down him and in the morning I picked him up and took him to the dentist. "There's no way you can play today," the dentist said, but he wouldn't hear of it. He was next in to bat, and he was sitting in the dressing room, with his mouth swollen and his nerve ends hanging out.
>
>   Maurice Hill came in. He was twelfth man, and he hadn't been playing on the Sunday at Torquay. "I don't think I can play today," he said. "I've got toothache." The dressing room erupted.

A wicket fell immediately. Close stepped out to bat and, in a painful daze, he found himself on the receiving end of a Robin Jackman bouncer that he top-edged for six: "That really brought me to my senses. After that I got my head down."

"When he came off at lunch," Brian Langford said. "I asked him how he was feeling. 'I shall be glad when I get my hundred,' he said. 'I'm a bit tired.'"

'He was not especially in form,' Alan Gibson wrote in *The Times*, 'and his runs did not come smoothly. But his hundred was the innings of a man determined to make runs.'

That first summer with Somerset he snapped up 34 catches, putting him third in the first-class list. He fielded mostly at short leg, where Peter Robinson, a slow left-arm bowler, had been previously:

> There wasn't a braver, more stupid fielder in the world than Brian. I was pleased when he came. Up till then I was doing bat-pad. "I'm going in there, lad," he said and I thought, "Thank God for that." I'd been trying to ditch the job for years.
>
> He used to get hit in the shins, and all he'd say was "Keep them up, lad." His legs sounded better than some bats. He got a nasty one at Kent. The lad Nicholls hit him in the collar bone. He just went off for a bit, had a fag and came back. He was unbelievable.

His bowling was little used, though it had its moments, as 'Robbo' recalls:

> Brian would bowl these little seamers, and he'd say, "I used to be as quick as Fred, you know." Ted Dexter made a comeback that year, playing in the Sunday League, and the first ball Brian bowled at him at Bath was an absolute long hop that Ted nailed straight to mid-wicket. "I always do Ted, lad," he said.

Somerset had never won a trophy, but they had been a good team in the mid-1960s, twice finishing third in the championship and reaching a Gillette Cup final. By 1969 they had lost many of their key players and were struggling, as Brian Langford, an off-spinner, remembered:

> I was called to a meeting at Glastonbury and told by Len Creed the vice-chairman that I was the captain. I was trying to work out afterwards if it was an honour or not. He said to me, "We don't expect you to win a game. We're going to be rock bottom. Just go and try your best." It was a battle. You don't mind getting runs scored off you if your own batsmen are scoring runs. But we weren't getting any runs that season.

"We were in the lifeboats," Peter Robinson says. "We had no opening bowlers. Brian and I would be bowling by twelve o'clock. Teams without bowling do struggle a bit. If we had even half a good morning, the wheels would come off between lunch and tea."

The situation improved in 1970 with the recruitment of Allan 'Jonah' Jones, a young and rather chaotic fast bowler from Sussex, and Tom Cartwright, county cricket's best medium-pacer from Warwickshire. Then in 1971 came Brian Close, bringing not only quality batting and fielding but long years of experience and an injection of Northern competitiveness.

"He was just what we needed," the all-rounder Graham Burgess says. "He'd played in great Yorkshire sides that were used to winning."

Close had been recruited by Bill Andrews, the Somerset coach. Andrews, an emotional man, gave long service to Somerset, claiming in later life that he had been sacked four times by the county: twice as player, twice as coach. He famously bowled Don Bradman, though the great batsman had scored 202 and was looking to get out, and he never tired of greeting people with an outstretched hand and the words "Shake the hand that bowled Bradman." Yet arguably his greatest contribution to Somerset cricket was to persuade Brian Close to come down to the south-west.

At a time when Close was in turmoil, reeling from his dismissal by Yorkshire and thinking of retirement, Andrews, acting with no authority from the committee, wrote to Brian and, getting no reply, followed up with two more letters, then a phone call. In his 1973 autobiography, inevitably called *The Hand That Bowled Bradman*, he wrote:

> I've always admired his leadership and tactical skill – and the stirring way he played for the county he adored, Yorkshire. I am of the opinion he would have been skippering England regularly today if he had apologised to the powers that be after an incident at Edgbaston. Brian lost the captaincy through this, but he had courage – because he considered he had done nothing wrong.
>
> Writing to him was an instinctive action on my part, but never did I doubt the wisdom or the ethics of what I'd done. Close was then forty, and already I could see him as manager, coach and captain.

Brian was approached by other counties, including Lancashire, Middlesex and Leicestershire who offered him good terms to play as Ray Illingworth's deputy. He was tempted, but Illingworth captaining Close? Over a round of golf the broadcaster Don Mosey told him firmly it would not work. "You want to lead from the front, and you know Raymond; he is very much his own man." Brian motored down to Somerset, where their enthusiasm won him over:

> They wanted to turn over a new leaf for the club and to make progress. As I drove back home to talk things over with my wife, the more I thought about joining the club, the more I liked the idea. Here was a place where I could do some good, as well as enjoy my last two or three years in first-class cricket, and perhaps show once again what I could do as a player without having the responsibilities I had had to shoulder.

Bill Andrews, a man who rarely stopped talking, admitted to becoming unusually quiet in the presence of the Yorkshireman:

> He had a strange effect on me. When I started to meet him more on small committees, I found myself rather subdued in his presence. We were once discussing the need to bring on a young reserve wicket-keeper in case of injury to Derek Taylor. I had a good young stumper up my sleeve. Close suddenly said: "I've kept wicket for England in a Test match."
>
> Chairman Colin Atkinson looked across at me and said: "Answer that one, Bill."

Brian Langford, with a bowling attack strengthened by the Australian leg-spinner Kerry O'Keeffe and the Barbadian swing-bowler Hallam Moseley, had become a capable captain. Freed of the cares of Yorkshire and its committee, Brian was happy to play under him – though he was not shy to offer members of the team "a few choice remarks on occasions". When Langford stood down at the end of the summer, there was only ever going to be one successor.

Graham Burgess has never forgotten something Brian said to him:

> He said, "You play cricket as you live your life. The people who play all the shots, you find they are the first in the bar at night; they give everything away in life. The ones who don't play shots, they don't buy the drinks."

Closey was a gambler in life, and that's how he played his cricket. Nine times out of ten it would work. The odd time he got panned for it, which was a great shame, as we needed somebody to take a gamble with the side we'd got.

Where he had Ray Illingworth at his side in the best Yorkshire years, now he had Tom Cartwright, to whom he paid tribute in *I Don't Bruise Easily*:

> Somerset players were not born and reared on success – winning was not the matter of life and death that it was to Yorkshire players. It was a good thing in some ways, but there were times when it was a disadvantage. Because they were not used to going all out for victory as a matter of course, the players were not geared to the intensity of concentration I regarded as the norm. It showed in fielding, it showed in batting and above all it showed in bowling.
>
> And that was where having Tom Cartwright in the side was so immensely valuable. He was a joy to watch as a bowler, a supreme artist, a master of accuracy, of variation and total concentration, and he did a great deal to teach our bowlers a new set of values.

"Brian was great in the three-day game," Peter Robinson says. "He'd set the declaration to give time to take ten wickets, no matter whether they'd got Kanhai or Sobers playing or what, and he'd find ways of getting people out." Brian Langford agreed:

> I remember one of his first games when I was still captain. I was bowling to Basil D'Oliveira. "He plays with his pad a lot," Closey said. "I'll go and stand in front." He stood right up close, and the third ball went straight into his hands.
>
> When he was captain, he was moving the field all the time. I was fielding mid-off in one game, and he moved me six times in one over. Robbo said, "It's your own fault. Don't look at him. If you look at him, he'll move you." Barrie Meyer was umpiring. We went off for lunch and Barrie said, "I'm the only bloke he hasn't moved."

As captain in three-day cricket he could force the pace of a game, but he was not averse to grinding out a result in a way that was not in the Somerset tradition. One such match, in his first year as captain, was at

Swansea, a game in which he locked horns with the Glamorgan Secretary Wilf Wooller, a man who in his long reign as county captain had had his share of run-ins with Yorkshire, especially in games in Wales which Wooller viewed as his personal fiefdom.

Bryan Stott has never forgotten a match at Neath when as a 19-year-old he went out to bat, with Yorkshire – needing 68 to win – on 18 for five:

Led by Wooller, the Glamorgan fielders were clustered all round me, talking away. It was a daunting experience.

It was the end of the second day, the extra half hour was taken, and we came off for bad light. Wilf, though, refused to leave the field. He stayed out there, still on the field of play, and the crowd in the rugby clubhouse started shouting and bawling. Then he began to walk towards the pavilion, and the spectators followed him like an army. He stood there, with the crowd baying, and the umpires inevitably brought us out again – in light that was worse than what it had been when we came off.

It was quite an atmosphere, and it did not get any better in the rugby club bar in the evening. Whilst a group of us were talking to Harold Williams, the Leeds United footballer, Freddie Trueman's voice suddenly carried across the room above the hubbub: "Welshmen, there wouldn't be any Welshmen if an Englishman hadn't tupped a nanny goat." We made a hasty getaway.

The next morning, when Billy Sutcliffe and I were coming out of the pavilion to bat, there was Wilf scrubbing the ball on the concrete steps. "What the bloody hell are you doing?" Billy said, and Wilf told him to bugger off. Billy took the ball to the umpires, and they just threw it back to Wilf. They didn't fancy an argument with him.

We lost a couple of wickets, and very soon heavy rain set in. It was pouring stair rods, I can remember the water running down behind my pads, but Wilf refused to come off. Eventually Don Shepherd, who was bowling, said, "Skipper, I can't hold the ball," at which point Wooller marched off the ground, and the rest of us, including the umpires, followed. That was our baptism in the ways of Wilf Wooller. It was another world from our Yorkshire second eleven games.

Brian Close, wise to the ways of Wooller, was not going to be intimidated. On the first day at Swansea, a Saturday, he persuaded the umpires, to the great frustration of the Glamorgan Secretary, that the square was too wet for the game to start till 2.30 in the afternoon, a decision that led to a public row between Wooller and the umpires. Then, in difficult conditions, the Somerset batsmen crawled to 113 for two off 72 overs.

They returned on the Monday, when Wooller's mood grew darker still. The Somerset captain led from the front, hitting a bright hundred, but his decision to continue batting after lunch provoked Wooller to announce over the tannoy that any dissatisfied spectator could have their entrance fee returned. Brian called this "bloody ridiculous", letting the innings run till three o'clock. It was a row that made the front pages of the *Guardian* and *Daily Telegraph*, but Somerset had the last laugh, bowling out Glamorgan before the close and enforcing the follow-on.

All that remained for Glamorgan on the Tuesday was to bat for a draw, which they failed to do, losing by an innings. Alan Jones, their opener, was at his most obdurate, batting 2¼ hours for 21, but he fell to the first ball of the only over bowled by the Somerset captain – 'caught at square leg off a groaning long hop'. Close, so reluctant to start on Saturday, even persuaded the umpires to play through rain. 'The sight of Wilf Wooller,' wrote John Reason in the *Telegraph*, 'mournfully viewing the proceedings from under the largest black umbrella in Swansea will be treasured as one of the memories of the season.'

This was not cricket as Somerset had known it.

"But he wasn't a good captain in the one-day game," Peter Robinson says. "He was still thinking he'd got to bowl them out. He wouldn't appreciate it at all if nothing appeared to be happening, if you were strangling it."

"One-day cricket," Tom Cartwright said, "is mostly about being clever in defence, and that just wasn't in his nature. He never defended in his life."

"He was a great captain when we were attacking," Brian Langford said, "but, when we were trying to defend, he'd get bored. Tom and I would build a bit of pressure. Then Closey would come on and bowl five or six overs of rubbish, and he'd take all the pressure off. I tell you, Tom used to do his nut."

Some remembered the occasion when he summoned up the burly non-bowler Richard Cooper who proceeded to bowl high full-tosses to the big-hitting Mike Procter, but Peter Robinson's memory goes straight to the Gillette Cup match against Leicestershire in 1973.

That summer the 41-year-old Jim Parks had come down from Sussex. Mostly he played as a specialist batsman, leaving the gloves in the capable hands of Derek Taylor, but sometimes in the one-day matches he wore them, as he did that day at Taunton.

Somerset made 212, a good score in those days, and some time after tea Leicestershire had slumped to 127 for seven. Tom Cartwright and Brian Langford had bowled out their overs and, though Chris Balderstone was still at the wicket, it seemed to be just a matter of how long it would take Allan Jones, Hallam Moseley and Graham 'Budgie' Burgess to mop up the tail.

Let them tell the story of the disaster that followed:

PETER ROBINSON: Jim Parks took a blow on the thumb, and he said he couldn't go on with the keeping. Brian Rose had done it a few times, but Closey said, "I'll do it. I kept in a Test match once."

TOM CARTWRIGHT: Before you could turn round, Closey was strapping the pads on. He couldn't wait for his chance; he never even tried to talk Jim round.

PETER ROBINSON: He caught a little skier off Budgie. "There you are, lad." But when Jonah came back on, Closey suddenly said, "These bloody gloves are too small" and took them off. And that was red rag to a bull to Jonah, who started bowling faster and faster.

GRAHAM BURGESS: As soon as he took the gloves off, Jonah – a bloody prat on the day – bowled a bouncer that went straight through Closey's hands.

TOM CARTWRIGHT: The only thing that would have incited Jonah more was if Closey had stood up to him. Jonah was bowling from the river end. Closey was trying to catch the ball as it went past him, and it was going straight through him, hitting the wall and coming all the way back to the middle. I said to him, "Just line the ball up with your head and take it in front of you." And he said, "Don't tell me how to keep, lad. I've done it in Test matches."

Fourteen byes were conceded, the last four bringing the visitors victory with an over to spare. 'By the bye Leicestershire are through,' was the *Times* headline. "It was like knocking somebody down for 14 rounds," Peter Robinson says, "and losing in the 15th." "It was a big match," Tom Cartwright said, "and in lots of ways it was farcical."

What undoubtedly made it worse for Brian was that his opposing captain was Ray Illingworth, someone he hardly ever got the better of in their encounters. On another occasion, in a Sunday League match at Yeovil's Westlands ground, Leicestershire's tail-ender Norman McVicker was on strike to Allan Jones with ten runs needed off the last two balls, and he hit both deliveries high over Graham Burgess's head at long-on. That evening Illingworth waited for a long time to say goodbye to his old captain, but he did not emerge from the Somerset changing room. "Tell Brian cheerio," he said finally.

The ultimate irony of Brian's career came in August 1972. The fixture list of the Australian tourists included three one-day internationals. The two teams had played one as a fill-in match when a Test had been washed out in 1970/71, but these were the first to be officially scheduled. Ray Illingworth, England's captain that summer, and Tony Lewis, due to lead in India in the winter, were both unfit – and, to the surprise of many, the selectors turned to Brian Close. The man sacked by Yorkshire for his negative attitude to limited-over cricket was now England's first one-day captain. He was told the news during a lunch break at Taunton, when he had just completed a century against Gloucestershire.

"It came as a bloody shock," he told John Arlott. "But it shouldn't have, should it? When you've been recalled seven times, you shouldn't be surprised at the eighth."

England won the series by two matches to one – though the defeat, if Brian is to be believed, was only because a plumb lbw was not given against the Australian opener Keith Stackpole. He could not be beaten.

*

By the summer of 1974 Tom Cartwright had replaced Bill Andrews as Somerset coach, and at his insistence they altered the recruitment policy. No longer would they sign players from other counties; now they would invest their limited resources in youth. Tom persuaded the committee to put aside £6,000 to employ six youngsters for the summer. First was Viv Richards, a young Antiguan who had completed a year's qualification while playing for Lansdown Cricket Club in Bath. The others were from all round the county: Ian Botham, Vic Marks, Peter Roebuck, Philip Slocombe and John Hook. All but John Hook would be at the heart of the side that won five one-day trophies between 1979 and 1983, the first in the county's history.

At Yorkshire Brian Close's eccentricities were not off the scale. He was playing with his contemporaries; he was always one of them. At Somerset it was different. He was like an overseas player, bringing all the strangeness of a foreign culture. He was an old man, too, one who had been playing long before the new youngsters were born. He played his cricket and lived his life in a style they had not encountered while growing up in the sleepier West Country.

Early stints as twelfth man seemed to be less about extra sweaters than trips to the bookmakers. "The main thing was to know the numbers for Joe Coral and Taunton Turf," Peter Robinson recalls. "And you'd have to ring up some stable lad. 'What have you got for Brian today?'"

"For one dog race he told me to put five pounds on number three," Peter Roebuck remembered, "and I put three pounds on number five. Even though it won, he still seemed disgruntled."

"Tom and he were a beautiful contrast," Vic Marks says. "One paying attention to detail and wanting to create all the good habits, the other a wild card, a maverick you thought was mad but whom you had to respect. I remember turning up 45 minutes late to a game once, I'd had a bit of a prang on the way, and Closey hadn't noticed."

"He'd struggle to know people's names," Peter Robinson says. "Keith Jennings made his debut in a Sunday League match. I thought, 'I hope he gets Keith on early.' Next thing you see is Rosey bowling. He probably didn't realise Keith was in the side to bowl till somebody told him."

Close and Cartwright. When I talked with Peter Roebuck, he compared the two with Churchill and Attlee, the leaders of Britain's wartime coalition. I shared the comparison with Brian's daughter Lynn, who thought it "brilliant", seeing immediately her father's similarities with Churchill. "He made pronouncements from on high, with the utter certainty that his way was the right way."

For Roebuck, the comparison captured both their widely diverging political views and their different inputs into their young charges:

> The two best pieces of advice I got in cricket were one from Tom, about the use of the left shoulder and dropping the bat down through the ball, and the other from Brian Close who said, "Players with lazy minds can't make it." Thirty years later, I find those two things are the core of the coaching I've done. I was very lucky to have those two influences – Close the great fighter, Cartwright the great technician.

Botham was lucky to have them, too. He used to combine Close's gambling and bravado with Tom's thorough professional sense that cricket was a craft, a battle of skills. Between them, because they were so different, Close and Cartwright brought out those characteristics in Ian. They may have come out anyway, for all I know. But Botham was lucky to have the two of them there.

Close and Botham took to one another, as Peter Roebuck recalled:

> From the very start Ian was fiercely competitive, determined to take the game to the opposition. His explosive exchanges with Brian Close brightened things up at Taunton. Once Ian stopped a ball brilliantly, surprising the batsmen who found themselves at the same end. Instead of trotting to the stumps to flick off a bail, Ian hurled the ball at the wickets, demolishing them. Close was furious, and rightly so, for the risk was foolish. There was much arm-waving and gesticulating before things simmered down. Two similar characters, Close and Botham, and their regard for each other grew with each row.

Viv Richards was another the captain set out to shape:

> It didn't take me long to be on the receiving end of one of his blasts. He pulled me to one side and said, "With all that bloody talent, why don't you graft a bit more?" That was telling me. No-one had summed me up so quickly and scathingly before. But he did it fairly – and with a hint of a smile on his face.
>
> He was being serious, though, about the way I played the game. I was still, I suppose, in attitude, really a weekend cricketer entertaining my mates in St John's.
>
> After his rollocking I went back to my shared flat and thought about what he'd said. Yes, I was inclined to be a lazy type on the field. I was apt to dream and lose myself during the game. And Brian Close was telling me, "Stop messing about. Change your attitude, Vivian. It isn't enough to have a natural talent." I think I got the message.

My word, yes, he did, becoming one of the most fiercely competitive cricketers, one who never drifted mentally. Botham and Richards, they were two of the game's all-time greats, and they were both moulded in their formative years by a man whom the Yorkshire committee thought was no good with youngsters.

He could draw on so much experience, such as the time when on a damp outfield a young player slipped while going for a catch. "Show me your boots," he told him in the dressing room and, with a quiet memory of the Roses match of 1950, he ran his hand down the smooth soles.

Brian never found committees easy, and in time the Somerset one became unhappy with him – unhappy that he was living in a hotel, not fulfilling his promise to settle in Somerset with his family, and at one point unhappy with his treatment of the youngsters. This came to a head during 1975, a summer in which it seems the committee were disappointed with the team's progress. It was a story which Henry Blofeld picked up in the *Guardian*, under the headline 'Clash of characters':

> In his Yorkshire days Close was nothing if not a demanding and uncompromising captain who expected his players to give him everything all the time. If they should wander out of place in the field, be slow into position before the start of an over or show that they had allowed a little success to go to their heads, he was always quick to put them back into line.
>
> One of the complaints I have heard of Close this season is that he has been too hard on the young players. He has shouted at them on the field of play and has been tough on them in the pavilion when they have offended his own high standards of what is required of a professional cricketer. Apparently a representative of the Somerset committee instructed him to be more mild with his players, and I could not help smiling when, each time I heard him issuing instructions to his fielders the other day at Folkestone, they were invariably followed or preceded by the word "please".

Against his natural instinct Brian Close refrained in one game from admonishing Ian Botham who was bowling badly and 'shouting at the fielders as if it was their fault'. It caused him to doubt whether to go on:

> I kept wondering whether it was worth the effort trying to improve things, trying to make promising players into good ones, trying to give the county some sort of future, when the committee didn't trust me enough to back me up and let me get on with it. I was sorely tempted to pack it all in, and I very nearly did.

It seemed there was even a possibility that the committee would dispense with his services at their next meeting, leaving Brian free – in Henry Blofeld's words – 'to pack his bags, settle in some other county town and give his last two years in cricket, wholeheartedly as always, to trying to pull up another ailing county side.'

> When his eyes crease and at the age of 44 he says with that familiar irrepressible chuckle, "I love this game, I've given my life to it, haven't I?", he is saying no more than the truth. He has still an endearing and unquenchable enthusiasm for the game of cricket.
>
> Obstinate, unbending, misunderstood, determined, unlucky, bloody-minded Yorkshireman. There has never been anyone quite like Brian Close, and when he's decided he's had enough, cricket will be the poorer. Let us hope he is not pushed to make that decision before he has to.

He stayed, of course, and the following June he was playing for England.

Above all, he wanted to give his adopted county its first trophy, but it did not work out. He was handicapped by the loss of Tom Cartwright to successive injuries for large parts of each of the seasons from 1974 to 1976, which he saw as a crippling blow to their chances of success.

Whenever they were in with a smell of a title, something went wrong, as it did so often in Brian's life. In 1974 they would have been Sunday League champions if they had won at Leicester – Ray Illingworth's Leicester – but rain at the midpoint of the game washed away that chance. Then in 1976, again in the Sunday League, they travelled to Cardiff, top of the table when the last round of matches started, and came away empty-handed.

Such was the cricket fervour in Somerset by this time that six thousand supporters arrived in coaches in Cardiff, reaching the ground before the gatemen had begun their shifts and taking their seats free of charge, only some of them contributing when the astonished Glamorgan Secretary Wilf Wooller sent round buckets inviting their coins. So packed and boisterous were the crowd that Alan Gibson wrote: 'Sophia Gardens might have been Bridgwater Carnival.'

Brian won the toss and invited Glamorgan to bat first, a decision he later regretted. Alan Jones, the veteran opener, was dropped by him at square leg on 21 – 'a low, stinging effort which went into and out of his hands like a bullet'– and went on to make 70, leading Glamorgan to a final total on the scoreboard of 190 for seven. At some point in Somerset's reply, though not spotted by all the West Country supporters, this was adjusted to 191. Even without Viv Richards, touring with the West Indies, it should have been an achievable score, but they lost early wickets, including Brian himself, caught on the square-leg boundary off the first full-blooded shot that he middled.

With Sussex losing at Edgbaston, they only needed a tie to pip Kent, playing at Maidstone, to the title. And they reached the last ball on 188 for eight: not two for a tie, as the scoreboard originally had it, but three. Graham Burgess was on strike to the left-arm seamer Malcolm Nash, with Colin Dredge at the non-striker's end. Graham remembers it well:

> Bill Alley was umpiring. I said to him, "How many to come?" "One left," he said. I thought the worst thing was if I missed it altogether. I said to Dredgy, "Whatever happens, we're going to run three, right?" I hit the ball over long-on, Alan Jones ran round to pick it up, I ran two and turned for three, and Dredgy, who was quicker than me, hesitated. I suppose he was out by about a yard. If he'd just kept going and not hesitated, maybe ...

Some in the crowd, according to Alan Gibson, thought Somerset had tied:

> They had at last won a major title after more than 100 years of county cricket! When the jubilant Somerset cheering had stopped, the announcer was heard, harrassed and apologetic, confirming that it was Glamorgan, after all, who had won. It was enough to make a Somerset man weep: though mostly, as they departed from the ground, they just swore.

They had failed by how much? 'Inches' in umpire Bill Alley's memory; 'two feet', in Brian Close's; 'about a yard' in Graham Burgess's; 'yards' in the *Guardian*, 'a hopeless attempt at a third run' in *The Times*.

Meanwhile, high in the air, the BBC helicopter carrying Peter Walker, Frank Keating and the Sunday League trophy had set off from Edgbaston, hoping to present the cup to the winners before they went off air. "I fancy Kent," their scorer Bill Frindall said, and on that basis they headed for Maidstone, landing on the roped-off square minutes before the programme's end, just as the last ball was bowled at Cardiff. The closing credits rolled up as a breathless and much relieved Peter Walker, amid great cheers, presented the trophy to the Kent captain Mike Denness. Back in Cardiff there were no cheers, only a disconsolate Brian Close:

> I made four mistakes. I put them in when I should have batted, I caught Alan Jones and then dropped him, I misfielded one and gave them an extra run, and I holed out to the first ball I hit in the middle. How can I blame anyone else?

"It was the only time I ever heard Closey say sorry after a match," Graham Burgess says.

In the *Guardian* Henry Blofeld called it 'a day to haunt Brian Close':

> He was everywhere in the field, cajoling and encouraging and even before the end of the Glamorgan innings completely covered in sweat. Few cricketers have had as many disappointments during their careers, and I know that he wanted to win this match as much as any he has ever played.

Viv Richards was back for the summer of 1977, when Ian Botham played his first Tests and Peter Roebuck and Vic Marks started to come through. Success was drawing near, and Close knew as much, not least in May when at Bath they beat the touring Australians for the first time in the county's history. There was a patient century by Brian Rose and wickets for a newcomer down from Littleborough in the Central Lancashire League, the six-foot-eight Barbadian Joel Garner.

"I was standing next to Closey in the slips when Joel was bowling," Graham Burgess recalls. "He said, 'Budgie, lad, if we've got this bloke next year, we'll win everything.' Perhaps we would have done if he had stayed. Closey was a very, very good captain."

Brian struggled all summer with fitness and form, announcing in July that the season, his 28th as a first-class cricketer, would be his last. The captaincy passed to Brian Rose, whom Close had come to trust, perhaps not least because of his keeping quiet about an incident between the two of them in the deserted Taunton dressing-room after the captain had taken a few blows from the West Indian quick bowler Wayne Daniel.

> I was about to go off for a shower when he said, " Rosey lad, you've got to help me." He started to take his trousers down, still with his pads on. I had the delightful task of taking his jockstrap off and, as I did so, I realised that he had a club cricketer's box on, one of those pink plastic jobs. And it had split, and then

shut, so that one large testicle was hanging out, trapped by the crack in the box. I knew the team doctor was in the pavilion, so I went to get him, complete with his black bag, but he was at a loss as to what to do. Then I dashed round to the groundsman's hut to see Don Price and borrowed the big screwdriver with a wide flat blade that he used for adjusting the mower.

Back in the dressing room, I showed it to Closey. He went even whiter. "Fucking hell, Rosey lad, what are you going to do with that?" But I put it in the crack of the box, twisted it to open the crack, and whipped his bollock back in, with a huge great wheal on it. I could see the relief on his face, but there was no word of thanks. Instead, he said, "You're not going to tell anybody, are you?" I didn't, or at least not until he had retired. I think it was what led him to recommend me as captain!

It would be Brian Rose's happy lot to lead the team to its first five trophies, though in that last summer Brian Close had one last chance to go out in glory. They reached the Gillette Cup semi-final, drawn away to Middlesex at Lord's, and with Garner available they fancied their chances.

Once more it all went wrong. Rain prevented play on any of the three scheduled days. Even with the teams postponing a championship match, they reached the morning of the sixth day still with no start. With further rain about to sweep in, the umpires opted for a 15-over match. Mike Smith won the toss for Middlesex, which Brian thought should have won him the Man of the Match award, and, with no restriction on the bowlers, Somerset collapsed against Wayne Daniel and Mike Selvey to 59 all out.

In a moment of despair, Brian told the press: "The whole thing typifies my life. It was a complete farce." Or, as Peter Roebuck recalled it:

Somerset players well remember his lament, as he realised that his last chance of success had withered and died, that 'my life has been a series of cock-ups.'

He was in a more philosophical state when he wrote his autobiography:

I very badly wanted to win something for Somerset, to repay a little to the county which had given me such a warm and sincere welcome when my cricket career seemed shattered. Unfortunately, I failed in the end but we had fun – and a few near misses. I hope their memories of me are as warm as mine of Somerset and its cricket.

17

A RUM FELLOW, THE HEMPEROR

Brian Close and Eric Morecambe, by Willie Rushton

"Spring is here once again," the comedian Eric Morecambe quipped, "and soon we will thrill to the sound of leather on Brian Close."

"It only hurts if you think it does," Brian would say after a fearful blow. "Pain? It's all in the mind." "It may well be," Ken Barrington once countered, "but it still bloody hurts."

"I could write a book about him," Peter Robinson says:

> I saw him walk down the wicket once to Andy Roberts, and he let the ball hit him on his chest. I said, "What are you doing?" "I just wanted to see how quick he was."
>
> I remember him saying about the Ali-Frazier fights, when Ali let Frazier hit him. "Well, I'd fight like that. How would they knock me down?" And he'd believe it.

"They reckon he fell asleep in the hotel one day with a fag on," Graham Burgess says, "and the fag burned out on his chest. You couldn't make it up."

There are so many stories about Brian Close, and they have done the rounds of after-dinner speeches so long that it's hard to know which ones are true, which exaggerated and which pure fiction.

Without helmet, shin pad or any protection he stood ridiculously close to the batsman, either at short leg or silly mid-off, and the balls would crash into him, some caught on the rebound by the keeper or slips. One, he claimed, hit him on the head and landed full toss on the pavilion steps. Another, cracking him dangerously close to his temple, was caught at slip. "Blimey, Brian, I dread to think what would have happened if that had hit you an inch or two lower," someone exclaimed, only to get the reply, "He'd have been caught in the gully."

Viv Richards remembers a thunderous cut by Mike Procter which Close, advancing slightly as if heading the ball, took smack on the forehead. He fell to the ground so dramatically they feared he might be dead – but no. "Did anyone take the catch?" he asked as he came round, then berated them for not doing so. "You pillocks, that was my ploy for you to catch it."

It was not only his own pain but that of others that he made light of. John Hampshire recalled a game at Middlesbrough where, as a youngster in the side, he was felled by a lifting ball from the West Indian fast bowler Charlie Griffith. Hit smack on his temple, he fell forward from the crease and was unconscious for a while. Eventually he staggered to his feet and was helped back to the dressing room where, laid out on the table with his team-mates hovering anxiously around him, he drifted in and out of consciousness.

> It's strange how odd, fleeting seconds of that befuddled state come back to me. Here I had a glimpse of priorities, Yorkshire cricket style. The face of captain D.B. Close appeared in the gallery above me. As I opened my eyes, he very earnestly imparted this advice: "Johnnie, if you ever get hit again, make sure to drop *inside* the crease, or they can run you out."

The only time anybody can remember Brian howling with pain occurred in the dressing room at Taunton, a moment that provoked great mirth all round, as Graham Burgess recalls:

> These lovely teas used to come in on a trolley, with a big metal teapot. Closey had just got out, and he was changing when the tea came in. All he had on was a towel. He leaned over the tray to help himself to the best cake, his towel slipped and he burnt his most delicate part on the boiling-hot teapot.

Another version of this moment has him leaning across the teapot not to reach a cake but to admonish a player, with the trademark jabbing of his forefinger. That might be right, as he was not a big cake-eater, living during the cricketing day on a diet of cigarettes and cups of tea.

Close the golfer is the subject of a good few stories: the balls that flew out from the trees with suspicious ease, the claiming of 'winter rules' when adjusting a lie, the dramatic explosions when a shot went badly wrong. Fred Trueman enjoyed telling these stories:

> He was known in golfing circles as a club thrower. He threw a club so hard once, it got stuck in a tree. He threw another to try and knock it down and finished up climbing the tree to get both of them. Another time he threw a club and lost it in the long grass.
>
> The best golfing story I've heard about him was told by Don Mosey. Closey once played a terrible shot when playing a foursome with Don. He threw the trolley, the bag, the clubs, the whole lot straight into the middle of a lake and stormed off, muttering about not wanting to play again.
>
> The rest carried on without him and passed the lake on the way back, only to find Closey, trousers rolled up to his knees in the middle of the water, retrieving the bag. "I thought you were never going to play golf again?" And Closey replied: "I'm bloody well not, but my car keys are in the bag."

Close the swimmer – 'the torpedo,' they nicknamed him – was another source of stories, which again Fred Trueman enjoyed telling. One involved an occasion on Yorkshire's tour of North America, when a few of them were sitting round the pool in Los Angeles:

> Suddenly Closey arrives clad in swimming trunks ready for his absolutely fantastic demonstrations. The first thing he did was to put a table at the edge of the swimming pool, take a run and dive straight over the top into the water. One or two of the lads, taking the mickey, gave him a round of applause. And of course he did it again, water flying all over the place.
>
> He then got a bit bolder, added another table, ran and dived over the top of two tables. As the daring grew, we finished up with chairs round the tables and Closey diving over the tables and the chairs. The edge of the swimming pool was tiled for

about four or five yards and, as Closey kept diving over the tables into the water, the tiles were getting wetter and wetter. Eventually – we knew it had to happen – up came Closey running like a hare, he slipped on the tiles, crashed into the tables and chairs, and the bloody lot went into the swimming pool!

It was one of the funniest things I've ever seen. To see Closey trying to retrieve chairs and tables from the deep end of a swimming pool is something I shall remember as long as I live.

Fred, who was never averse to elaborating a story, reckoned there was a point when, dissatisfied with the height of the diving board, Brian went up to the balcony of his room and dived in from there. A man in the room below thought he had fallen by accident, telephoned the hotel switchboard and the emergency services arrived.

During a visit by the Somerset team to the Roman Baths in Bath, Brian dived into the water, only to crack his head on the bottom. "I didn't realise it was so shallow, lad," he said when he emerged with a bruised forehead.

Once at Westcliff in Essex he managed to walk through a plate-glass door, sending fragments everywhere yet escaping with one minor cut.

According to Ray Illingworth, Brian could be surprisingly clumsy at times. Before his marriage to Vivien, he would often eat at the Illingworths' house, but his visits proved more expensive to the money-conscious Ray than just the price of the meal.

One week he pushed his chair back from the table, fell back and broke the chair leg. The next week the same thing happened again. After that he gave the chairs a rest – which was just as well, as we were down to two – but on his next visit, as he was yawning and stretching, he pushed his fist into a light fitting. He was fast becoming a luxury I couldn't afford.

Whatever the sport, Brian was good at it – the best in his own mind – and not only cricket, football, golf, boxing and snooker. Once, when introduced to a woman who had been a top table tennis player, he said, "I've played a lot, you know. I don't believe I've ever lost a game." He probably said the same of his squash, even after a game against Somerset's Mervyn Kitchen when, match point down, he suddenly announced "Right, that's my lot" and walked off the court.

According to Ray Illingworth, there was a time when Brian became fascinated by the sport of wrestling:

> I used to share a room with him until he suddenly started taking an interest in wrestling. He would insist on practising a half-nelson at seven in the morning.

Brian's inability to admit that he could be wrong or that something was his own fault provided stories, too, as Peter Robinson recalls:

> He had more excuses than anybody. He dropped a skier in the deep once. "It just came down quickly at the last minute," he said. When he got out, we used to sit and wait for what excuse he was going to come back with. "Do you know why I got out today?" "Why's that?" "I never had my chewing gum in." Another time he played an awful shot just before lunch and got out – and, when I came in, he looked at me: "Your running between the wickets is diabolical. And another thing, why didn't you tell me it was one o'clock lunch?"

"He'd always have a reason for everything," Tom Cartwright said. "Every time he came back after getting out, I'd light a cigarette for him and put it straight in his mouth. If you could stop him speaking for five minutes, you'd be all right."

To his regret Brian never hit a double-century, having excuses for the two times he got close, both in 1960. First, on 198 at The Oval, he chased a wide ball and was caught in the covers, claiming the ball had landed in a rough patch created by the bowlers' follow-through. Then on 184 at Scarborough, off Bomber Wells, he was out to a 'miracle catch' taken by Merv Winfield running round at square leg and sticking out a hand:

> Stamping back to the pavilion, cursing myself at every step, I had to pass the hugely grinning Bomber. "Ar, Closey," he said. "Tricked you again. Caught in my leg-trap!"

The best of these stories of excuses is the day at Trent Bridge when he went in on a hat-trick to face the Nottinghamshire left-armer Barry Stead. Richard Cooper was the departing batsman, lbw. "What's it doing?" Brian asked him, getting the reply from a batsman who had faced just one ball, "It's swinging." Let Peter Roebuck tell the tale as it was handed down to him:

204

Nottingham set an attacking field for the hat-trick ball as Close took guard. Amazingly Close swung lustily at his first ball, skying it straight to the solitary outfielder, Nirmal Nannan. Amidst astounded celebrations Close strode from the field, stormed into the changing room and roared at Cooper, "Tha told me it were swingin', but tha never said it were seaming, too!" Brian Close could outstare any mere facts.

Playing in a charity match in a stately home, he batted scratchily and was out for not many. The next man in, facing the same bowler, proceeded to hit three gigantic sixes into the next field. "Stupid berk," Brian muttered. "I could have done that, but I didn't want to lose the ball."

In another such match Imran Khan hit Brian back over his head for three perfect straight sixes, only for Brian to snatch his sweater at the end of the over and say, "That'll do for me. I could never bowl at bloody sloggers."

His competitive spirit never dimmed, however insignificant the game. For some years Brian was a regular in a pro-am cricket festival organised by Fred Rumsey in Barbados. English tourists paid to play in teams, each captained by a star Test cricketer and including the odd local. Trying to prevent the Bajans from coming out to bat, Brian told his team to drop all the catches offered by the tourists. "He might have been a former captain of England," Fred said, "but I had to tell him off."

The journalist David Hopps recalls a match in the 1980s when Close captained the Yorkshire committee against the local media. In what was intended to be a light-hearted, bridge-building game, Brian hit a quick fifty, then marshalled his team in the field to the point where the journalists needed 37 from the last over – safe enough for him to entrust the ball to the Club President, Viscount Mountgarret. The over started with two wides, one bouncing three times, followed by a ball that was despatched over midwicket for a huge six. It was too much for Brian, who strode with intimidating purpose towards the former Captain in the Irish Guards: "Bloody pull yourself together ... my lord."

He was never quite at ease among aristocracy. Tom Cartwright had a memory of an Old England game at Eaton Hall in Cheshire, the country house of the Duke of Westminster, where Brian created a scene by stubbing out his cigarette in a highly valuable ornament.

Brian could be a worrier, and the worries could keep him awake. There is a story that he once rang the Yorkshire bowler Tony Nicholson at two o'clock in the morning, wanting to talk through something that had happened the previous day. "Skipper, do you know what time it is?" the half-asleep Nicholson protested, at which Brian is said to have turned to his wife, "Viv, Tony wants to know what time it is. Clock's on your side."

You never knew what to expect with Brian, and that was part of the fun. Frank Keating, drawing on Dickens' *Pickwick Papers*, said just this at the end of an affectionate profile of him:

> He is, as Sam Weller said so lovingly of Mr P, "a rum sort of fellow, the hemperor. For one reason you never know what he's going to get hup to next."

The Somerset players remember a time when Garry Sobers was coming out to bat for Nottinghamshire. Summoned to gather round by their captain, they were expecting some masterstroke of tactical genius like the time he caught him first ball in a Test match at The Oval. Instead, in all earnestness, he informed them, "This lad's a left-hander."

Everybody was called lad, even the women. They say that when his wife and Vivian Richards first met, he introduced them to each other with the words: "Viv lad, meet Viv lad."

Perhaps we should finish the stories with the only occasion anybody remembered him being lost for words, a tale that the writer David Foot told well. Somerset were playing at Bath at the same time as Peter O'Toole was appearing at the Theatre Royal in the city. O'Toole, born in Yorkshire and cricket-mad, turned up at the game and sought out David, whom he knew from his days in rep in Bristol.

> "I've got a special request," he said over a pint glass. "Can you arrange for me to have a chat with Closey at the close of play?" He said it with schoolboy earnestness. Yet here he was, an international film star, asking me to have a word in Brian Close's ear. I introduced them, and it was hard to tell which of them was the more star-struck.

18

BEHOLD YOU LIVE, GRANDAD

The eighty minutes at Old Trafford, in the closing overs of play on Saturday 10 July 1976, were as memorable and dramatic as any in the long career of Brian Close.

In the summer of 1963, as a 32-year-old at the peak of his game, he had withstood the pace of Wes Hall to take England to the brink of victory at Lord's. Now, at the age of 45, his reflexes inevitably slower, he was facing an even faster West Indian bowler, Michael Holding, for seven successive overs from the Warwick Road end – on a pitch of uneven bounce, in poor light, with the West Indian supporters in the crowd at their most exuberantly noisy and barely a ball on a full enough length for him to play on the front foot.

With no helmet he jerked his head away from a delivery that reared up and missed him by a whisker. With no thigh pad or chest protector, just a thin towel tucked into his trousers, he took six or more blows on his body, summoning all his legendary courage not to telegraph any pain. Yet even this was not possible, as twice his knees juddered. So concerned was his young protégé Viv Richards that at one point he asked "Are you all right, cappy?", only to get the shortest and most dismissive of replies. It was a battle, and in his own perverse way the old warrior was relishing it. As he once said, "It's sympathy that makes you soft."

"It was like being caught at the wrong end of a coconut shy," he told Chris Lander of the *Daily Mirror*. "I didn't know where I was going to be struck next. There's no doubt that Michael Holding is the fastest bowler in the world. He's a yard and a half quicker than Wes Hall was on the 1963 tour."

He said the opposite in his filmed interview with me: Hall was the quicker. But by then he was in the land of memories, not fresh bruises.

The ordeal, in the words of Peter Roebuck, 'demonstrated his resilience, his tenacious refusal to back down one inch. It was as if his very manhood was being challenged.' Roebuck, with Graham Burgess and Mervyn Kitchen, watched the highlights that evening in a hotel bedroom: 'We were diving under the sheets as if it were a Hitchcock movie. And we were 100 miles away!'

Bill Alley had umpired the previous summer when the Australian Jeff Thomson, often said to be the quickest of the 1970s, had bowled. He told reporters that Holding was "the fastest I've seen whilst umpiring top cricket. He's really let them slip in this Test."

At the other end from Close, facing Andy Roberts and Wayne Daniel, was the 39-year-old John Edrich, another gutsy left-hander, though it seems he did not have his partner's stomach for the fight. "One fucking Test too far," he told Close in one mid-wicket conference.

"Don't make me laugh, John," Brian said. "My ribs are agony already."

What a pair they were – a combined age of 84 and the best England could offer to open the batting against three young, super-fit fast bowlers. Close, facing Holding, took the worst of it, but Edrich was the one who was disenchanted, as John Woodcock observed:

> "I have just about had enough of this" sums up how Edrich looks. "You can hit me as hard as you like, but you're wasting your time" is the impression that Close likes to give.
>
> As an example of unflinching courage it was the equal of anything a heavyweight boxer displays. To bring Close back into this England side at the start of this series was, I thought, a pity; yet I would have backed no one else to have matched him for defiance.

Late in Holding's bombardment, too late in the view of some observers, umpire Alley stepped in to tell him to bowl fewer bouncers, but it seems that Brian was not impressed by that, as he explained in the filmed interview: "The bouncers weren't the ones hitting us. I tell you, when we got off the field that night, we didn't buy Bill a drink."

David Steele, supposed to be next man in, was on the physio's table, suffering from a migraine. His slot at number three had passed to Bob Woolmer. "I'll repay you one day," Steele had said, only to get the reply, "I just hope I live to see it."

Seventeen overs were bowled in those 80 minutes, with the score at the end of it 21 for no wicket, including nine no balls and a wide. John Edrich, with two fours, was on 10, Brian Close on 1. Holding's seven overs, all bowled at Close, were maidens. When they returned to the dressing room, the atmosphere, Brian said, was "like a morgue, with the bodies all sitting upright". Pat Pocock, padded up as nightwatchman, recalled the silence:

> When they came in, the whole dressing room stood back and stared in genuine awe. Suddenly Edrich broke into a great gust of laughter. He was looking across the ground at the scoreboard. "Do you know what your score is, Closey?" he said. "One! All that for one!"

Brian was so stiff that he could not get down to take off his boots. "Here, lad, give me a hand" he said to David Steele. "I'm a bit bruised up here."

The England physio, seeing the state of Brian's bare torso, wanted him to go for an x-ray, but "Nay, lad," he said. "Just give us a Scotch." He swallowed it in one gulp and headed into the showers.

That evening Brian needed a long session with a pain-killing freeze spray just so that he could lie down in bed, let alone sleep. And there was a battle to resume on Monday morning.

*

The first innings of his 1976 Test comeback, at Trent Bridge, had not gone well. Unlike at Taunton, when he batted his way back into the England team, he was groping to cope with the pace of Wayne Daniel, as Tony Lewis described in the *Sunday Telegraph*:

> Brian Close came in. His bald head gleamed in the sunlight, his jaws jutted; he approached yet another comeback innings with familiar, even tread. The large West Indian contingent loved him. "Behold you live, Grandad. Grandad live for ever more!" Yes, the tension he knew, but not quite the speed this time. He was dropped by Greenidge at second slip off the first ball – a fast but straightforward chance. Daniel was not disappointed for long, because a couple of runs later Close was gone. It was just a touch to the keeper, but a touch was enough.

In the second innings he came in after lunch on the last day. England, set 339 for victory, were on 55 for two, with the captain's instructions to play for the draw. He edged his first ball from Daniel just short of slip, then settled to his task, playing out time with John Edrich in a game that, amid slow handclaps, drifted into a lifeless draw. In the latter stages, after the West Indians had abandoned the challenge, he faced innocuous spin bowling, which, given he was in the team 'as a bastion against extreme

209

pace', was in the words of Michael Melford in the *Daily Telegraph* 'like inviting Yehudi Menuhin to play the trumpet'. His unbeaten 36 kept him in the side for the second Test.

At Lord's England lost Wood and Steele early on the first day, and Brian joined Mike Brearley at 31 for two. At first, John Arlott wrote in the *Guardian*, 'his bat seemed all edges.' He was 'made to feel at home by a couple of thunderous blows on the body', but he gradually settled, adding 84 for the third wicket before his partner was bowled by Roberts. John Woodcock, a sceptic about his recall, was moved by his performance:

> Having got to 50, I thought the old man would battle on to an emotional, indeed memorable hundred. So carefully and comfortably was he playing that there seemed no reason for him to get out. He looked as if he had been brought up from Stonehenge for the day. In another 46 years, when he retires, we shall have to place him there, to be gazed on as one of the rocks of ancient Britain.

Then on 60, in a moment that typified his career, Brian smacked an inviting full toss from the spinner Jumadeen into the covers and watched in disgust as Vanburn Holder took an outstanding diving catch. England were all out for 250, his 60 the only fifty of the innings.

Brian was in the best of spirits when he sat and chatted to Chris Lander at the end of the day:

> Close revealed great red and mauve bruises around his upper body. And he laughed away the pain of those 90mph thunderbolts. He joked about one bruise which left the imprint of the seam just below his rib cage. "That one left everything but the maker's name," he said. "They call me the balding old blighter, the Wharfedale Bull and all sorts of other things. I'm just pleased I showed I could still do it in a Test. It brought back memories of the day Wes Hall and Charlie Griffith dug them in at me on this ground. I never imagined I would be back doing it again. This innings was more important because a good many people in cricket refused to believe my reactions were up to this sort of bowling."

England gained the upper hand next day, bowling out the West Indies for 182, but Saturday was lost to rain, making the task of winning harder. In the second innings Wood retired hurt after a blow on the hand, Brearley and nightwatchman Pocock fell cheaply, and once more Close came in to bat in a crisis. This time he scored 46, falling to another fine catch by Holder, and David Steele 64, the only two men to pass 30 in a total of 254. His match aggregate of 104 runs was the best in the England side.

Frank Keating was mingling among the crowd where Peter O'Toole – 'looking gorgeously seedy in green cord, unshaven, blacktoothed, with only the Gauloise in a long holder giving the game away' – watched with admiration.

> Steele was hit two awful blows in the box by Roberts and hopped about, rubbing himself in a frenzy. Close was hit in the box, too, but he just thought of his upbringing and Maurice Leyland's dictum about fast bowling: "None of us likes it, but we don't all of us let on."

The match was drawn, and the teams, still locked 0-0 in the series, moved on to Old Trafford. England made two changes to the batting. Brearley and Wood, the openers, were dropped, to be replaced by Edrich, himself dropped at Lord's, and the Lancastrian Frank Hayes.

Brian had no problem with Tony Greig as a person – 'He's a likeable chap, a pretty dynamic sort of personality' – but he was no fan of his captaincy. He checked himself from saying too much in our filmed interview: "I could tell you some tales, but I daren't. I literally daren't. It's not fair."

He thought Greig lacked tactical acumen, and he did not think he had the right players in the side. He pressed to no avail for the inclusion of Essex's John Lever, thinking Viv Richards (who scored 829 runs in four Tests that summer) had a weakness against left-arm seamers. He was frustrated that he never got a bowl, having devised with the keeper Alan Knott a ploy for dismissing Richards. And he was appalled by the lack of close catchers around the bat. At one team meeting, they say, he even suggested they could dismiss Alvin Kallicharran by his standing right up close at short leg and getting Pocock to bowl a leg-stump full toss. The batsman, a known sweeper, would crash the ball into his body, and another fielder would take the catch on the rebound.

In one story, possibly apocryphal, Greig asked Brian his opinion about players who could strengthen the Test team, and Brian offered Ray Illingworth: "And if the two of us played, we wouldn't need you."

By the end of the Third Test, the press were questioning Greig's position. His 'grovel' comment had fired up the West Indians, who were targeting him so successfully that he had scored only 38 runs in five innings and taken three wickets for 172.

Before that Third Test the two of them had a meeting in the hotel, as Brian recalled in our filmed interview:

> He called across to me: "Closey, Closey." Christ, I thought, we're back in the old amateur days; they used to call you by your surname. "Yes, skipper, what's happening?" "Come and have a cup of tea in my room." Well, I found his room, and I sat down on the bed. He said, "Brian, the selectors and I have been talking, and we want you to open the innings in this match."
>
> I said, "You must be joking. The last time I opened the innings in first-class cricket was bloody years ago. I've pulled you round twice already in this series. Against the West Indies anything might happen with the new ball. You've got to have somebody experienced enough to pull it round if it does go wrong. Anyway, what's Bob Woolmer in the side for?"
>
> "Oh," he said, "we think he's got a lot of Test cricket left in him, and we don't want him killed off." So I opened the innings with John Edrich.

At Lord's England had Old and Snow, two quick bowlers, to take the new ball. At Old Trafford they had Mike Hendrick and newcomer Mike Selvey, both distinctly medium-pace. Brian, comparing the two attacks, was not being wholly unkind in calling it a contest between cannons and pea-shooters. Despite an innings of 134 by Gordon Greenidge, Hendrick and Selvey bowled well on the first day to dismiss the West Indies for just 211. It looked a poor score but, when the visitors' much quicker bowlers set to work on the surface, it quickly became enormous. Brian fell early for 2, lbw to one that kept low from Wayne Daniel, Edrich soon followed, and it was just as Brian predicted. Nobody with experience was there to turn it round, and they were all out for 71.

West Indies took control of the match, with centuries from Greenidge (again) and Richards, and their captain Clive Lloyd declared after tea on Saturday on 441 for five, setting England 552 for victory. Greig's great theory, to thwart the West Indies in the early Tests and wait for their morale to collapse, was not going to plan.

At one point on Saturday evening Brian had urged his partner to hang on in. "You know what Manchester's like," he said hopefully. "It might rain on Monday and Tuesday." But no such relief was on offer on Monday morning when the bowlers opted for a fuller length. Edrich and Close took the score to 54 before Edrich was bowled by Daniel. Six runs later Roberts, working up a full pace, sent Brian's off-stump cartwheeling backwards, and Woolmer followed, lbw next ball. Brian made 20, Edrich 24, the two top scorers, as the innings collapsed to 126 all out. The margin of defeat, an overwhelming 425 runs, has been exceeded by England only twice in Test history – in Australia in 1928/29 and in India in 2023/24 – and never at home.

The day after the Test Somerset were playing a Gillette Cup match against Warwickshire at Edgbaston. Early in his innings Brian was struck a fierce blow by Bob Willis. The ball hit one of the rawest of his Test match wounds, and he was unable to hide the hurt, going perilously close to dropping to his knees. As John Woodcock put it, 'It was not a case of Willis being faster than Holding and Roberts but simply that even granite yields if hammered often enough.' In pain great enough to prevent him from taking the field later, he went on to hit an aggressive 69, the best innings of the day, and won the Man of the Match award.

With the next Test at Headingley Brian hoped he had done enough to stay in the team. He had scored 166 runs in the series, at an average of 33; only David Steele had scored more. But it was not to be. "Edrich and Close did a bloody good job at Old Trafford," selector Charlie Elliott explained. "It's just that the moment has arrived when we've got to think in terms of getting some openers for the future."

In Brian's world he would have stayed in the team and been appointed captain in place of Greig. 'We Could Have Beaten West Indies', he called the chapter in *I Don't Bruise Easily*. But he knew in his heart his time was over. The newspapermen, with the exception of John Woodcock, were calling for him to be 'pensioned off', in one case describing his return as 'a ludicrous experiment'.

"It was expected after all the pressure from the national press," Brian said when the team was announced. "Of course I'm disappointed, but I'm grateful to have been given the chance for England again. It's a pity that I can't play at Headingley, when we might have given them a bit of their own back."

The selectors opted for a top four of Woolmer, Steele, Hayes and the 35-year-old Chris Balderstone. This time England lost by only 55 runs, but the top order again let them down: 32 for three in the first innings, 23 for three in the second.

Brian's strange, on-off Test career was finally over. It did not end in cricketing glory but, my word, it cemented his reputation as one of the bravest men ever to play the game. And he never complained, as others did, about the West Indian bowling that evening. "It was great fun," he told his biographer Alan Hill. "A trying time, but you enjoy those battles."

*

The West Indians loved the way he played his cricket. In 2010 he was invited to Hartford in Connecticut to be inducted into a Cricket Hall of Fame created by the West Indian and Indian communities there – a rare Englishman in their long roll call of the greats of West Indian and Indian cricket. His visit was the subject of a delightful piece by Benj Moorehead in *The Wisden Cricketer*:

> At last his time comes. But not before a dramatic introduction from the MC Rudolph Cohen, a member of the West Indies 1966 party that toured England. Sparing no detail, Cohen talks about the dismissal of Sobers in the Oval Test. Sobers, he explains, tried to turn the ball finer than he might have because he didn't want to injure Brian Close who, needless to say, was crouched at short leg and took the catch.
>
> "I don't know what match you were talking about," Brian says when he gets to the podium, "but I certainly wasn't playing in it." Laughter. Brian's speech is unscripted, unabashed and hugely popular. "I captained England seven times and never lost a match so they sacked me." It was almost stand-up.
>
> After the speeches Brian raises his glass and offers a toast that goes exceptionally well: "As we say in Yorkshire: to all of us, them 'n' us, me 'n' all!"

In 2015, hearing that Brian was close to death, Michael Holding, on commentary duty at Headingley, sought him out for a final reunion, putting his arm around him affectionately, the two of them forever linked by the memory of that evening at Old Trafford.

I wonder. Would Brian really have been such a liability if he had captained England in the Caribbean?

19

JUST A GREAT SOFT THING REALLY

In 1993, accompanied by Vivien, Brian led a Lord's Taverners team on a tour of Kenya, a happy trip where celebrities Tim Rice, Richard Stilgoe and Bob 'the Cat' Bevan mingled with Derek Pringle, Farokh Engineer, Mark Nicholas and Fred Rumsey. As captain of the team Brian was called on to give a speech at the Muthaiga Country Club, famous as the setting of the 'White Mischief' murder.

As a speaker he was not in Fred Trueman's class, nor in fairness did he charge as exorbitant a fee, but he had a great fund of stories and opinions and he could hold an audience in his spell. He had a standard opening line: "Being here with you tonight I feel just like a castrated glow-worm – de-lighted." Then, without notes and with little or no preparation, he would go where the mood took him. He knew what people wanted to hear, and he could judge when it was appropriate to broaden the Yorkshire vowels and add a few 'bloody's, even a 'bugger' or two – old-fashioned swearing. That night at the Muthaiga Club he was in fine form, ending with an uplifting statement about the joy of living. "I've decided that when I can no longer play cricket, play golf and make love, that's when I'll give up," he said. From the back of the room, quick as a flash, came a female voice: "Two to go then, darling."

*

Many were Brian's overseas tours, and almost always he was invited to captain them, even when the party included international stars such as Ian Chappell, Glenn Turner, Tony Greig and Graeme Pollock.

He was a resolute opponent of ostracising South Africa, believing that maintaining the contact was a better way to influence the regime. History may have proved him wrong, but at least he practised what he preached. In October 1973, on a tour to South Africa organised by the businessman Derrick Robins, he led a team that included two 'honorary whites', the West Indian John Shepherd and the Pakistani Younis Ahmed, and among their fixtures they made history as the first international team to play in the township of Soweto.

In March 1975 he returned on a second Robins tour, again with Shepherd and Younis, and again they played in Soweto, a game watched by '3,000 excited and vociferous schoolboys'. Then, in a surprising move, the government allowed two 'non-whites' to be selected in the South African Board President's XI against the tourists, the first time a mixed-race side had represented the country. When one of them, the 19-year-old Edward Habane, took the final wicket to seal victory, he was carried shoulder-high from the field by his team-mates. It might only have been window-dressing, designed to appease the critics of apartheid, but the tourists left with the hope that their visits were doing some good.

The hope was fleeting. SACBOC, the body governing 'non-white' cricket, were adamant that there should be 'no normal cricket in an abnormal society' and banned the two players. One, Dickie Conrad, was already serving a controversial ban from the previous year for sneaking through a 'whites only' entrance to see the Robins XI against an all-white team. He wanted, he said, to watch and learn from his cricketing hero, Brian Close.

The following year the children of Soweto, some of whom who had been at the cricket, staged a demonstration against the use of the Afrikaans language for the teaching of key subjects in their schools. In an act of chilling brutality hundreds were shot dead, the world recoiled in horror, and the sporting boycott of South Africa was tightened.

John Murray, who was on the first of these two Robins tours, reflected on the decision in 1967 to strip Brian of the England captaincy:

> It was said that his temperament would not allow him to carry the flag on an overseas tour. Having experienced his captaincy in South Africa – the tour was nothing but a great success – I am convinced that he would have carried that flag with honour.

Though he retired from county cricket in 1977, Brian went on playing for many years. After Somerset came a year as the professional for Todmorden in the Lancashire League, often playing both days of the weekend, a year that he enjoyed greatly, sometimes taking his young family to the matches. The next year he played for Scarborough, captaining them to victory in the national club championship, a knock-out competition which was sponsored by John Haig, the whisky distillers. At Lord's, after a two-wicket victory achieved with two balls to spare, he once more held aloft a trophy, his spirit undimmed by the passing of the years. And there to witness the day was his great champion Alan Gibson: 'It was grand to see the Old Bald Blighter again, looking the same age as he has for the last twenty years.'

There followed a spell with his home club Baildon, a coaching assignment with the Scotland team – and countless charity matches here, there and everywhere: for Old England, Lord's Taverners, David English's Bunbury team, the Barbados cricket festivals, trips to Australia, America, Africa.

"I'm thinking of burning my boots so they can't ask me to turn out again," he told his biographer Alan Hill early in 2002, but the Cricket Archive website lists him as playing in August that year for the Lord's Taverners in Suffolk. At the age of 71 he opened the batting with the England footballer Russell Osman, retiring after scoring 18 in an opening partnership of 76. There may well have been games after that. He loved playing cricket; despite what he said to Alan Hill, he never wanted it to be over.

For three years, from 1979, he was an England selector, with a brief to watch county games in the North and Midlands. When Mike Brearley stood down as captain, the four of them – Alec Bedser, Ken Barrington, Charlie Elliott and Brian – settled on Ian Botham to succeed him, a choice recommended by Brearley himself. You might think that, as Botham's former captain, Brian's opinion would have been pivotal, but he argued hard against the decision, then urged the young Botham to turn it down. "You'll make a great captain in four or five years," he told him, "but if you take the job now you'll have the worst bloody year of your life." To his dismay he was proved right, holding the recommendation against Brearley when the other selectors voted to recall the former captain.

Brian resumed his first-class career in 1982 by taking on the annual fixture in the Scarborough Festival, captaining D.B. Close's XI against the touring team. He was in his element with this; he knew everybody there, and he revelled in being the elder statesman. Against the New Zealanders in 1986, at the age of 55, he made his last first-class appearance. Needing ten runs to join the august list, published each year in *Wisden*, of batsmen who have scored 35,000 runs, he was out for four, getting a fine touch on a ball down leg and walking without a glance at the umpire. Despite having a head for figures, he could not quote his career record like Fred Trueman and Geoff Boycott did. Personal statistics never mattered to him. He played for the love of the battle.

He remains the oldest first-class cricketer of the last fifty years. In that time only one other Englishman has played beyond the age of 50: the 51-year-old Raymond Illingworth. Spread across five decades, his career span of 37 years, from 18 to 55, is the twelfth longest of all time – and the longest of the post-war era, four years greater than Fred Titmus who played from 16 to 49. In his first season Brian batted against the Glamorgan off-spinner Johnnie Clay, whose debut had been in 1921; in his last he took the wicket of the New Zealander Ken Rutherford who was still playing in the year 2000.

One who could have gone on longer, setting who knows what records, was the 45-year-old Geoffrey Boycott. Playing for DB Close's XI in that match at Scarborough, he went out to bat in the second innings, needing 90 runs for his 1,000 for the season and was bowled for 21. He had one more opportunity, against Northamptonshire, to reach the target for the 24th successive time which, with three more 1,000s in overseas seasons, would have taken him within one of the record set by WG Grace and Frank Woolley. But in his only innings he was run out for 61, finishing on 992. A fracture of his left hand had kept him out of several games that summer and, to his great annoyance, he was not immediately selected when fit to return, a failure of communication for which Brian, as Chairman of Cricket, was responsible, not reaching the phone in time because – once again – his car had broken down.

A fortnight later amid great bitterness Boycott's career was over, his contract terminated by Yorkshire. "We couldn't carry on with a cult figure grinding out his personal glory while the rest of the players made up the numbers," Brian told the press. "He always puts himself before the club."

Boycott's autobiography appeared the next year, with a 28-page closing chapter recounting every detail of his sacking. It was an ugly business, and the wounds had not healed ten years later when the two of them appeared as witnesses in a libel trial between Imran Khan on the one side and Ian Botham and Allan Lamb on the other. Close declined to answer when asked if he thought Boycott an honest man; Boycott, in response, called Close "a bitter and angry man trying to get his own back" for things he, Boycott, had written about him.

Brian could become angry. His temper would flare sometimes in the dressing room when he would pin a member of his team against the wall and shout at him. Just occasionally it would flare at home; once he broke a standard lamp across his knee. But the rage would pass as quickly as it flared up, and within minutes life would go on as if it had never happened. Boycott's description of Brian as 'a bitter and angry man wanting to get his own back' does not fit with anything I have been told about him. But perhaps the long drawn-out saga around Boycott brought out the worst of everybody at Yorkshire.

With his great reputation and his sharp cricketing brain Brian was in many respects an ideal Chairman of Cricket, but the world of committees was not a natural habitat for him, certainly not in that turbulent time of pro- and anti-Boycott factions. He did not prepare methodically for the meetings and, though he was happy enough to exchange opinions in a lively argument, he was never comfortable with the political intriguing. He would say what he thought, naïvely assuming that everybody else was doing the same.

He also found it hard to move with the times. The cricket of his day was always better, and his thoughts on the failure of Yorkshire to tap into the talent of the county's British Asians were rarely helpful. On one occasion he tried to explain their absence from the higher levels of Yorkshire cricket by saying they had more children and therefore could not afford the equipment or the coaching.

I remember ringing him in the late 1990s. It was the first time I had spoken to him, and all I wanted was a quote from him about Ken Taylor's artwork which he offered enthusiastically. But he stayed on the phone and was quickly into his stride, running down the modern game:

> Look at it now. Captains take a bowler off or put him on, they have to go and have a five-minute chat, placing the field and all that. We used to do that between balls. And if a fellow didn't look as if he was taking wickets, "Right, put your sweater on." Another bowler was straight on. We had variety in the attack. We gave the batsmen different problems all the time. But they don't know how to do it now because of the influence of the one-day game. "Oh well, we've so many overs to bowl so we'll take our time." I told them thirty years ago. It's been the ruination of cricket.

When Ian MacLaurin was appointed Chairman of the England and Wales Cricket Board in 1997, Brian was asked by his former team-mate Roy Booth what he thought of the appointment. "I don't know," he said. "He's been a good business man and that. I've written him a letter. I've said, you'd do well to meet me so I can put you wise to a few things."

"Has he arranged a meeting with you yet?"

"No. I've had a letter back, saying he's pretty busy, but he hopes to see me some time in the future."

From the way Roy repeated the conversation to me, I think he knew that Ian MacLaurin, with his modernising agenda, was not looking to be 'made wise' by the former England captain.

Brian was happier in action, leading men from the front – as he had a further chance to do in the 1990s when the county established an academy programme and Brian, now well into his sixties, took on captaincy of the youngsters. The journalist David Warner recalls watching his first game in charge of them. Coming in down the order, he batted with as much determination as if once more the County Championship was at stake. Called for a quick single, he threw himself headlong over the line, emerging covered in dust. Some of his team may have had grandfathers his age, but they knew his reputation and they were inspired by him. "He was great," a young Ryan Sidebottom told his dad, "but doesn't he swear a lot?"

Another father, seeing the old man speaking to his son while they batted together, asked eagerly, "What did he say to you?", only to get the reply, "He said he was dying for a bloody fag."

In the nets he thought nothing of batting without pads on. "That's the way you learn to hit the ball, lad," he told the young Michael Vaughan. "If you don't, you'll soon end up with a broken kneecap."

He was less successful in imparting his cricketing knowledge to his son Lance, who was put off by his father's impatience and short fuse: "If he told you something, he expected you to be able to do it straightaway." Lance played club cricket in Yorkshire and in Kent, but he did not enjoy the burden of being pointed out as 'Closey's lad' and saved his serious sport for the game of rugby.

Nevertheless, as a teenager, Lance was persuaded several times to accompany his father to charity matches. Always he had to bring his kit – just in case, as often happened, a celebrity did not turn up.

> We'd be playing in front of ten thousand people sometimes. And when we came off the field, we would be swarmed by kids wanting our autographs. I would sign, and two seconds later they'd ask, "Who are you again?"
>
> Usually I would bat at number eleven and field third man at both ends, but I did get three for six against an Oxford University side, bowling dodgy left-arm spin. And I taught Richard Branson how to put his pads on properly.

*

In 2001, thirty-three years on from the last of Brian's triumphs, Yorkshire were County Champions again. It had been a long wait, and they had sacrificed their Yorkshire-born creed to get there. Several had begun life outside the county, including leading run-scorer Darren Lehmann, an Australian, and top wicket-taker Steve Kirby, a Lancastrian. That was all forgotten in the celebrations, and fittingly, when the team went down to London to receive the trophy at Buckingham Palace from the Duke of Edinburgh, they took Brian Close with them.

Whenever they met, the Duke would make a bee-line for Brian. They had in common a certain disregard for excessive etiquette and stuffy convention. When it came to the taking of the team photograph, with the Duke in the middle of the front row, Brian stood aside, knowing he had no role in the county's success, but the Duke insisted on his joining them.

The success was a one-off, with the county next year relegated to the second division where they languished for three years. It was too much for Brian to bear, and at the age of 75 he strode into the Chief Executive's office and offered his services on a twelve-month contract to "sort them out". He could shake them up, put some life back into them, give them some purpose in the field. When I was told the story, I half-imagined him donning his whites and leading them out at Headingley. He still had that self-belief, that defiance of reality. He could not be beaten.

In 2006, shortly after the death of Fred Trueman, Brian and Ray Illingworth appeared in an episode of the ITV police drama *Heartbeat*. They were cast as two Cricket Veterans, watching a village match umpired by Dickie Bird. When late in the day a young woman came out to bat, the camera cut to the two of them. "What's the game coming to?" a cloth-capped Brian said. "I wonder what Fred would say." Ray duly chuckled – an endearing portrait of two elderly men who, through all the turmoil of Yorkshire cricket, retained an affectionate respect for each other.

In 2008 Yorkshire County Cricket Club invited Brian to become its President, only the third professional cricketer after Len Hutton and Bob Appleyard to hold the office. The club that had sacked him in 1970 was now awarding him its highest honour, and with pride he undertook his duties in his own inimitable style. He held the position for two years, the last hurrah of a Yorkshire career that had started back in the 1940s when he was just a weaver's son from a council house, entering a world that was way beyond his ken.

*

His golf lasted for several years after his cricket ended, with a buggy to help him round the course when the walking grew difficult. He played at Hollins Hall in Baildon, where each year he organised a Brian Close Celebrity Golf Classic, raising thousands of pounds for the treatment of heart disease. He worked hard to bring business to the club, so much so that when his golfing days were finally over he remained a special guest, regularly using its gym. Whenever he dropped in, they set the television to the channel of his choice, served him with free cups of tea and coffee and, even after the ban on indoor smoking, got out his ashtray and allowed him to puff away.

He got through sixty cigarettes a day, and attempts to persuade him to give up got nowhere. "It's my only pleasure in life," he would protest. "You can't take that away from me." He was still smoking forty a day when he was undergoing radiotherapy for lung cancer. At Headingley, in the exclusive Hawke Suite, he would hide his fag behind his back, convincing himself that it had not been noticed. A ring of smoke would form above his head, there would be a strong smell of nicotine in the air, but even as an old man he was still 'Closey'; for the most part, with one or two notable exceptions, the people there chose to turn a blind eye.

His smoking habit took its toll on the family finances, but worse was the gambling on horses. In his prime he had contacts with trainers and jockeys at several stables, and his losses were never that great, but these contacts grew fewer as he slipped into old age, with one well-known television commentator telling him not to ring again.

He still craved the adrenalin rush of winning, the excitement that he experienced as a teenager at the Melbourne Cup, and, with his serious cricket-playing days over, the thrill of the horses grew more central to his life. At one point, agreeing to cut down, he closed his telephone accounts, but that only led to his spending more time at the bookmaker's shop, where Geoff Cope often encountered him on the pavement:

> Some of his ashes were scattered outside the bookies at Guiseley because that's where he lived at the end. He'd be there in winter in a light-medium sweater, stood outside with no coat on, with a plastic cup of coffee. His hand would be shaking, his cigarette would be shaking. "Brian, why don't you go inside?" "You young 'uns, you don't know what it's like. You're brought up soft." He'd always give me that line.

Brian relished the moments when, with his super-speedy mental arithmetic, he leant on the kitchen top, cigarette in one hand, betting slips in the other, and tallied up his winnings. If he returned from the bookies with a pocket full of rolled notes, he was always generous, never saving it to cover his outgoings on the bad days. "When I win lots of money, I'll buy everybody a house," he would say, but it never happened. Instead, to make ends meet, he and Vivien were forced to sell some of their garden, then they had to downsize to a smaller house.

He was given stints of television and radio commentary, but at important moments he was missing, not watching the cricket but following the racing in the Ladbrokes tent. Soon enough the invitations dried up.

His principal occupation after cricket was selling insurance, which he did well, though he knew he was trading more on his name than his financial expertise. For all his ability with numbers he was never good with his own money. He was too trusting of others, too often taken advantage of.

He was generous with his time, always willing to give interviews and answer questions about his life. Early in the 1970s, after he had completed his first season with Somerset, the New Zealander Norman Harris visited the Closes at their house at Baildon, writing a perceptive portrait for the *Observer*'s colour supplement. The feature ends with a description of the scene on the front lawn when the photographer is taking pictures:

> Brian romps with his dog. Vivien watches, smiling. Young Lance is there, too, an independent child who refuses to say a word to the visitors or to give up a lethal pair of scissors he has seized. Brian Close continues his play with his boxer dog Skipper. He seems happy to carry on all morning, if the photographer wants, regardless of the dog hair and saliva gathering on his business suit. Skipper keeps bouncing in the air like a new-shorn lamb, while roaring like a lion. Don't be fooled by him, says Close: he does his best to look ferocious and makes a lot of noise, but he's just a great soft thing really.

The family always had a dog. The first three were boxers, all called Skipper. The last was a terrier-cross, Jasper, who grew old with him. Walking with a stick in his final years Brian would take him round the local streets each day, never bothering to pick up the poo – another regulation, like the ban on indoor smoking and the speed limits on the roads, that he preferred to disregard. The neighbours all knew who he was so he collected a few fixed penalty notices.

Apart from a short Easter break each year in the Lake District, with friends Gerry and Jan Waller, whose daughter Kath married Ian Botham, he rarely went on family holidays. Ian joined them several times in the Lake District, Lance remembering the rivalry between the two men:

> My father bought a little inflatable dinghy that we sailed on Ullswater, and the next year Ian turned up with a bigger one. So we had to get a bigger one still with an engine, which Ian then topped with an even more powerful one. We finished up with a speedboat with a 60-horsepower engine, and we only used it once a year.

The two men had much in common, which Kath came to realise after a few years of, as she put it, 'living with a legend':

> I loved and admired Brian, but it was clear how difficult he was to live with. I can see many of the traits in Ian that I saw then in Brian: the selfish single-mindedness which is so difficult to incorporate into a family situation; the inability to see through people; and the great generosity, not just in financial terms but in the depth of affection they both show towards the people they like.

Once, when Vivien on her own took the two children on a coach trip to the South of France, they got back to Victoria Station, only to discover on ringing home that Brian had forgotten he was supposed to be picking them up. He drove down as fast as he could, but the episode was not untypical of him. As a teenager in the 1980s Lynn often accompanied him to cricket and golf, sometimes caddying for him, but "I always had to keep my eye on the car at the end of the day, as he'd have been perfectly capable of going home without me."

On the long car journeys to the golf and cricket, through the fog of cigarette smoke, Brian would listen with great interest when Lynn talked to him about history and literature, subjects he had given up at a young age at school. But he did not read books or go to the theatre, and he did not keep up with the popular music that Lynn listened to.

> He once sat next to Mick Jagger at a cricket match, and he didn't know who he was. At some point he cottoned on and got

him to sign some things for me. But I wasn't really bothered. It wasn't my sort of music.

He would have enjoyed other things if he had known them when he was young. But he wasn't keen on admitting when he didn't know about things.

"He wasn't a good Dad," Lynn says with considerable affection, "but he was mine. He was very much his own person."

At one point she and her husband Mark, facing the prospect of homelessness, turned up hoping they could stay till things got sorted out. Vivien, always the more practical one, saw difficulties in such an arrangement, but Brian responded immediately and decisively. "Don't be silly. You must come and live with us. Shut up, Vivien." And he gave Lynn a great hug. "It was one of the few occasions I can remember him doing so."

The arrangement lasted six months, during which Brian enjoyed the chance of man-to-man sporting chats with Mark. The sessions of d-i-y were less fun. "He dropped a hammer on my head a few times," Mark says. "He was so strong," Lynn says, "and he had this idea he could do everything by brute strength. He would never do it properly."

When he was diagnosed with cancer, he refused to use the word, talking of 'a lung infection' or 'a sprained rib'. "He was still fit and strong," Lynn says, "still thinking he could shake off his illness. I'd go to see him in hospital when he was on oxygen, and he'd be furious if I didn't bring cigarettes."

The one thing he did give up, to their surprise, was driving. He backed out of the drive one day, smacked into a car coming down the hill and decided of his own volition that his days at the wheel were over.

He had a magnificent physique, without ever doing much to keep himself fit. In the pre-season Easter holidays in the Lake District he would don several layers of clothing and a scarf, run for a mile or two to work up a sweat, then have a hot bath. That was his training. He never put on weight, the cigarettes saw to that. His built-in fitness kept him going, even when the cancer was taking its final grip. He was still walking up and down stairs till a day or two before he died.

The end, surprisingly quick, came on the evening of Sunday 13 September 2015. A man who for so long had seemed indestructible slipped away quietly in his own bed at home.

In the months that followed they needed six coats of paint to rid the house of the smell of his cigarettes.

20

ONE HELL OF A LIFE

Between Brian Close's first match in 1949 and his last in 1976, England took part in 244 Tests, in only 22 of which, spread across 11 series, did Brian appear. He could have played against Australia 71 times, and he did so only twice: at Melbourne in 1950 and Old Trafford in 1961. Both times, on cricket's greatest stage, the manner of his failure earned him near-universal condemnation.

It was not the career predicted for him when he burst on the scene as a prodigiously talented 18-year-old: the youngest cricketer to be capped by Yorkshire, the youngest to do the double, the youngest to play for England. His obituary in *Wisden* ended with the verdict of Doug Insole: "Of all the cricketers who were around at that time, his career was the most disappointing. He had more ability in every aspect of the game."

Did it all happen too quickly for him? Did that carefree teenager who loved every moment of his first summer with Yorkshire have the joy knocked out of him during his lonely six months in Australia? Post-war England was desperate for a new generation of cricketers to emerge, and he was undoubtedly promoted before he was ready. National Service deprived him of a second summer with Yorkshire, and he was ill-equipped both as an immature cricketer and as an inexperienced young man for the long tour of Australia. The hurt never left him.

If he had not failed his Army medical in February 1949, if he had done his 18 months of National Service then, he would have come into cricket as a 20-year-old in 1951 and would never have had to carry the baggage of that 'youngest ever' tag or of his failure in Australia. His career might have played out in a more conventional way.

Yet there was something in his character that makes it unlikely he would ever have followed a conventional path through life, ever have settled comfortably into the traditional, no-nonsense ways of Yorkshire cricket. He would always have had an impulsive streak, a yearning to take risks, to do things his own way. The rules of the road would never have been followed too obediently.

The Old Trafford Test in 1961, when he made such a mess of trying to sweep Richie Benaud's leg-spin, could so easily have been the end of his Test career. He was thirty years old, he had been given seven chances by England, and he had a batting average under 18, with not a single fifty to his name. He had great talent but he lacked maturity of judgement, that was the general view. At Yorkshire the men who ran the club thought him unstable, undependable, too much of a maverick. They were most reluctant to entrust him with the captaincy.

In 1963, with no clear alternative, Yorkshire held their breath and put him in charge. And it was the making of him. It turned out that he was a born leader, respected by his men and brimming with tactical nous. He inherited a side that had grown used to winning, and they continued to do so. His own form took him back into the England team in 1963, when he became a national hero with a formidably brave innings against the West Indian pacemen at Lord's. In 1966 he was a spectacular success when he was summoned back to the England side as captain. These were his golden years.

How badly it ended, with both England and Yorkshire. In neither case did he see the danger on the road ahead of him. With typical stubbornness he was adamant that he had done nothing wrong at Edgbaston, and he could not bring himself to speak the words of apology that the men at Lord's expected of him. Call him defiant, or call him daft. Either way he gave succour to his enemies and lost the greatest prize in English cricket, the captaincy of the national team.

It was a tragedy for Brian and, perhaps also, for English cricket – the years of his dynamic and inspiring captaincy cut short. Did the offence justify the punishment, or was it a stitch-up by the cricket establishment, a greater injustice – if the wider political ramifications are stripped out – than the one suffered by Basil D'Oliveira the following year? With his brand of risk-taking cricket and his friendship with Garry Sobers, Brian could have been a great success in the Caribbean.

The loss of the Yorkshire captaincy hit him even harder, and it too was unforeseen. Yet there were reasons for it: his dislike of the one-day game, his loyalty to the older players at the expense of youth, the medical report suggesting he would not play much longer. Yorkshire, refusing to employ overseas players, were starting to struggle; it is hard to see how they could have won further trophies if Brian had spent his last years with them, rather than with Somerset.

What a wonderful finale those years in the West Country were. As the key batsman in a much weaker side, he showed what runs he might have scored if he had played for himself, not the team, at Yorkshire. And, past the age of forty, away from the intense pressures of a county that expected and demanded success, he loved his role as the 'Old Bald Blighter', adding a fresh competitiveness to the easier-going ways of Somerset cricket.

Some outstanding youngsters were emerging, best of all Viv Richards and Ian Botham, and he left his mark on them. The long years in the game, the rollercoaster of his career with its triumphs and disasters, had taught him so much, and he imparted his accumulated wisdom in his own distinctive style: gruff and unyielding on the outside but never unkind in the way the senior players in Australia had been unkind to him. He was not a touchy-feely man, not naturally empathetic towards others, but in his undimmed enthusiasm and his care for his team he was a captain the young Somerset cricketers loved to play for. There were mad moments when it all went pear-shaped, but it was never going to be dull.

'A brilliant genius and thick at the same time' was Ken Biddulph's summary of him. As a sportsman, with a superb physique and innate ball sense, he could have been a superstar of the game. As a captain, with his tactical acumen and his ability to motivate men, he could have been the greatest of all England captains. Yet too many things went wrong throughout his career, and a fair few of them were down to his own nature: his recklessness, his refusal ever to accept fault, his inability to adapt to changing times, his naïvety when dealing with those who ran the game.

In his last playing years his idiosyncrasies turned him into one of the game's greatest characters, his legendary bravery epitomised by that evening at Old Trafford when at the age of 45 he ducked and swayed as Michael Holding sent down thunderbolts at him. That, and the extraordinary innings at Lord's when he came down the wicket to Wes Hall, is how we have come to remember him: the most courageous cricketer of them all, the hardest of men. Yet that was just one aspect of his character and of his achievements.

The cars he wrote off, the cigarettes he smoked, the horses he lost money on, they left him in old age in relative poverty. But they were all of a piece with his character, defiantly going his own way through life. On the cricket field he was full of imagination, but in other ways he had tunnel vision, locked into habits and attitudes that did not change – and did not want to. That was the hard side of him. Yet there was also a kindness, a generosity, a lack of ill-will that made him a very lovable man.

He carried so many scars – not the physical ones to his body, they were just pain that you could switch off, but the emotional ones: the tour of Australia, the pillorying of his innings against Benaud, the losses of the England and Yorkshire captaincies. He went through them all in our filmed interview, as he did so many times in interviews over the years. The wounds had not healed, but he had learned to live with them.

*

Let us end by giving Brian the final word, as he always wanted.

As our interview drew to a close, he broke off from a diatribe about the softness of modern cricketers – "I mean, we didn't even wear vests" – to speak of the love of the game that he and his fellow cricketers had shared.

> Every one of us enjoyed it. Participating. Competing. And helping others. Winning for your team. Having some achievement at the end of it that you could share with other people. It was just a great lifetime experience.

He said how, if it had not been for his military service, he might have gone to university and never been a sportsman. Then he looked down, gathering his emotions, and reflected on the way it had all turned out.

> It's been a life full of enjoyment, I suppose, and a few sad moments. I've laughed at them many a time when I've shared my experiences with people.

Raising his head he broke into a slightly manic laugh, then fell again into silent thought before delivering one final line.

> It's been one hell of a life.

With his bushy eyebrows and dome-like forehead, he looked for a moment as resolute as he had been when facing Wes Hall and Michael Holding. Then his pale blue eyes twinkled, and his face creased into another laugh.

He had had his knocks, but nothing was going to beat him.

A BRIEF STATISTICAL DIGEST

All figures are from the Cricket Archive website

TEST CRICKET

(1949-1976)

BATTING AND FIELDING

M	I	NO	Runs	HS	Ave	100	50	Ct
22	37	2	887	70	25.34	-	4	24

BOWLING

Overs	Mdns	Runs	Wkts	Best	Ave	5wi
199.4	56	532	18	4-35	29.55	-

(7 overs were eight-ball)

FIRST-CLASS CRICKET

(1949-1986)

BATTING AND FIELDING

M	I	NO	Runs	HS	Ave	100	50	Ct	St
786	1225	173	34994	198	33.26	52	171	813	1

BOWLING

Overs	Mdns	Runs	Wkts	Best	Ave	5wi	10wm
11629.1	3602	30947	1171	8-41	26.42	43	3

(98.2 overs were eight-ball)

ONE-DAY (LIST A) CRICKET

(1963-1977)

BATTING AND FIELDING

M	I	NO	Runs	HS	Ave	100	50	Ct
164	156	11	3458	131	23.84	2	11	53

BOWLING

Overs	Mdns	Runs	Wkts	Best	Ave	4wi
378.1	54	1446	65	4- 9	22.24	2

BEST PERFORMANCES IN FIRST-CLASS CRICKET

SCORES OF 150+

198	Yorkshire v Surrey	The Oval	1960
184	Yorkshire v Nottinghamshire	Scarborough	1960
164	Yorkshire v Combined Services	Harrogate	1954
161	Yorkshire v Northamptonshire	Northampton	1963
154	Yorkshire v Nottinghamshire	Trent Bridge	1959
153	Somerset v Middlesex	Lord's	1973

SEVEN OR MORE WICKETS IN AN INNINGS

19	6	41	8	Yorkshire v Kent	Headingley	1959
23.5	7	43	8	Yorkshire v Essex	Headingley	1960
24.4	9	62	7	Yorkshire v Essex	Bradford	1955

ELEVEN WICKETS IN A MATCH

42	16	116	11	Yorkshire v Kent	Gillingham	1965

CAREER RECORDS

TEST CRICKET

At 18 years 149 days, Brian Close is the second youngest man to play for England. Rehan Ahmed, at 18 years 126 days in 2022, is the youngest.

At 45 years 140 days he is the oldest to play for England since Gubby Allen in 1948.

His career span of 26 years 356 days is second to Wilfred Rhodes (30 years 315 days) among Test cricketers of all countries.

FIRST-CLASS CRICKET

Brian Close's 786 appearances place him 10th in the all-time list. Since the war, only Fred Titmus (792) and Ray Illingworth (787) have played more.

His 812 catches as a fielder (not keeping wicket) place him 5th in the all-time list. Since the war, only Tony Lock (831) has taken more.

His 359 matches as captain place him 8th on the all-time list. Since the war, only Mike Smith (404) and Wilf Wooller (360) have captained more.

His career span of 37 years 114 days is the longest of any post-war English cricketer.

CAPTAINCY

Only four men have led a county to four or more championship titles: Lord Hawke (Yorkshire, 8, 1893-1908), Brian Sellers (Yorkshire, 6, 1933-1946), Stuart Surridge (Surrey, 5, 1952-1956) and Brian Close (Yorkshire, 4, 1963-1968).

FIRST-CLASS CRICKET

BATTING AND FIELDING

HOME	M	I	NO	Runs	HS	Ave	100	50	Ct
1949	31	50	10	1098	88*	27.45		4	19
1950	4	7	1	202	92*	33.66		2	5
1951	6	12	1	384	135*	34.90	1	2	5
1952	33	45	9	1192	87*	33.11		8	27
1953	2	2	1	14	10	14.00			1
1954	31	43	7	1320	164	36.66	2	7	25
1955	32	53	5	1330	143	27.70	2	5	38
1956	27	37	5	802	88	25.06		3	23
1957	34	56	4	1666	120	32.03	4	6	37
1958	34	53	5	1497	120	31.18	2	7	33
1959	33	56	3	1879	154	35.45	5	8	37
1960	36	51	3	1699	198	35.39	3	8	44
1961	37	64	8	1985	132	35.44	5	9	47
1962	29	46	6	1447	142*	36.17	3	7	30
1963	31	50	3	1529	161	32.53	1	10	27
1964	36	55	7	1455	100*	30.31	1	8	48 +
1965	30	46	7	1127	117*	28.89	3	2	31
1966	34	56	11	1331	115*	29.57	3	6	46
1967	23	32	4	884	98	31.57		8	29
1968	27	34	8	660	77*	25.38		3	34
1969	20	27	4	812	146	35.30	1	4	10
1970	20	28	2	949	128	36.50	1	6	20
1971	26	42	10	1389	116*	43.40	5	6	34
1972	20	33	6	1396	135	51.70	3	7	17
1973	21	32	5	1096	153	40.59	3	3	21
1974	24	40	9	1153	114*	37.19	1	5	25
1975	22	38	6	1284	138*	40.12	1	8	14
1976	20	34	5	1137	88	39.20		8	17
1977	16	25	2	438	87	19.04		2	19
Occasional matches									
1978-1986	6	10	4	170	51	28.33		1	5
OVERSEAS									
1950/51 (Aus)	9	13	3	231	108*	23.10	1		9
1955/56 (Pak)	12	20	1	684	92	36.00		5	12
Minor tours									
1959-1975	20	35	8	754	102	27.92	1	3	24
Total	**786**	**1225**	**173**	**34994**	**198**	**33.26**	**52**	**171**	**813**

+ 1 stumping as a stand-in wicket-keeper in 1964

BOWLING

HOME	Overs	Mdns	Runs	Wkts	Best	Ave	5wi	10wm
1949	1245	324	3150	113	6-47	27.87	6	
1950	153.1	46	386	20	6-61	19.30	1	1
1951	101.4	37	246	4	1-22	61.50		
1952	1107.4	331	2746	114	6-69	24.08	6	
1953	45	19	105	3	2-61	35.00		
1954	534	138	1474	66	6-38	22.33	4	
1955	871.4	257	2274	97	7-62	23.44	5	
1956	266.5	75	674	24	4-27	28.08		
1957	289	92	787	32	5-29	24.59	1	
1958	342.1	85	921	34	4-30	27.08		
1959	757	210	2162	88	8-41	24.57	5	
1960	611.3	207	1493	64	8-43	23.32	3	
1961	615	220	1716	67	6-55	25.61	3	
1962	413.5	164	929	32	3- 4	29.03		
1963	425.2	134	1176	43	6-55	27.34	1	1
1964	563.5	199	1360	52	6-29	26.15	1	
1965	527.2	202	1217	58	6-49	20.98	4	1
1966	563.3	201	1362	60	6-27	22.70	2	
1967	372.1	142	870	29	4-68	30.00		
1968	340	140	772	32	4-87	24.12		
1969	115	47	282	7	1- 4	40.29		
1970	34	10	95	2	1-15	47.50		
1971	39	11	160	5	3-20	32.00		
1972	35	10	128	3	2-77	42.66		
1973	159.5	29	560	10	2- 3	56.00		
1974	104	30	287	14	5-70	20.50	1	
1975	294.1	87	931	29	4-22	32.10		
1976	163.1	36	605	15	3-35	40.33		
1977	0.2	-	8	-	-	-		
Occasional matches								
1978-1986	27.1	3	142	5	2-33	28.40		
OVERSEAS								
1950/51 (Aus)	98.2 +	9	475	13	3-81	36.53		
1955/56 (Pak)	145	57	313	11	2-40	28.45		
Minor tours								
1959-1975	268.5	50	1143	25	4-36	45.64		
Total	**11629.1**	**3602**	**30947**	**1171**	**8-41**	**26.42**	**43**	**3**

+ The overs in 1950/51 were eight-ball

Acknowledgements

This book has been born out of many conversations over more than a quarter of a century. I would like to thank all those, living and dead, who have given their time in talking to me, first and foremost Brian Close himself, whom I interviewed at length twice and spoke to more briefly on several other occasions. I am also most grateful to Lynn and Lance, Brian's two children, for sharing with me some of their memories of their father.

I am greatly indebted to Ken Taylor not only for the many insights he has shared with me over the years but for his permission to reproduce his two drawings of Brian. The fact that I have dedicated a whole chapter to him will tell you how much I value his reflections.

I would also like to thank the following people:
David Allen, Keith Andrew, Bob Appleyard, Graham Atkinson, Bob Barber, John Barclay, Alec Bedser, Ken Biddulph, Jimmy Binks, Dickie Bird, Roy Booth, Graham Burgess, Donald Carr, Bob Carter, Tom Cartwright, Geoff Cope, Geoff Edrich, Tom Graveney, David Green (Derbyshire), Mark Hainsworth, Wes Hall, Maurice Hallam, Geoffrey Howard, Raymond Illingworth, Peter Jenkins, Brian Langford, Eddie Leadbeater, Ted Lester, Vic Marks, Arthur Milton, Alan Oakman, Charles Palmer, Jim Parks, Richard Parry, Pat Pocock, Mike Procter, Peter Robinson, Peter Roebuck, Brian Rose, Fred Rumsey, Patrick Shervington, Reg Simpson, Terry Spencer, Micky Stewart, Bryan Stott, Bob Taylor, Derek Ufton, Martin Veal, Peter Walker, 'Bomber' Wells, Don Wilson and Vic Wilson.

I would especially like to thank David Warner, for many years the cricket correspondent of the *Bradford Telegraph & Argus* and the kindest of men, and Ron Deaton, whose work on the preservation of Yorkshire's cricket history has not had the recognition it deserves. The two of them have given me access to the many letters Brian Close wrote to his friend John Anderson in the early years of his sporting career. Much, though not all, of what I have used from these letters has appeared in the excellent book they created out of these letters:

David Warner & Ron Deaton: *Just A Few Lines* (Great Northern, 2020)

Both David and Ron have been immensely generous in reading my manuscript and offering helpful comments, as have Stephen Brenkley, Stephen Lamb, Simon Lister, Douglas Miller, Richard Whitehead and David Woodhouse, all of whose judgements I value greatly. In some cases I have done the same for their books, part of a world of mutual collaboration which is so heartwarming in the potentially lonely life of the author.

I am most grateful to Neil Robinson and Alan Rees, of the MCC Library at Lord's, who shared with me all the documents relating to Brian Close's loss of the England captaincy in 1967. Time did not permit me to read every one of the hundreds of letters, mostly angry, that MCC received.

I am delighted that this book is being published by Fairfield Books, my old publishing company. Matt Thacker and his team are doing a splendid job of carrying forward the flame to a new generation of cricket book readers. It is a pleasure to continue to be associated with the venture.

I have read and made use of the following books:

Bill Alley: *Standing the Test of Time* (Empire Publications, 1999)

Bill Andrews: *The Hand That Bowled Bradman* (Macdonald, 1973)

John Arlott: *Days at the Cricket* (Longmans, Green & Co, 1951)

John Arlott: *Cricket Journal 2* (William Heinemann, 1959)

John Arlott: *Cricket Journal 4* (William Heinemann, 1961)

J.S. Barker: *Summer Spectacular* (Collins, 1963)

Richie Benaud: *A Tale of Two Tests* (Hodder & Stoughton, 1962)

Richie Benaud: *Willow Patterns* (Hodder & Stoughton, 1969)

Ian Botham: *Botham's Century* (Collins Willow, 2001)

Ken Barrington: *Running into Hundreds* (Stanley Paul, 1963)

Ian Botham: *Head On – The Autobiography* (Ebury Press, 2007)

Kathy Botham: *Living with a Legend* (Grafton Books, 1987)

Geoffrey Boycott: *The Autobiography* (Macmillan, 1987)

Geoffrey Boycott & Jon Hotten: *Being Geoffrey Boycott* (Fairfield Books, 2022)

Freddie Brown: *Cricket Musketeer* (Nicholas Kaye, 1954)

John Callaghan: *Yorkshire Cricket Greats* (Sportsprint, 1990)

John Clarke: *Cricket with a Swing* (Stanley Paul, 1963)

John Clarke & Brian Scovell: *Everything That's Cricket* (Stanley Paul, 1966)

Brian Close: *Close on Cricket* (Stanley Paul, 1966)

Brian Close: *Close to Cricket* (Stanley Paul, 1968)

Brian Close: *I Don't Bruise Easily* (Macdonald & Jane's, 1978)

Andrew Collomosse: *Magnificent Seven* (Great Northern Books, 2010)

Jack Fingleton: *Brown and Company* (Collins, 1951)

Charles Fortune: *The Australians in England 1961* (Robert Hale, 1961)

Tom Graveney: *Cricket Over Forty* (Pelham, 1970)

John Hampshire: *Family Argument* (George Allen & Unwin, 1983)

Alan Hill: *Brian Close – Cricket's Lionheart* (Methuen, 2002)

Alan Hill: *Johnny Wardle – Cricket Conjuror* (David & Charles, 1988)

Richard Hoggart: *The Uses of Literacy* (Chatto & Windus, 1957)

Martin Howe: *Norman Yardley* (ACS Publications, 2015)

Len Hutton: *Fifty Years in Cricket* (Stanley Paul, 1984)

Brian Jackson & Denys Marsden: *Education and the Working Class* (Routledge, 1962)

John Kay: *Ashes to Hassett* (John Sherratt & Son, 1951)

J.M. Kilburn: *A History of Yorkshire Cricket* (Stanley Paul, 1970)

J.M. Kilburn: *Thanks to Cricket* (Stanley Paul, 1972)

Alan Knott: *It's Knott Cricket* (Macmillan, 1985)

Jim Laker: *The Australian Tour of 1961* (Frederick Muller, 1961)
Ray Lindwall: *The Challenging Tests* (Pelham Books, 1961)
Peter May: *A Game Enjoyed* (Stanley Paul, 1985)
Don Mosey: *Boycott* (Methuen, 1985)
Don Mosey: *We Don't Play It For Fun* (Methuen, 1988)
Pat Pocock: *Percy* (Clifford Frost Publications, 1987)
Stuart Rayner: *The War of the White Roses* (Pitch, 2016)
Viv Richards & David Foot: *Viv Richards* (World's Work, 1979)
Viv Richards: *Sir Vivian* (Michael Joseph, 2000)
R.A. Roberts: *Fight for the Ashes 1961* (George G. Harrap, 1961)
Peter Roebuck: *Slices of Cricket* (George Allen & Unwin, 1982)
Brian Rose: *Rosey* (Fairfield Books, 2019)
Alan Ross: *The West Indies at Lord's* (Eyre & Spottiswoode, 1963)
Mark Rowe: *Brian Sellers* (ACS Publications, 2017)
Fred Rumsey: *Sense of Humour, Sense of Justice* (Fairfield Books, 2019)
Garry Sobers: *My Autobiography* (Headline, 2002)
Jon Spurling: *Rebels for the Cause* (Mainstream, 2004)
Rob Steen: *This Sporting Life – Cricket* (David & Charles, 1999)
David Steele: *Come In Number 3* (Pelham Books, 1977)
E.W. Swanton: *Elusive Victory* (Hodder & Stoughton, 1951)
E.W. Swanton: *Swanton in Australia* (Collins, 1975)
Fred Trueman: *As It Was* (Macmillan, 2004)
Fred Trueman & Don Mosey: *Champion Times* (Dalesman Publishing, 1994)
Fred Trueman: *The Thoughts of Trueman Now* (Macdonald & Jane's, 1978)
Peter Walker: *Cricket Conversations* (Pelham Books, 1978)
Johnny Wardle: *Happy Go Johnny* (Robert Hale, 1957)
Chris Waters: *Fred Trueman* (Aurum Press, 2011)
E.M. Wellings: *No Ashes for England* (Evans Brothers, 1951)
Chris Westcott: *Class Of '59* (Mainstream, 2000)
Simon Wilde: *England: The Biography* (Simon & Schuster, 2019)
Don Wilson: *Mad Jack* (Kingswood Press, 1992)
Ian Wooldridge: *Cricket, Lovely Cricket* (Robert Hale, 1963)
Norman Yardley: *Cricket Campaigns* (Stanley Paul, 1949)
Various authors: *Brian Close – Souvenir Testimonial Brochure* (1976)
Wisden Cricketers' Almanack

I have quoted from a number of newspapers and magazines:
The Cricketer, The Times, Sunday Times, Guardian, Observer, Daily Telegraph, Daily Express, Daily Mail, Daily Mirror, Sunday Mirror, Sunday Dispatch, The People, Bradford Observer, Bradford Telegraph & Argus, Bristol Evening Post, Hull Daily Mail, Manchester Evening News, Western Daily Press, Yorkshire Evening Post, Yorkshire Post.

INDEX

Adcock, Neil 65
Alcock, George 105
Allen, David 93-5,97-8,115-6
Allen, Gubby 7,10,149,157
Alley, Bill 19,197,208
Ames, Les 149,154,156
Amiss, Dennis 11,134
Anderson, John 30-1,36,39,
    47,53-4,60,63-4,138
Andrew, Keith 110
Andrews, Bill 186-7,192
Appleyard, Bob 24-5,27,58,61,
    64,69,77,79-80,82-3,221
Arlott, John 41-2,90,94,192,210
Asif Iqbal 166
Aspinall, Ron 167
Atkinson, Colin 187
Atkinson, Graham 104
Attlee, Clement 29,193
Bailey, Trevor
    32,48,50,54,65,102-3,132
Bairstow, David 22
Balderstone, Chris 191,214
Barber, Bob 134-5,137
Barker, JS 114
Barrington, Ken
    15-6,66-7,97-8,112-4,127,
    136,149-50,154,159,200,217
Barstow, Stan 139
Bedser, Alec 15-6,40,48,50,
    52,80,149,217
Bedser, Eric 34,52
Benaud, Richie 91-2,94-8,128,
    162,165,227,229
Berry, Bob 38
Best, George 124
Bevan, Bob 215
Biddulph, Ken 18-23,27,76,228
Binks, Jimmy
    70-1,86,111,167,176,178
Bird, Dickie 172,221
Birkenshaw, Jack 88
Blackburn, Derek 82,100
Blofeld, Henry 11-2,195-6,198
Bolus, Brian 103
Booth, Roy 23,176-7,219-20
Botham, Ian 11-2,76,192,
    194-5,217-8,224,228
Botham, Kath 224
Bowes, Bill 35-6,99,118
Boycott, Geoff
    11,26-7,103,106-7,111,119,
    124,128-9,132-4,150,152,
    155,158,166,181-2,217-9
Bradman, Don 165,186

Braine, John 139
Branson, Richard 220
Bray, Charles 116
Brearley, Mike
    14,169,174,210-1,217
Brennan, Don 60
Brookes, Dennis 41
Brown, David 127
Brown, Freddie 36-7,39-41,46,
    48,51-3,56,58-9,66
Brown, Tony 122
Burgess, Graham 186-7,191-2,
    197-8,200-1,207
Burnet, Ronnie 20-1,26,82-3,
    85-9,100,105,168
Butcher, Basil 135
Callaghan, John 25
Callas, Maria 124
Calthorpe, Freddie 148
Cardus, Neville 14
Carey, Mike 168
Carr, Donald 68-9,148-9
Carter, Bob 177
Cartwright, Joan 74
Cartwright, Tom 73-4,152,155,
    184,186,188,190-4,196,204-5
Castell, Alan 71-2
Chapman, Brian 95,159
Chapman, Percy 148
Chappell, Greg 166
Chappell, Ian 215
Charlton, Bobby 124
Churchill, Winston 139,193
Clark, David 153-4,156
Clay, Johnnie 218
Close, Harry 31,36
Close, Lance 220,223-4
Close, Lynn 131,193,224-5
Close, Vivien 26-7,72,129-31,
    159,181,203,206,215,223-5
Clough, Brian 141
Cohen, Rudolph 214
Compton, Denis
    21,33,42,47,49,52,53,144
Conrad, Dickie 216
Cooper, Richard 190,204-5
Cope, Andrew 24-5
Cope, Geoff 11,24-5,73,78,
    146-7,169,171,173-9,180,222
Cope, June 24
Cowan, Mike 103
Cowdrey, Colin 17,25,65,
    91,115-6,126-8,134,137,142,
    142,149,151,157-8,160-1,163-5
Coxon, Alex 31,41-2,61

Creed, Len 185
Crowther, Leslie 129
Daniel, Wayne
    11-2,198-9,208-9,212-3
Davidson, Alan 93-4,98
Denness, Mike 11,15,198
Dewes, John 31,41,44,49-51
Dexter, Ted
    25,91,94-5,110-1,113,
    118,128,162,179,185
Dickens, Charles 206
Doggart, Hubert 31,40
D'Oliveira, Basil 127,133,157,
    163,176,188,227
Dollery, Tom 40
Douglas-Home, Alec 149,156-7
Dredge, Colin 75,197
Eastham, George 144
Edinburgh, Duke of 139,221
Edrich, Bill 38,41,48
Edrich, Geoff 38
Edrich, John 14,134,208-9,212-3
Elliott, Charlie 15,154,217
Engineer, Farokh 166,215
English, David 217
Evans, Godfrey 41,47
Feather, Robin 100
Fingleton, Jack 45-6
Foot, David 206
Fortune, Charles 95
Fox, Marcus 143
Frazier, Joe 200
Freeman, Tich 61
Frindall, Bill 197
Furniss, Mr 103
Gaitskell, Hugh 100
Garner, Joel 198-9
Gaskell, Albert 167-8
Gibbs, Lance
    112,115,126,166,182
Gibson, Alan
    9,12-4,54,185,196-7,216-7
Gilligan, Arthur 154,156
Gimblett, Harold 41
Gladwin, Cliff 143
Goodway, Cyril 154
Gothard, Eddie 154,156
Grace, WG 218
Graveney, Tom 35,110,126,
    133,135-6,144,164-5
Gray, Laurie 154
Green, Michael 52
Greenidge, Gordon 13,209,212
Greig, Tony
    10,14-7,40,112,211-3,215

Grieves, Ken 110
Griffith, Billy 35,39,149,154
Griffith, Charlie 113-6,118,
 127-8,136-7,201,210
Grout, Wally 95
Habane, Edward 216
Hainsworth, Mark 224-5
Hall, Wes 23,25,112-6,
 118,207-8,210,228
Hallam, Maurice 80
Halliday, Harry 145
Hallows, Charlie 145
Hammond, Wally 148
Hampshire, John 103,111,168,201
Hanif Mohammad 149,159
Harris, Lord 148
Harris, Norman 183-4,223
Harvey, Neil 92
Hawke, Lord 148
Hayes, Frank 211,214
Heath, Edward 139
Heine, Peter 65
Hendrick, Mike 212
Hesketh, Clifford 83
Higgs, Ken 127,133,136
Hill, Alan 23,70,214,217
Hill, Jimmy 144,146
Hill, Maurice 184
Hirst, George 24
Hobbs, Jack 148
Hoggart, Raymond 139-40
Holder, Vanburn 210-1
Holding, Michael
 11-2,207-8,213-4,228
Hook, John 192
Hopps, David 205
Howard, Geoffrey 59,67-9,142
Hutton, Len
 15-6,24,26,31-2,36,44,49,
 56-7,79-81,89,114,125,133,
 136,141,144,148,151,164,221
Hutton, Richard 152-3,155,168
Idris Begh 68
Ikin, Jack 65
Illingworth, Ray
 25,29,77-80,83,85,87,101,108,
 111,127,133-5,147,164,168-70,
 174-6,178,181-2,184,187-8,
 192,196,203-4,211,217,221
Imran Khan 205,218
Insole, Doug 40,133-4,149-50,
 153-4,157-8,160-1,163,226
Iverson, Jack 44-5
Jackman, Robin 166,168,184
Jackson, Brian 140
Jackson, Les 25,37,41-2,92
Jagger, Mick 224-5

Jardine, Douglas 148
Jennings, Keith 193
Johnson, Ian 46,49
Johnston, Bill 46
Jones, Alan 190,196-8
Jones, Allan 186,191-2
Jones, Jeff 127
Jorden, Tony 155
Jumadeen, Raphick 210
Kallicharran, Alvin 182,211
Kanhai, Rohan 115,166,182,188
Kardar, AH 68-9
Kay, John 132-3
Keating, Frank
 23,27,197,206,211
Kenyon, Don 149-50,153
Kilburn, Jim 33-4,36,99-100,
 108-9,117,161,167
Kilgour, Colonel 59
Kirby, Steve 221
Kitchen, Mervyn 203,207
Knight, Barry 144
Knott, Alan 149,211
Laker, Jim
 15,34,36-7,80,90-1,94-6
Lamb, Allan 218
Lander, Chris 207,210
Langford, Brian
 20-2,86,184-5,187-8,190-1
Larter, David 110
Law, Denis 119,124
Lawry, Bill 92
Leadbeater, Eddie 39,57,61,78
Lehmann, Darren 221
Lester, Ted 28,39,41,82
Lever, John 211
Lewis, Tony 135,209
Leyland, Maurice 211
Lillee, Dennis 10-1,15
Lindwall, Ray 49,69,94,96
Lister, Lionel 180
Lloyd, Clive 212
Loader, Peter 80
Lock, Tony 66,80,93,148,151
Long, Arnold 166-8
Lowson, Frank 30-4,57,83
McCool, Colin 19
McDonald, Mr 31
McIntyre, Arthur 49-50
Mackay, Ken 97
McKenzie, Garth 93
MacLaurin, Ian 219-20
McVicker, Norman 192
Majid Khan 166
Makepeace, Harry 38
Mann, George 36,40
Manning, Jl 58

Margery 138
Marks, Vic 192-3,198
Marlar, Robin 11,86-7
Marsden, Denys 140
Marshall, Roy 151
Matthews, Stanley 144
May, Peter 25,36,57,86,91,
 93-5,98,149-50,153,165
Melford, Michael 14,17,210
Menuhin, Yehudi 210
Mercer, Tony 129
Meyer, Barrie 188
Milburn, Colin 127,134,149,164
Miller, Keith 162
Milton, Arthur 24
Monckton, Walter 139
Moorehead, Benj 214
Morecambe, Eric 200
Morris, Robert 31
Mortimore, John 122
Moseley, Hallam 187,191
Mosey, Don
 20,104,106,108,187,202
Mountgarret, Viscount 205
Muhammad Ali 200
Murray, Deryck 113,115,182
Murray, John 134,136,216
Nannan, Nirmal 205
Nash, John 52,60,62
Nash, Malcolm 197
Nicholas, Mark 215
Nicholls, David 185
Nicholson, Tony
 111,133,152,168,177,205-6
Norfolk, Duke of 111
Nurse, Seymour 127
Oakman, Alan 110
O'Keeffe, Kerry 187
Old, Chris 172,179,212
O'Neill, Norman 96-7
Osman, Russell 217
O'Toole, Peter 206,211
Padgett, Doug 88
Padmore, Albert 12-3
Palmer, Charles 58
Paris, Cecil 154
Parker, Jack 34
Parkhouse, Gilbert 44,49,52-3
Parkinson, Michael
 141,150,154,162,166
Parks, Jim 66,68,86,114,
 118,134,157,191
Pawle, Gerald 183
Pocock, Captain 73
Pocock, Pat 209,211
Pollock, Graeme 215
Pope, George 176

Powell, Enoch 139
Preston, Norman 141
Pretlove, John 141
Price, Don 199
Price, John 134-5
Prideaux, Roger 164
Pringle, Derek 215
Procter, Mike 114,166,190
Ranjitsinhji, KS 32
Reason, John 164,190
Rehan Ahmed 7,12
Rhodes, Wilfred 7
Rice, Tim 215
Richard II 13-4
Richards, Barry 166
Richards, Viv 74-5,192,194-5,
197-8,201,206-7,211-2,228
Richardson, Peter 66,70
Richardson, Tom 114
Roberts, Andy
11-2,200,208,210,213
Roberts, Ron 93,128-9
Robertson, Jack 41
Robertson-Glasgow, RC 49
Robins, Derrick 215-6
Robinson, Peter 16,74,183,
185-6,188,190-1,193,200,204
Roebuck, Peter
75,192-3,198-9,204-5,207-8
Roope, Graham 11
Root, Fred 143
Rose, Brian 191,193,198-9
Ross, Alan 113
Rowbotham, Denys
37,65,106,110,116,118
Rumsey, Fred 145-7,163,205,215
Rutherford, Ken 218
Ryan, Mel 101
Sainsbury, Peter 68
Savile, Jimmy 141
Scovell, Brian 16,135-7
Sealey, Derek 37
Sellers, Brian 39,41,77,79,84,
89,100,102-3,118,146-7,154,
156,166,169,171-2,178,182
Selvey, Mike 166,199,212
Shackleton, Derek 71-2,115-6
Shakespeare, William 13,161
Shankly, Bill 119-20
Sharpe, Phil 88,104,106-7,
120-1,152,168
Shepherd, Don 189
Shepherd, John 166,215-6
Sheppard, David 35,41,49,51
Sidebottom, Ryan 220

Sillitoe, Alan 139
Simpson, Reg 44,46-9,53,125
Slocombe, Philip 192
Smart, Lorna 61-2
Smith, Mike (Mdx) 199
Smith, Mike (Wwks)
126,134,149,153,156,160
Smith, Peter 32
Snow, John 134-6,212
Sobers, Garry
124,126-7,129,134-7,160,
165-6,172,188,206,214,227
Spencer, Terry 79,82
Stackpole, Keith 192
Statham, Brian 92-3
Stead, Barry 204
Steele, David 14-5,208,
209-11,213-4
Stewart, Micky 35-6,59,100,
117,132,151,157,168,182
Stilgoe, Richard 215
Storey, David 139
Stott, Bryan 81-4,86-8,
102-3,106,189
Subba Row, Raman 92,95-7
Sutcliffe, Billy 81-2,84,189
Sutcliffe, Herbert 32,81-2,84,
102,114,141
Swanton, Jim
38,41,45-6,55,66,154
Swetman, Roy 69
Tallon, Don 44
Tattersall, Roy 145
Taylor, Bob 142
Taylor, Derek 187,191
Taylor, Jeff 119,123-4
Taylor, Ken
20,23,62,81,88,102,106-8
119-25,132-3,140,144-6,
152,167,170,174,178,219
Tendulkar, Sachin 33
Tennyson, Lord 148
Thicknesse, John 153,157-8
Thomson, Ian 87
Thomson, Jeff 10-1,15
Titmus, Fred 66,92,114-5,127,
134,151,157,218
Todd, Eric 100
Trueman, Fred
15,24,26,29-31,56-9,61-2,64,
75-6,78-9,82-5,87,90,92-4,
97,101-5,107-8,111-2,115,
117-9,123,128-9,133-4,141,
147-8,152-3,167-8,170-8,
189,202-3,215,217,221

Turner, Glenn 215
Turner, Mike 147
Tyson, Frank 58,65
Ufton, Derek 142
Underwood, Derek 11,127,134
Vaughan, Michael 26,220
Veal, Martin 180
Walker, Peter 135,193,197-8
Waller, Gerry 224
Waller, Jan 224
Wardle, Johnny
20-1,61,77-8,81-4,104
Warner, David 130,220
Warner, Pelham 100
Warr, John 40-2,53
Washbrook, Cyril
40,44,46-7,49-50,52
Waterhouse, Keith 139
Watson, Willie 62,65,82,91
Webb, Maurice 35
Weller, Sam 206
Wellings, Lyn 45,47,49,52
Wells, Bomber 170-1,204
Westminster, Duke of 204
Wharton, Alan 161
White, Crawford
148,153,160-1,163-4,181
Whitehead, Richard 133
Wight, Peter 104-5
Williams, Andy 130
Williams, Harold 189
Willis, Bob 213
Wilson, Don 22,84,87,101,
107-8,133,167,179,181
Wilson, Harold
100,140-1,143,162
Wilson, Vic 25,79,83-4,
88-9,99-108,171
Winfield, Merv 204
Wood, Barry 14,210-1
Woodcock, John
14-7,65-6,90-1,95,98,116,
118,127-8,136-7,152-4,
158,164,208,210,213
Wooldridge, Ian 115
Wooller, Wilf 162,189-90,196
Woolley, Frank 30,218
Woolmer, Bob 14,212-4
Worrell, Frank 115-6,128,165
Worsley, William 177-8
Yardley, Norman
38-41,60,64-5,78-9,81,96
Younis Ahmed 167,215-6

BOOKS BY STEPHEN CHALKE

Runs in the Memory – County Cricket in the 1950s *(1997)*

Caught in the Memory – County Cricket in the 1960s *(1999)*

One More Run *(2000), with Bryan 'Bomber' Wells*

At the Heart of English Cricket – The Life and Memories of Geoffrey Howard *(2001)*

Guess My Story – The Life and Opinions of Keith Andrew, Cricketer *(2003)*

No Coward Soul – The Remarkable Story of Bob Appleyard *(2003)*

A Sporting Scrapbook – The Wimbledon Club 1854-2004 *(2004)*

Ken Taylor – Drawn to Sport *(2006)*

A Summer of Plenty – George Herbert Hirst in 1906 *(2006)*

Tom Cartwright – The Flame Still Burns *(2007)*

Five Five Five – Holmes and Sutcliffe in 1932 *(2007)*

The Way It Was – Glimpses of English Cricket's Past *(2008)*

A Long Half Hour *(2010)*

Now I'm 62 – The Diary of an Ageing Cricketer *(2010)*

Micky Stewart and the Changing Face of Cricket *(2012)*

Gentlemen, Gypsies and Jesters – The Wonderful World of Wandering Cricket *(2013), with Anthony Gibson*

Summer's Crown – The Story of Cricket's County Championship *(2015)*

Team Mates *(2016), with John Barclay*

In Sunshine and in Shadow – Geoff Cope and Yorkshire Cricket *(2017)*

Cricketing Allsorts *(2018)*

Through the Remembered Gate *(2019)*

Horse and Cart to Helicopter – Lansdown Cricket Club 1825-2020 *(2020), with John Dixon, David Dolman & David Taylor*

Punchy's Hampshire Years – Cricket and Dancing *(2021), with Alan Rayment*

Yes ... No ... Wait ... Sorry! *(2022, quiz book), with Chris Coley*

Footprints – David Foot's Lifetime of Writing (2023)

If you need help in tracking down any of these titles, please contact Stephen Chalke
at **stephen.chalke@hotmail.co.uk** or on **01174 523760**